Sexuality and Slavery

GENDER *AND* SLAVERY

Sexuality and Slavery

RECLAIMING
INTIMATE HISTORIES
IN THE AMERICAS

EDITED BY
Daina Ramey Berry
AND
Leslie M. Harris

The University of Georgia Press
ATHENS

A Sarah Mills Hodge Fund Publication
This publication is made possible, in part, through a grant from the
Hodge Foundation in memory of its founder, Sarah Mills Hodge,
who devoted her life to the relief and education of
African Americans in Savannah, Georgia.

Chapter 7 was originally published, in somewhat different form, as the
article "The Sexual Abuse of Black Men under American Slavery," by
Thomas A. Foster, in *Journal of the History of Sexuality* 20, no. 3 (2011):
445–64. Copyright © 2011 by the University of Texas Press. All rights
reserved. Used by permission. Chapter 9 was originally published,
in somewhat different form, as "What's Love Got to Do with It?
Concubinage and Enslaved Black Women and Girls in the Antebellum
South," by Brenda E. Stevenson, *Journal of African American History* 98, no. 1
(2013): 99–125. Used with the permission of the Association for the Study of
African American Life and History, www.asalh.org.

Designed by Kaelin Chappell Broaddus
Set in 10.5/13.5 Garamond Premier Pro
by Graphic Composition, Inc.
Bogart, Georgia

Most University of Georgia Press titles are
available from popular e-book vendors.

Printed digitally

Library of Congress Cataloging-in-Publication Data

Names: Berry, Daina Ramey, editor. |
Harris, Leslie M. (Leslie Maria), 1965– editor.
Title: Sexuality and slavery : reclaiming intimate histories in the Americas /
edited by Daina Ramey Berry and Leslie M. Harris.
Description: Athens, Georgia : University of Georgia Press, [2018] |
Series: Gender and slavery | Includes bibliographical references and index.
Identifiers: LCCN 2018003955| ISBN 9780820354033 (hardcover : alk. paper) |
ISBN 9780820354040 (pbk. : alk. paper) | ISBN 9780820354026 (ebook)
Subjects: LCSH: Slaves—Sexual behavior—History. |
Slavery—America—History. | Women slaves—America—Social conditions. |
Slaves—America—Social conditions.
Classification: LCC HT1048 .S49 2018 | DDC 306.77086/25—dc23
LC record available at https://lccn.loc.gov/2018003955

CONTENTS

FOREWORD

CATHERINE CLINTON

It was with great regret that I was unable to attend a conference organized by Daina Ramey Berry and Leslie Harris at the University of Texas in Austin in 2011. The audience of three hundred showed that a new generation of scholars and students is responding to clarion calls to highlight neglected aspects of the African American past. The following year, a selection of the conference presenters workshopped their papers at a closed meeting with invited critics at New York University, which I was pleased to attend. The stellar lineup of historians in both venues were working on sexuality and slavery, across a vast period of time and space, scattered across diverse cultures and geographies, and tackling foundational topics. I had always dreamed a book might address these key aspects, and I felt uplifted by the energy these articulate and dramatic researchers generated. Although those inspirational marathons of new research and spirited exchanges cannot be captured between two covers, the present volume joins essays from both meetings with additional essays solicited by the editors, gathering new momentum for this topic.

Forty years ago, when I undertook my first investigations of slavery, slavery studies seemed to catch fire within and outside the academy. People were glued to their television sets watching Alex Haley's ancestors portrayed in the blockbuster miniseries *Roots*. Reviews of *Time on the Cross* appeared in *Time* magazine. The number of publications in the field nearly tripled from the 1960s to the 1970s. A handful of award-winning studies blazed onto the scene—from Stanley Elkins to Eugene Genovese, from John Blassingame to Herbert Gutman to Orlando Patterson. From economics to demography to the cultural turn, from community studies to microhistories to transnational works, these scholars were poised to investigate almost every aspect of slavery's past. There seemed only one unifying factor for all of these diverse scholarly trends: the persistent neglect of gender. This glaring omission was an ongoing dilemma, but after the 1980s, sparks began to fly. In the wake of Jacqueline Jones's *Labor of Sorrow, Labor of Love: Black Women, Work, and the Family, from Slavery to the Present* (1985) and Deborah Gray White's *Ar'n't I a Woman? Female Slaves in the Plantation South* (1985), a

Skewed to reflect patriarchal projections.

new generation of historians was unleashed on the archives, on the academy, and the rising tide of black women's history became a force to be reckoned with.

By the turn of the twenty-first century, a cadre of determined interrogators questioned not only women's absence from historical accounts but also the way in which sexual issues were skewed to reflect patriarchal projections. The meta-narrative primarily defining slavery as an economic issue was challenged. No longer would these fresh and vibrant academics allow the trivializing of personal and social aspects of slavery's corrosive impact. The minimizing of violence and sexual exploitation within the historical reframing of slavery during the remarkable revisionism of the 1970s has been replaced by serious engagement with gender and sex, intimacy and identity. But these sweeping changes within the American historical canon, the project of integrating desire and resistance, intimacy and exploitation deserves to be moved front and center.

Once obligatory gender analysis began to appear with regularity, women's work in the field of slavery studies began to introduce more complex appreciation of matrifocal legacies, concepts of demarcation and labels of illicit that transcended previous usages, aspects of masculinity, and sex role subversions within slave communities brought up from the footnotes. Naturally, scholars began to disagree, and this only enriched an already burgeoning field.

This anthology assembles the best and brightest stars in the field, emerging voices whose cutting-edge criticality and provocative suggestions can reshape the historical landscapes of bondsmen and women on land and sea, on islands and mainland, within memory and competing communities.

I am awed by the bounty of detailed analysis of individual lives and collective experience, of those struggling to redefine citizenship and identity, and those resisting enslavement within a system stacked against them. Men and women are highlighted at their most vulnerable on the pages within. Several essays rely on a master's or mistress's self-serving accounts—with acidic detection of alternate meanings for those scratches from nibs dipped in ink and dissemblance. But tales of resilience and the survivalist struggles of those fighting against the system of bondage are featured as well. Essayists draw on a range of riveting accounts—from physicians' and travelers' accounts, from official records or voices of the enslaved themselves, through court records and published narratives or buried evidence in scattered archival repositories. Most impressive is how this new generation can scour the world, in digital or physical searches, tapping into the vast array of materials available, and weave fascinating tales of slavery.

In the face of glacial resistance among American historians to recognize that we need to look to the past in order to guarantee the future, I stand in wonder of the immense talent represented here. I am grateful to witness such new and invigorating campaigns of revitalization and to have such sharing colleagues working toward making past lives matter—lives that once were abandoned at the side of the road along history's fast lane. Our authors allow the rest of us to celebrate (however briefly in the face of historic challenges ahead) and to wish our imaginations could have foretold such a prophecy.

* metanarrative →
what other metanarratives ...

* survivalist struggles of those
fighting against the system of bondage

Decision Points

ACKNOWLEDGMENTS

This book originated in a 2011 conference hosted by the Institute for Historical Studies at the University of Texas. Our thanks to History Department Chair Alan Tully, Director Julie Hardwick, and Program Coordinator Courtney Meador for providing such a wonderful space and the logistical acumen to support our work, and to the attendees for their insightful questions and comments. In 2012, many of the contributors to the volume workshopped their papers over a weekend sponsored by the New York University Department of Social and Cultural Analysis and the City University of New York Graduate Center. Thanks to Jennifer L. Morgan and Herman Bennett for organizing these meetings. Throughout the life of this project, Catherine Clinton has provided stalwart intellectual and personal support as we worked to bring the volume to publication. Brenda Brooten, Pero Dagbovie, Jacqueline Jones, Wilma King, and Jennifer L. Morgan offered strong intellectual support for this project. We are also grateful to Emory University, Northwestern University, and the University of Texas for granting financial support toward the completion of this volume.

Anonymous readers for Oxford University Press and the University of Georgia Press provided valuable feedback on the essays in the volume. Special thanks go to Sharon Block, who suggested that we include the opening essay in the volume from our late colleague and friend Stephanie M. H. Camp, and who took the lead in securing permissions for the images therein and for editing the essay with careful attention to Stephanie's voice and intent. We are also grateful to the *Journal of the History of Sexuality* and the *Journal of African American History* for permission to reprint Thomas Foster's and Brenda Stevenson's articles.

The University of Georgia Press staff, especially Lisa Bayer, Katherine Grace LaMantia, Jordan Stepp, and Jon Davies, have been patient with us through unforeseen delays. We are pleased that they suggested this book serve as the inaugural project for the new Gender and Slavery series. J. E. Morgan provided expert assistance in securing the cover image, and Deborah Oliver's copyediting made this a better volume. We also wish to thank Nancy Gerth for completing the index and taking the time to highlight key topics covered in this work.

Last but not least, working on this volume confirmed for each of us the impor-tance of scholarly collaboration in building and deepening historical knowledge. The essays presented here represent only part of the network of scholars that grew stronger as a result of our work together. They offer new ways to consider the intimate lives of the enslaved and those who claimed ownership of them. We are grateful to have been part of this endeavor.

Sexuality and Slavery

INTRODUCTION

DAINA RAMEY BERRY
AND LESLIE M. HARRIS

My heart yearned for my wife and children, from whom I
had now been separated more than four years.

—CHARLES BALL, *Slavery in the United States*

No matter whether the slave girl be as black as ebony or as fair as her mistress.
In either case, there is no shadow of law to protect her from insult, from violence,
or even from death; all these are inflicted by fiends who bear the shape of men.

—HARRIET JACOBS, *Incidents in the Life of a Slave Girl*

This volume adds to a growing literature that seeks to place sexuality at the center of slavery studies in the Americas. By sexuality, we mean the range of emotional and physical practices that have grown up around human reproduction and non-reproductive intimate expression, practices rooted in cultural beliefs and reflective and expressive of love but also of oppressive power. Until the second half of the twentieth century, few histories treated the history of sexuality seriously. In mainstream slavery studies, historians viewed sexual practices within slave communities with disdain or contempt; upheld stereotypes of black male rapists and lascivious enslaved women; and discounted formerly enslaved peoples' accounts of—or ignored completely enslavers' use of—sexual coercion as a tool of power over enslaved people.[1] Only with the full recognition of African American history as a distinct field of study, and the rise of feminist histories that first critiqued sex as a tool of patriarchy and then fully explored the variety of sexualities, did the study of sexuality within slavery begin to gain legitimacy.[2] Even then, the most fruitful studies of sexuality were cloaked within studies of slave families or, less often, focused on the sexual abuse of enslaved women by slave-owning men.[3] In many mainstream histories of slavery, scholars have marginalized or simply overlooked the importance of sexual practices and emotional intimacy within slave communities and between enslaved people and enslavers. Until recently, scholars interested in the historiography of sexuality and slavery have had to look at two different bodies of literature. Early writers of women's history addressed intimacy and abuse, focusing their efforts mainly on one racial or ethnic group of women or on a binary analysis of how black and white women interacted.[4] Those who wrote about racial and ethnic history emphasized interracial violence and often overlooked the impact of intra-racial conflict.[5] However, with the rise of women's, race, and ethnic studies departments and campus units in the 1960s and 1970s came a body of work that focused on women's and men's gendered histories. The long-term impact is an explosion of works of gender history, with new and important studies being done on men and masculinity as well as on women and sexuality.[6]

Sexual intimacy comprised a core terrain of struggle between slaveholders and the enslaved. As Jennifer L. Morgan and many other scholars have demonstrated, sexual practices were linked throughout the Americas to the question of how enslaved populations might reproduce, literally, wealth for slaveholders and their descendants in the form of children.[7] Sexuality was also linked to the imposition onto slave communities of enslavers' cultural and religious beliefs about the proper role of sexuality. Conversely, many Europeans believed that people of African descent had no norms around sexual practice and thus were available for slave owners to enact their own emotional and sexual fantasies in relationships with enslaved people. In either case, members of the slaveholding class often deployed their power by intervening in the most intimate areas of slave life.[8]

But placing sexual intimacy at the center of slavery studies also reinforces the very human connections and relationships that were at the heart of slavery—the intimacy of day-to-day contact on slave ships, on plantations, and in urban areas, and how those contacts led to emotional relationships. Sexual intimacy was one part of a continuum of emotional intimacies that scholars and the general public have struggled to understand. What was possible in terms of emotional and sexual intimacy under slavery? How were enslaved people able to form families amid a system that limited autonomy so dramatically and violently? Could relationships between enslaved people and enslavers entail non-abusive emotional intimacy?

It is not surprising that we today seek to understand more deeply the context and meaning of sexuality practices historically. While the commercialization of sex in our culture has made knowledge of sex seemingly ubiquitous, the meaning of physical and emotional love and intimacy as well as the boundaries of abuse remain cloaked in a fog of confusion for many. Stories of sexual abuse enabled by extreme differentials of power—gendered, economic, social, and age—predominate in a culture starved for healthy expressions of sexual intimacy. Our time putting together this volume was bracketed in 2011 by the exposure of decades of child sexual abuse by Penn State assistant football coach Jerry Sandusky, and in 2016 by the exposure of a recording of presidential candidate Donald Trump describing how he used his wealth and fame to force himself physically on women, including grabbing their vulvas. The broad public disdained both events as unacceptable, even as both instances were enabled by the colleagues of the men at the center of these scandals. As this book went to press, the exposure of numerous cases of sexual harassment and misconduct perpetrated by a range of powerful men emphasized the ways in which sexuality has continued to be a central dynamic in the maintenance of power in modern society. The hundreds of women and men who stepped forward against their predators had one thing in common: the power dynamic between them and their alleged assailants silenced them at the time of the initial act. Indeed, what is striking about most of these cases is that they reference actions that occurred as much as forty years ago, indicating the continuing difficulty of pursuing remedies for sexual harassment as it occurs.

While these stories remain in the headlines, human trafficking has also gained widespread attention in the past decade as a contemporary form of slavery. This modern human slave trade involves sex tourism, prostitution, pornography, forced marriage, sweatshop work, and migrant farming operations that exist all over the world. As a result, we continue to puzzle through what actions like these say about the health of our society as a whole.

This volume offers no easy solutions to our current conditions. But the complicated sexual map we live amid today does have roots in the past. Understanding the power dynamics of slavery and their impact on intimacy may give us some clarity with which to view our current condition. More telling is that even given the oppression of slavery, men and women still found their way, and sometimes struggled their way, to healthy expressions of loving partnerships of all kinds. If they were able to do so with so much stacked against them, we can learn from their examples and move toward a richer understanding of the complexities of human interaction.

Constructing a history of sexuality and slavery faces the same methodological and archival challenges as any history of intimacy, and indeed for any history. Political concerns have limited research into this particular history: racist interpretations and the widespread, historical stereotyping of black sexuality that dates back to initial contact between Europeans and Africans have long distorted this topic, while the fear of replicating such distortions has at times led to a profound silence. These essays demonstrate how scholars can successfully construct histories of enslaved people's experiences and interpretations of sexuality. The contributors explore consensual sexual intimacy and expression within slave communities, as well as sexual relationships across lines of race, status, and power. The use of sexuality as a tool of control, exploitation, and repression, but also as an expression of autonomy, resistance, and defiance is addressed. The chapters of this book also discuss the politics of constructing such histories, the archival and methodological challenges to this research, and the regional differences and similarities across the Americas through historical, legal, and feminist frameworks. As we define sexuality broadly—inclusive of consensual intimacy, coercive exploitation, and the range of positions in between—we seek to complicate our understanding of the intimacy of power.

The balance between creating respectful portrayals without reinscribing exploitation represents one of the many challenges of this work. The archive represents another. Enslaved people left relatively few written records, but autobiographical and other forms of testimony—interviews, letters—from enslaved and free, white and black, also provide hints into the history of intimacy. These firsthand accounts reveal as much in their silences as they do in direct statements. We also know a lot about slavery from plantation records and legal and government documents. Writing the history of sexuality and slavery involves finding creative ways to work against archival gaps without propagating planter mentalities. Developing a counter-narrative is one essential goal for scholars who write in either of these fields.

In chapter 10, by Jim Downs, we learn that many of the writers who tackle this subject are novelists, poets, and artists, who are afforded more freedom to imagine than historians who must study extant documents to satisfy a profession wedded to a high level of empiricism. Downs's essay is a call to welcome the interpretive possibilities that artists embrace, and yet our other essayists (and Downs himself) demonstrate via their research how much remains to be excavated from the archives, and how much can be said empirically. Each historian rebuilds the archives she or he visits by the very act of asking new questions of the documents therein. If we open ourselves up to how we as scholars produce and consume scholarship on sexuality and slavery, our emotions take us on an alternative journey through the historical record, one that can often lead to different interpretations and new analytical perspectives of legal proceedings according to Bianca Premo (chapter 4) and Maria Fuentes (chapter 3). Through these documents we witness people freeing and enslaving others, acknowledging and ignoring them, and we also see racialized and gendered black bodies.

Using a gendered lens, the chapters in this volume address women but also men and masculinity, the complexities of men's choices, and men's potential for abuse at the hands of others. From Thomas Foster (chapter 7) and David Doddington (chapter 8), we learn about husbands longing for intimacy with their wives and fathers seeking to parent within an institution that often prevented the full expression of both. More familiar stories of exploited enslaved women are cast in a different light by Stephanie Jones-Rogers (chapter 6), as she describes situations in which the abusers were white women. Her essay and some of the others offered here encourage us to pause and check our assumptions, reminding us to look in all directions for the sources of such abuse. Interference in the sexual lives of the enslaved could also be a tool of power unrelated to reproduction. Although Harriet Jacobs is our most eloquent witness to the ways in which white male power could find expression in the manipulation of enslaved people's intimate lives, and the sexual abuse of enslaved women by white men, Jacobs's narrative is only one account among many that detail the ways in which enslaved men and women were subject to the sexualization of power in slaveholding societies.

This history is not only about painful or destructive intimacy. It is also about pleasure and love. In the face of widespread control of their intimate lives, enslaved people—sometimes successfully—worked to obstruct such intrusions and regain control of their intimate lives according to Jessica Millward (chapter 5) and Brenda Stevenson (chapter 9). Some also used sexuality and reproduction as a weapon in the war to create autonomous lives. Such struggles were not always successful, and many came at great cost. Thus in the end, the superstructure of slavery reflected only one element of intimate relationships among enslaved men and women. As in any society, sexuality could also be a terrain of struggle *within* slave communities. Amid the confines of slavery, black men and women shaped their own experiences, meanings, and knowledge of love, sex, eroticism, intimacy, and power. They did not always agree on these meanings. Intimate conflicts within slave communities attest to their fundamental humanity.

This book will be in good company with other edited collections from international conferences and projects on the subject of slavery and sexuality broadly defined.[9] Although the enslaved did not receive sufficient reverence for their bodies and experiences during their lives, we are invigorated by the current state of scholarship. We hope that the chapters in this book challenge your assumptions, engage your emotions, and encourage you to approach your work with respect and care.

NOTES

1. The epigraphs are from Charles Ball, *Slavery in the United States: A Narrative of the Life and Adventures of Charles Ball, a Black Man* (New York: John S. Taylor, 1837), 387 [electronic edition, Documenting the American South, http://docsouth.unc.edu /neh/ballslavery/ball.html]); Harriet Jacobs, *Incidents in the Life of a Slave Girl, Writ-*

ten by Herself, edited by Lydia Maria Child (Boston: Published for the author, 1861), 45. Dismissive accounts include U. B. Phillips, *American Negro Slavery: A Survey of the Supply, Employment and Control of Negro Labor as Determined by the Plantation Regime* (New York: D. Appleton, 1918), 5–6, 254, 298–99, 360–62, 454–64; Kenneth Stampp, *The Peculiar Institution: Slavery in the Ante-Bellum South* (New York: Knopf, 1956), 326–27, 340, 342–47. In general, these mainstream historians ignored the fugitive slave narratives, WPA narratives, and other sources in which formerly enslaved people and others detailed sexual abuse as well as emotional intimacy in slavery.

2. John Blassingame's recuperative projects, which began in the 1960s, restored the place of enslaved people's perspectives and are central to enabling histories of sexuality. See especially *Slave Testimony: Two Centuries of Letters, Speeches, Interviews, and Autobiographies* (Baton Rouge: Louisiana State University Press, 1977).

3. Herbert Gutman's *The Black Family in Slavery and Freedom, 1750–1925* (New York: Pantheon, 1976) addressed issues of intimacy but within a project aimed at recovering heteronormative, male-dominated, marriage-based family structures. Through the end of the twentieth century, scholars worked to expand this limited view. See for example Deborah Gray White, *Ar'n't I a Woman? Female Slaves in the Plantation South* (New York: Norton, 1985); Ann Patton Malone, *Sweet Chariot: Slave Family and Household Structure in Nineteenth-Century Louisiana* (Chapel Hill: University of North Carolina Press, 1992); Brenda E. Stevenson, *Life in Black and White: Family and Community in the Slave South* (New York: Oxford University Press, 1997); Frances Smith Foster, *Love and Marriage in Early African America* (Boston: Northeastern University Press, 2007); and Tera Hunter, *Bound in Wedlock: Slave and Free Black Marriage in the Nineteenth Century* (Cambridge, Mass.: Harvard University Press, 2017). Works that named sexuality as their central theme (as opposed to women's, family, or marriage history) were fewer and included Catherine Clinton and Michele Gillespie, eds., *The Devil's Lane: Sex and Race in the Early South* (New York: Oxford University Press, 1997); and Thelma Jennings, "'Us Colored Women Had to Go through a Plenty': Sexual Exploitation of African-American Slave Women," *Journal of Women's History* 1, no. 3 (1990): 45–74.

4. See for example the work of historians Ann Firor Scott, Elizabeth Fox-Genovese, Catherine Clinton, Gerda Lerner, Marli F. Weiner, and Thavolia Glymph, who all write about women in plantation households. Thelma Jennings, Deborah Gray White, Darlene Clark Hine, and Wilma King published about various aspects of black women's lives, enslaved and free.

5. Notable exceptions include Brenda E. Stevenson, "Distress and Discord in Virginia Slave Families, 1830–1860," in *In Joy and in Sorrow: Women, Family and Marriage in the Victorian South*, ed. Carol Bleser (New York: Oxford University Press, 1991), 103–24; Christine Daniels and Michael V. Kennedy, eds., *Over the Threshold: Intimate Violence in Early America* (New York: Routledge, 1999); Adrienne D. Davis, "Slavery and the Roots of Sexual Harassment," in *Directions in Sexual Harassment Law*, ed. Catherine MacKinnon and Reva B. Siegel (New Haven: Yale University Press, 2003), 457–79; and Thavolia Glymph, *Out of the House of Bondage: The Transformation of the Plantation Household* (Cambridge: Cambridge University Press, 2008).

6. On manhood, see essays in this volume by Thomas Foster and David Dodding-ton. Hilary Beckles, "Black Masculinity in the Caribbean," in *Interrogating Caribbean Masculinities: Theoretical and Empirical Analyses*, ed. Rhoda E. Reddock (Kingston, Jamaica: University of the West Indies, 2004), 225–44; Darlene Clark Hine and Ear-nestine Jenkins, eds., *A Question of Manhood: A Reader in U.S. Black Men's History of Masculinity*, vol. 1: *"Manhood Rights": The Construction of Black Male History and Manhood, 1750–1870* (Bloomington: Indiana University Press, 1999); Edward Bap-tist, "The Absent Subject: African American Masculinity and Forced Migration to the Antebellum Plantation Frontier," in *Southern Manhood: Perspectives on Masculinity in the Old South*, ed. Craig Thompson Friend and Lorri Glover (Athens: University of Georgia Press, 2004), 136–73; Sara Roth, "'How a Slave Was Made a Man': Nego-tiating Black Violence and Masculinity in Antebellum Slave Narratives," *Slavery and Abolition* 28, no. 2 (2007): 255–75; Lydia Plath and Sergio Lussana, eds., *Black and White Masculinity in the American South, 1800–2000* (Newcastle upon Tyne, U.K.: Cambridge Scholars, 2009); Sergio Lussana, "To See Who Was Best on the Plantation: Enslaved Fighting Contests and Masculinity in the Antebellum Plantation South," *Journal of Southern History* 76, no. 4 (2010): 901–22; Kevin Dawson, "Enslaved Swim-mers and Divers in the Atlantic World," *Journal of American History* 92, no. 4 (2006): 1327–55; and Kenneth Marshall, *Manhood Enslaved: Bondmen in Eighteenth- and Early Nineteenth-Century New Jersey* (Rochester, N.Y.: University of Rochester Press, 2011).

7. For studies that center reproduction, see Kathleen Brown, *Good Wives, Nasty Wenches, and Anxious Patriarchs: Gender, Race, and Power in Colonial Virginia* (Chapel Hill: University of North Carolina Press, 1996); Jennifer L. Morgan, *Laboring Women: Reproduction and Gender in New World Slavery* (Philadelphia: University of Pennsyl-vania Press, 2004); Edward Baptist, "'Cuffy,' 'Fancy Maids,' and 'One-Eyed Men': Rape, Commodification and the Domestic Slave Trade in the United States," *American His-torical Review* 106, no. 5 (2001): 1619–50; Adrienne D. Davis, "'Don't Let Nobody Bother Yo' Principle': The Sexual Economy of American Slavery," in *Sister Circle: Black Women and Work*, ed. Sharon Harley (New Brunswick: Rutgers University Press, 2002), 103–27; Daina Ramey Berry, *Swing the Sickle for the Harvest Is Ripe: Gender and Slavery in Antebellum Georgia* (Urbana: University of Illinois Press, 2007) and *The Price for Their Pound of Flesh: The Value of the Enslaved, from Womb to Grave, in the Building of a Nation* (Boston: Beacon, 2017); Marie Jenkins Schwartz, *Birthing a Slave: Motherhood and Medicine in the Antebellum South* (Cambridge, Mass.: Harvard University Press, 2010); Edward Donoghue, *Black Breeding Machines: The Breeding of Negro Slaves in the Diaspora* (Bloomington, Ind.: AuthorHouse, 2008); Gregory Smithers, *Slave Breeding: Sex, Violence and Memory in American History* (Gainesville: University Press of Florida, 2012); and Sasha Turner, *Contested Bodies: Pregnancy, Childrearing, and Slavery in Ja-maica* (Philadelphia: University of Pennsylvania Press, 2017).

8. For studies of rape, see Diane Miller Sommerville, *Rape and Race in the Nineteenth-Century South* (Chapel Hill: University of North Carolina Press, 2004); Sharon Block, *Rape and Sexual Power in Early America* (Chapel Hill: University of North Carolina Press, 2006); Wendy Warren, "The Cause of Her Grief: The Rape of

a Slave in Early New England," *Journal of Women's History* 93, no. 4 (2007): 1031–49; and Estelle B. Freedman, *Redefining Rape: Sexual Violence in the Era of Suffrage and Segregation* (Cambridge, Mass.: Harvard University Press, 2013).

9. See, for example, Gwyn Campbell and Elizabeth Elbourne, eds., *Sex, Power, and Slavery* (Athens: Ohio University Press, 2015); Jennifer L. Morgan, Jennifer Brier, and Jim Downs, eds., *Connexions: Histories of Race and Sex in North America* (Champaign: University of Illinois Press, 2016); Bernadette Brooten, ed., *Beyond Slavery: Overcoming Its Religious and Sexual Ideals* (Boston: Palgrave, 2010). Queer theory and historiography are growing in the area of slavery studies through the Black Sexualities Project at Washington University in St. Louis and the Queering Slavery Working Group helmed by Jessica Marie Johnson and Vanessa Holden.

CHAPTER I

Early European Views
of African Bodies

Beauty

STEPHANIE M. H. CAMP

Though she was black, that was amply recompenc'd by the Softness of her
Skin, the beautiful Proportion and exact Symmetry of each Part of her Body,
and the natural, pleasant and inartificial Method of her Behaviours.

—WILLIAM SMITH, *A New Voyage in Guinea* (1744)

Early modern European travelers in Africa did not consistently generalize about
a place called Africa and people called Africans. Neither the place nor the people
existed for Europeans prior to the Atlantic slave trade and, especially, European
colonialism in Africa in the nineteenth century. Within African imaginations,
too, "Africa" came into existence through the slave trade and colonization. Previously, people of the sub-Saharan continent identified as members of kinship,
political, and linguistic groups. European travelers to West and Central Africa
helped to invent "Africa" (and African Americans) when they purchased people
who had been severed from the family relationships and the linguistic and political affiliations that gave them identities as persons. In place of these former
selves, slave traders imposed a new identity: enslaved "African" chattel. In time,
the identity "slave" would define African Americans just as "African" would define the people of the subcontinent.

But in Africa during the 1600s and 1700s, these identities were very much
still in the process of becoming. English involvement in the slave trade produced
paradoxical experiences. On the one hand, it gave the mariners, merchants, and
sailors who worked in the trade every possible reason to malign the people they
bought and sold. And so they did—prolifically. At the same time, the trade gave
some Englishmen (and other European men) the opportunity to spend time,
sometimes years, in Africa. During that time, they had experiences that challenged what they thought they knew about gender norms, about women, and
about Africa. European writers recorded their conflicts over sexual practices in
particular, offering evidence of some of the ways that West African definitions of

"The Virginia Planters Best Tobacco" and "The Tobacco Pipe Makers"
advertisements depict partially naked female slaves.
The Colonial Williamsburg Foundation, Museum Purchase.

what made bodies beautiful differed significantly from European ideals, as well as from what Europeans knew of Africans. Many Europeans recoiled from these challenges to their worldview, but others, after an initial shock of disgust, found it difficult to sustain their repugnance over time. They came to see African bodies as diverse: black and tawny, female and male, slave and free, rich and poor.

When the traveler Richard Jobson traveled along the Gambia River on "Guinea Company" (the slave trading Royal African Company) business in the 1620s, he met people he called Fulbie (Fulbe). Quickly interpreting them through their bodies, Jobson was pleased to note that they "goe clothed." He then scoped out the differences between men and women and tried to figure out who, if anyone, was beautiful. Jobson approvingly noted that the Fulbe were "Tawny," not "blacke," and "handsome." The women more so than the men: Fulbe women were "streight, upright, and excellently" well formed. They were blessed with "good features, with a long blacke haire, much more loose then the blacke women have." They tended to their hair fastidiously, just as they did to their clothes and their dairy work. Being quite "neate and cleane" in their habits, should they be caught in any "nastinesse," Fulbe women, like good English women at home, blushed with embarrassment. They worked, like Irish women, with cattle, but were much tidier than Irish women. Theirs was a "cleanlinesse [with which] your

Irish women hath no acquaintance." Jobson linked "Tawny" skin, "long [...], long" hair and straight bodies with "handsome" women, and he made a point of distinguishing the lighter-colored Fulbe from "blacke women" in general as well as from the "perfectly blacke, both men and women" Mandinka. In Jobson's view, Africans came in multiple colors: tawny, black, and "perfectly black." Not only were Africans not all one people, they were not yet all black. And, in Jobson's estimation, the lighter brown skin of some Africans enhanced their beauty.[1] Eurafricans and brown-skinned Africans received much praise for being beautiful.

But dark brown and black Africans were far from unrecognized by European men for their beauty. For instance, during his time in the Cape Verde Islands in the late 1640s, Richard Ligon met the most beautiful woman he had ever seen. She was "a *Negro*," the mistress of a Portuguese settler and a woman "of the greatest beauty and majesty that ever I saw." In his account, Ligon dreamily detailed her body's exquisite form ("her stature [was] large, and excellently shap'd, well favour'd, full ey'd, and admirably grac'd"), the cloth and color of her clothing (she wore a head wrap of "green Taffety, strip'd with white and Philiamort," a "Peticoat of Orange Tawny and Sky color; not done with Strait striped, but wav'd; and upon that a mantle of purple silk"), her jewelry, her boots. And her eyes! A decade had passed since his voyage, but Ligon had never forgotten their exotic allure. "Her eyes were her richest Jewels, for they were the largest, and most oriental that I have ever seen." Her smile was a paragon—and not, Ligon insisted, simply because all Africans had white teeth. That misconception was a "Common error." But hers were indeed "exactly white, and clean." Ligon's "black Swan" spoke "graceful[ly]," her voice "unit[ing] and confirm[ing] a perfection in all the rest." Hers was a "perfection" that exceeded the grace and nobility of British royalty. The woman was possessed of "far greater Majesty, and gracefulness, than I have seen [in] Queen *Anne*." Ligon's readers must have been quite surprised to read a favorable comparison between their queen and an African concubine.[2] Then again, it was not exactly easy in the middle of the seventeenth century to know what to expect when it came to representations of Africa. It was an age of intense contradictions.

Later in his travels, Ligon surprised his sixty-plus-year-old self with the force of the admiration and desire he felt for some of the "many pretty young *Negro* Virgins" he met later on his voyage. There were two "Negro" women, in particular, who took Ligon's breath away. The two women were "Sisters and Twins" and their "shapes," "Parts," "motions" and hair were "perfection" itself. Indeed, they were works of art. True, Ligon admitted, their shapes "would have puzzl'd Albert Durer," the German Renaissance painter known for his mathematical approach to proportion. And Titian, the Italian painter revered for his soft, fleshy representations of the human form and harmonious use of color, would have been perplexed by their muscles and "Colouring." Still, the women "were excellent," possessed of a "beauty no Painter can express." The twins were unlike North Africans, East Africans, or Gambians, "who are thick lipt, short nos'd and [who had] uncommonly low foreheads." In what ways the twins were different from these others, Ligon did little to clarify; he did not describe their facial features, bodies, or skin color. He did, however, detail their hair and their "motion," both of which he found irresistible. They wore their hair neither shorn nor cornrowed, but loose in what Ligon deemed "a due proportion of length." Their "natural Curls [...] appear as Wyers [wires]," and the women bedecked their corkscrew curls with ribbons, beads, and flowers. The occasional braid twisted adorably onto their cheeks. Their motions? "The highest." Grace in movement was "the highest part of beauty," and the twins had mastered it. Ligon was surprised to find in Africa such living embodiments of "beauty," "innocence," and "grace."[3]

The emerging stereotype about African women's rugged reproductive capacity was not wholly devoid of admiration of African women's stoicism and physical strength, especially when European men (inevitably) compared African women to European women. In light of what they thought they witnessed in (or read about) Africa, some male writers came to see European women as annoyingly weak. Pieter de Marees announced in 1602, for instance: "the women here are of a cruder nature and stronger posture than the Females in our lands in Europe."[4] In this double backhanded compliment, de Marees hitched together African and English women, loading both with the burden of embodying British civility and its constitutive opposite, African savagery.

Charles Wheeler, an English trader who lived in Guinea for a decade in the employ of the Royal African Company in the 1710s and 1720s, shared Marees's perception of the ease with which African women produced children, as well as his regard for it. "One Happiness, which those of this Part of the World enjoy before those of *Europe*," Wheeler told William Smith, who later wrote about his travels, "is their Labours. These are Times with them so easy, so kind, so natural and so good, that they have no Need of Midwives, Doctors, Nurses, &c. and I have known Women go to Bed over Night, bring forth a Child and be abroad the next Day by Noon." Wheeler admiringly attributed the good times that African women enjoyed during pregnancy and childbirth to their "natural" state of being. Citing the "Black Lady" with whom he lived during his decade on the coast, he (and she) credited above all women's "Chastity" during pregnancy and menstruation. "You White People," Wheeler's Black Lady told him, "do not observe this Rule, [and] there are among you, Lepers, Sickly, Diseased, Ricketty,

Frantick, Enthusiastic, Paralytic, Apopletic, &c." European clothing made matters worse. English women's "Stays, and Multiplicity of Garments [. . . as well as] the Multitude of other Distempers and damnable Inconveniences, [which they] through Pride and Luxury, had brought upon themselves" produced the "hard Labours" they suffered so terribly loudly. In Wheeler's and his lady's interpretation, civility and its sartorial demands distorted women's bodies and led to painful parturition. African women's lighter, looser clothing, "so contriv'd as to confine no one Part of the Body," rewarded them with easier pregnancies and more dignified birth experiences. The natural manner in which African women gave birth extended to the care of newborns—with beautifully healthful results. No special "Provision [. . .] of any Necessaries" were made for newborns, and "yet all its Limbs grow vigorous and proportionate." William Smith had lifted this last sentence from Willem Bosman's influential 1705 book, but with an important addition: Smith thought that it was the coddling of infants in Europe that "makes so many crooked People." The "vigorous and proportionate" limbs of African infants were born of unconstrained, natural female bodies. African women's natural state rewarded them with ease in childbirth and straight-limbed children. African women, from Bosman's, Wheeler's, and Smith's points of view, were innocents unscarred by the curse of Eve.[5]

The same slave trade that pricked English interest in Africa and contempt for Africans also elicited its seeming opposite: a need to engage with Africans and to know something about them. In order to make their purchases, male travelers simultaneously recognized, fantasized, and reshaped local identities. They perceived, as we have seen, differences among Africans—differences of culture, of skill, and in their bodies. European travelers were not incapable of recognizing human beauty in Africa. Even slave traders were capable of recognizing it, but with a twist. Slave traders interpreted bodies through a merchant's mindset: set to turn some African people into property, they perceived beauty with the slave market in mind. In the mid-seventeenth century, Richard Ligon knew that the buyers of slaves in Barbados saw Africans as more than simply monstrous or hardy. Barbadian planters chose slaves "as they do Horses in a Market; the strongest, youthfullest, and most beautiful yield the greatest prices."

The naval doctor John Atkins agreed. "*Slaves* differ in their Goodness," Atkins opined in 1735. Based on his travels in "Negro-land" (West Africa), he found "those from the *Gold Coast* are accounted best, being cleanest limbed, and more docible" (though he thought they were also "more prompt to Revenge, and murder"). Slave sellers in Africa and in the Americas embellished Africans' bodies in order to make them appear healthier, stronger, more beautiful. The reality of starved, exhausted, and likely ill bodies had no place in the market. Sellers

washed the stain of urine, feces, and blood from the slaves' skin, shaved and de-
loused their hair, and rubbed them with "Negro Oyle" (palm oil) or lard to make
their skin glisten and hide the effects of the captives' traumatic forced migrations.
Improving slaves' appearance of vitality was an essential part of getting them sold
"to Advantage." Indeed, the historian of the slave trade Stephanie E. Smallwood
has called the aesthetic preparation of the slaves' bodies for sale the part that
"would matter most in the captives' upcoming performance" in the market.[6] It
was to no slave trader's advantage to insist that Africans were a uniformly revolt-
ing people. The irony, of course, is that slavery's logic of commodification evacuated beauty of the power it often held. Commodified and enslaved beauty was
anything but powerful.

Some English travelers thought they discerned a difference between African
women and men, a difference in the aesthetic value of their bodies. Of those who
compared men and women, most insisted that the men were far better made,
smoother, and above all more symmetrical than the women. With some exceptions, African women, who challenged European gender norms so profoundly,
were viewed as more unevenly made than men were.[7] Their physiques, it was
frequently claimed, had been disfigured by field work, pregnancy, and breast-
feeding. The traveler Francis Moore claimed that the women he saw during his
travels along the River Gambia in the 1720s were asymmetrically made with "one
Breast [. . .] generally larger than the other." The surgeon John Atkins, who had
denounced the women of "Negro-land" for their distended breasts, nonetheless admired the male bodies he encountered. The men were "well-limbed, clean
Fellows, flattish nosed, [. . .] seldom distorted." The women were simply "not
nigh so well shaped as the Men." "Childing, and their Breasts always pendulous,
stretches them so unseemly a Length and Bigness," he wrote, seemingly with nose
wrinkled.[8]

Richard Ligon also perceived distinctions between African men and women.
For all that he admired the beauty of many of the women he met in Africa, his
tone changed dramatically once he reached Barbados. During the late 1640s
when he lived in that slave colony, Ligon made a point of being "very strict" with
himself "in observing the shapes of these people." Enslaved men were choice,
like cuts of meat: "the men, they are very well timber'd, that is broad between the
shoulders, full breasted, well filleted, and clean leg'd." The women, on the other
hand, were decidedly "not" on same order of beauty. According to Ligon, African men's bodies were symmetrical, but women's bodies were irregular. Enslaved
men's bodies "h[e]ld good" with the rules laid out by the "Master of Propor-
tions," the artist Albrecht Dürer, in his 1522 study of geometry, *Four Books on Mea-
surement*. Ligon applied his interpretation of Dürer's study to his "observation"

of enslaved men in Barbados and concluded that their shoulders, chests, and legs were placed and sized in balanced proportion to one another. In sharp contrast to African men's elegant proportionality, enslaved African women's bodies were out of whack. According to Ligon's reading of Dürer's work, women should have "twice the length of the face to the breadth of the shoulders, and twice the length of her own head to the breadth of her hips." By these measures of corporeal harmony, Barbadian slave women were "faulty; for I have seen very few of them, whose hips have been broader than their shoulders, unless they have been very fat." Young women's breasts were "very large" and unnaturally pert, "strutting out so hard and firm, as no leaping, jumping, or stirring, will cause them to shake any more." Older women had borne children, nursed them, and carried them with "cloaths [. . .] which come upon their breasts" and pressed them "very hard." Formerly firm breasts aged and drooped. They "hang down below their Navels, so that when they stoop at their common work of weeding, they hang almost down to the ground." Drawing on centuries of European fantasies of monstrous races in Africa, Ligon perceived "that at a distance, you would think they had six legs."[9] African men, in Ligon's account, were paragons of proportionality, but African women were distorted almost beyond human form.

Ligon's change of mind came about just as the English were becoming increasingly involved in the African trade in people. Indeed, Ligon's transformation happened on a journey along a slave trade route ending in the slave society of Barbados. His perceptions of black bodies there must have been deeply stained by their debasement. Just as Ligon's attitudes changed with exposure to the trade in people, the tone of English discussions of Africa changed in the middle of the seventeenth century. Scholars of racial difference in the early modern Atlantic world have detected a decline in the contradictions after about the mid-seventeenth century, and a rise of more uniformly negative appraisals of Africa and Africans.[10]

Despite the general shift in tone, however, there remained a good deal of inconsistency on the specific question of beauty well into the eighteenth century, the era of deep English involvement in the Atlantic slave trade. The inconsistency extended even to African women, who continued to be seen in contradictory ways. Even during a time when contempt for dark skin was extremely widespread, it was not universal. There was no consensus among Englishmen that blackness was uniformly the very antithesis of beauty. Until a trip to East Africa in the 1760s and 1770s, the traveler James Bruce "had always connected the idea of perfect beauty with a fair complexion." But upon seeing East African women, he had to think again. The women there were so lovely to him. One in particular was "a woman of the most beautiful form, the most delicate skin, and the most lovely composition of features" he had ever seen. The sight of her was an epiphany. "At once" Bruce became "convinced that almost the *all* of beauty consists in elegance of figure, in the fineness and polish of the skin, in grace of movement, and the expression of the countenance."[11] Based on what he observed during a trip he made to Camp Palmas (the coasts of Côte d'Ivoire, Ghana, and Benin) in 1786 and 1800, the ship captain John Adams told his readers that "Fantee women are well-formed, and many of them are not wanting in personal beauty." What "beauty" meant to Adams was fairly specific: "their features are small, their limbs finely rounded, their hands and feet small, and their teeth uniformly white and even." Fantee women had an elaborate daily toilette. Adams got the impression that they "often" took "an hour or two" and used "no inconsiderable degree of skill" to wash their bodies ("from head to foot every day") and teeth, moisturize and perfume their skin, dress, and style their hair. These gorgeous and fastidious women were, Adams pointedly noted, dark skinned. The men weren't too shabby, either. Adams thought they were "black as jet, muscular, and well-formed." Elsewhere in West Africa, he encountered others who were "very black" or "extremely black" and also "good-looking" or "a fine race of people." Indeed, when he compared another group of people, a group who were "not of so deep a black as those of the Fantee," he found them merely "inoffensive." They were nothing to compare to the beautiful Fantee, whose skin was a "deep" black.[12]

Bruce and Adams were but two examples. Plenty of other Englishmen came to the same conclusion: black could be beautiful. The entrepreneur Joseph Hawkins lived among and traded with the Igbo people in the late eighteenth century. He perceived them as "considerably blacker than the natives of the lower CONGO country" who had "a yellowish tinge [...] owing, I suppose, to their greater intercourse with the whites." Mixture with whites may have lightened black skin, but it did not brighten it; rather, it cast a "yellowish tinge" into the skin. The dark skin of the Igbo, on the other hand, was one element of their overall "well formed, [...] upright" bodies, along with their "strait" limbs.[13] And when Alexander Falconbridge, a doctor who worked on slave ships, met the young wife of a Sierra Leonean "King" during a voyage in the 1790s, his reaction was conflicted. Though he contemptuously referred to her as a "Peginee" (picaninny), he also found her to be "most beautiful." He also met an African "Queen" who, he thought, must have "been a good looking woman in her youthful days."[14] In his 1791 account of his travels in Sierra Leone, John Matthews described a number of the peoples he met there (the "Bullams, Timmaneys, and Bagoes") as having "a good black [color], straight limbs, and pleasing features." Noting the aesthetics of the female bodies he saw, Matthews professed, "many of their women are really handsome" as well as "exceedingly clean." Gray-bearded elders made "a most venerable appearance."[15]

Likewise, while "tawny" Africans garnered their share of admiration from European men, not everyone agreed that light-colored (but nonwhite) skin was so very comely. In 1726 the Royal African Company sent the mapmaker William Smith to survey a portion of the West African coast. Once there, he had a very strong reaction against the "MULLATOES" of coastal Sierra Leone. A treacherous "Bastard Brood" in general, they were also "frightfully ugly, when they grow in Years, especially the women." In 1705, Willem Bosman wrote that "the whole brood" of mixed-race Africans were "far from handsome" when young, and they only got uglier with age. "When old, [they] are only fit to fright children in their beds." Time "speckled" their bodies with "white, brown, and yellow spots, like the tigers, which they also resemble in their barbarous nature."[16] To the long list of animals that Africans of all shades were supposed to resemble—toads, wolves, goats, apes—we may now add tigers.

Clashing interpretations of African bodies also persisted in continental travel writing. Take, for example, the work of the French traveler and physician François Bernier, a pioneer in the field of racial classification. In 1684, Bernier broke with past European practices of sorting humanity by country or region, and proposed, instead, a "new division of the earth" which divided the world's people into "four or five Types of Race among men whose distinctive traits are so obvious." And by "obvious," Bernier meant visible in the form of the body. Bernier has been credited with originating a modern idea of race (i.e., the idea that race is rooted in biological classifications).

Yet, despite his rather absolute take on racial difference, when it came to the question of "the beauty of women" in Africa, Bernier reminded his readers, "there are lovely ones and ugly ones to be found everywhere." There were African women who were black and beautiful. "Among the Blacks of Africa I have also seen some very beautiful women who did not have thick lips and snub noses," the latter being two of the essential features of Bernier's African "type." These women were "of such an astonishing beauty that they put in the shade" the goddess Venus—but only when they had an "aquiline nose, small mouth, coral lips, ivory teeth, large bright eyes, gentle features, and a bosom and everything else of utter perfection." These dark-skinned women were, in Bernier's eyes, undeniably lovely. At one point in his travels, Bernier claimed, he witnessed a number of Africa's beauties "completely naked, waiting to be sold" in a slave market. "I can tell you," Bernier informed his reader, "there could be nothing lovelier in the world to see—but they were extremely expensive because they were being sold at three times the price of the others." The black women in Bernier's description were "lovely"—"nothing lovelier"—in a very different way than were Ligon's "black Swan," Jobson's "Tawny" Fulbe women, or even the free women that Bernier had seen. These women possessed "perfect" features (the aforementioned "aquiline nose, small mouth, coral lips, ivory teeth, large bright eyes, gentle features, and a bosom and everything else of utter perfection"), and they were slaves, a fact that subjected them to being stripped nude and put up for sale. Their commodified beauty was a rare and valuable combination. Consequently, they were "extremely expensive."[17]

Bernier thought "brown ones," such as the women "in the Indies" could also be "lovely." Despite the tendency in France for yellow skin to be seen as sickly, the "yellow" and "very light tallow" of South Asian women was "highly valued" among them, and Bernier "found them very much to my liking too." The distinction was that "this slight yellowishness if bright and sparkling, [was] quite different from the nasty livid pallor of someone with jaundice." Bernier asked his reader to "imagine a beautiful young daughter of France contracted jaundice— but instead of her sick, pallid face, and her yellowish, faded, listless eyes, think of her having a healthy, soft and smiling face with beautiful bright eyes full of love: that is something like the idea I want to give you."[18] The man who divided humanity into a handful of biologically distinct races was the same man who insisted that feminine beauty could be found everywhere around the globe, at times offering comparisons that favored "brown ones" over French beauties.

Whether dark or yellow, speckled or spotted, dull skin was the antithesis of beautiful skin. It was important to male writers that skin be smooth, even-colored, transparent, and glowing. "Liveliness" was the word many Englishmen used to express this ideal of feminine skin. Dull, dingy skin (whether light or dark) was unattractive, whereas bright skin (sometimes even if it was dark) was lovely, the implied difference being the life that shone through. The light brown or "tawny" skin that some European men found so pretty struck others as dingy, perhaps a little sickly. John Adams, who esteemed black-skinned women and men so highly, thought that some Africans had a "yellow, bilious cast" to their skin. He did not come right out and say it was unappealing, but his comparison of their skin to bile clearly was not complimentary.[19] "The natives of the lower CONGO country" had what Joseph Hawkins, a sailor, could only describe as a "yellowish tinge" to their skin. And when the slave trader William Snelgrave met a very light-skinned African woman, one "so white, [she was] equal to our English Women," he was puzzled by her appearance. Her hair was "wooly, [. . .] like the blackest of the Natives." Her features were "the same" color as her hair: black. But her skin—it seemed so white. He searched and searched for the thing that set her skin apart from English skin, the thing that would reveal its non-whiteness. Then he found it: its dull tone. It was "not so lively a Colour" as that of English roses.[20]

The eighteenth-century French naturalist Georges Louis Buffon, whose writings on race were enormously influential in Europe and the United States (historians have dubbed him the father of modern racism), saw more than color when he looked at Africans' skin. He saw tone and texture, and in these he could see beauty. Buffon admired the beauty of the people he called Jaloff, referring to those who lived in southern Senegal within the Jolof empire. They were, he said, one of Africa's darker people and among the world's beautiful people. "They are all very black, well-proportioned" and tall. "Their features are less harsh than those of the other Negroes; and some of them there are, especially among the female sex, whose features are far from irregular." It was easy for Buffon to admire these women and men for "with respect to beauty, they have the same ideas as ourselves." Which was to say that "they consider fine eyes, a well-made nose and mouth, and lips of a proportional smallness." Really, the only difference between the Senegalese and "us" was the "exceedingly black, and exceedingly glossy" color and tone of the former's skin. Lively, dark, and glossy Senegalese skin was admirably "delicate" and "soft."[21]

But he also made a point of excluding dark skin color from his summary of overall Senegalese beauty: "colour alone excepted, we find among them women as handsome as in any other country of the world." Buffon was just as contradictory about other West African peoples who, "like those of Senegal," were "well made, and very black." Like the "Jaloff," "the negroes of the island of Gorée, and of the Cape de Verde coast" were "glossy" and prideful of their color, which they "prized" far above the skin of those "who are not the same as much as white men despise the tawny." Indeed, these were the very "negroes" that he found to be "more beautiful" than, for instance, the Aboriginal people of Australia precisely because of the healthy look of their "exceedingly black" skin. "Copper-colour" was, Buffon believed, a sure sign of sickness. Buffon seemed to be amused by West Africans' belief "that, because they are the blackest, they are the most beautiful of men." But he did not exactly contradict the idea, either.[22]

Liveliness and glossiness were visible in the skin and evident in personalities as charm. Like liveliness, charm helped beautify female bodies in English minds. Both animated personalities, especially women's, and had the power to make women of any color into beauties. Charles Wheeler, who worked for the Royal African Company in Guinea for ten years in the early 1700s, adored his African lover for "the natural, pleasant and inartificial Method of her behaviours. She was not forward, nor yet coy."[23] John Matthews shared the feeling in his 1791 ac-

count of a voyage to Sierra Leone. In his view, comeliness was linked to personality. Describing a number of the people he met during his voyage in terms that
mixed descriptions of their bodies with descriptions of their character, Matthews
considered some of them to be "a stout, active, and personable race; of a good
black, straight limbs, and pleasing features; and rather above the middle size."
One group, the "Timmaneys," he found to be particularly "remarkable for an
open, ingenuous countenance; and many of their women are really handsome."[24]
Charm, sincerity, hospitality all could beautify African bodies, making them
"pleasing" and "really handsome."

Englishmen who read French travel writing would have found a similar pattern of thought. It did not hurt West African women's depiction in French writings that they were seen as possessing a gay temperament and a sexual predilec-
tion for European men. The Jaloff were, according to Georges Buffon, usually
very gay, lively, and amorous. They "are very fond of white men whom they ex-
ert every assiduity to please, both to gratify themselves, and to obtain presents
which may flatter their vanity," Buffon explained.[25] Likewise, François Leguat's
seventeenth-century report on his travels described Senegalese women in flattering tones. The "female negroes there," were, by Leguat's description, "some of
them perfect beauties" possessed of "fine and soft" skin, "black and open" eyes
and an "easy, free air, that is highly agreeable."[26]

So, for more than a few European writers, African women were sweet, easygo-
ing, and delightful. These attributes were embodied in their legendarily soft skin.
It was so silky, it sometimes even compensated, in English descriptions, for other
African failings. Some Englishmen in Africa, especially those who lived there
for some time, learned to view female beauty as a complex of bodily attributes,
as something not easily reducible to the light/dark dichotomy. During his decade's residence in Guinea, Charles Wheeler got to know a woman who cut "no
despicable Figure" even "though she was black." She possessed other qualities:
"softness of her Skin, the Beautiful Proportion and exact Symmetry of each Part
of her Body, and the natural, pleasant and inartificial Method of her Behaviors."
These made up for, in Wheeler's heart, her skin color. Like other male travelers,
Wheeler had a few additional words for her "lovely Breasts, whose Softness to the
Touch nothing can exceed." In even more sensual tones, the poet Thomas Gray,
back in the seventeenth century, had asked in his commonplace book "whether
White or Black [skin] be best?" He answered his own question. "The Black in
softness doth excel." More precisely, black women's "Lovely Breasts" were graced
with a "Softness to the Touch [that] nothing can exceed."[27] So much talk of soft
African skin. Which raises the question: how did he, and the others, know that
African women's skin and bosoms felt so very soft?

The open secret among European men traveling to or settling in the slave trading regions of West and Central Africa was the fact of sexual relationships between many European men and African women. Whatever contradictory messages about African bodies they published once home in Europe, many, *many* male travelers to Africa had sexual relationships with local women during their sojourns. European men found their preconceptions about African family formations and sexual practices challenged by their experiences in Africa. The Royal African Company trader Charles Wheeler admitted that, when he first arrived in Guinea, he was ignorant of "the local people and their social & cultural practices." He "soon" learned to appreciate the people's culture and their comeliness. While Wheeler listened to his companion's explanation of the reasons for sexual companionship to be provided to guests, he was distracted by her beauty. "During this Conversation," he later recalled, "and whilst we were at Supper, I could not forbear viewing my Fair with an amorous Eye, her Hair was done up in a Ringlet, set with precious Stones, from whence divers Locks of Hair beset with Diamonds descended from behind, and loosely play'd upon her jetty Breasts and Shoulders."[28]

Being the first Europeans to arrive, the Portuguese were the first to make themselves at home in West Africa. Richard Jobson reported on the "*Molatoes*" he saw during his 1620–21 voyage along the River Gambia, where the Portuguese had been exploring since about 1450. They were the offspring of Portuguese settlers and the "countrey blacke women" to whom they were married (according to local custom, if not Portuguese law) or with whom they lived. Richard Ligon made a similar observation at the Cape Verde Islands, where he found a Portuguese man living with "his family consisting" of "three negroes" and "a *Mollatto* of his own getting." By the late seventeenth century, the English had muscled their way into the Africa trade and therefore into relationships with African people, including sexual relationships with women. A 1682 dispatch from a Royal African Company officer reported from an English settlement in Sierra Leone that "Every man hath his whore ffor whom they steal &c." There were "whores" who lived with their lovers and prostitutes who didn't, though the latter could become the former. Francis Moore, who traveled in Gambia in the early 1720s, knew the prices that prostitutes charged there to be "a little Coral, or a Silk Handkerchief"—both were handy for trade or body ornamentation. But if "any White Man has a Fancy to any of them, and is able to maintain them," he could live with her "in the Nature of a Wife," even "without the Ceremony of Matrimony." Well into the nineteenth century, European and white American men who traveled to Africa connected with local women. During his trip to West Africa in the 1850s, the American Methodist minister Charles W. Thomas disapproved of the "concubinage, and other vices indulged in by a majority of the white residents here." He thought their decadence undermined the good work Christian missionaries tried to do.[29]

From West African points of view, sexual relationships between African women and European men were highly structured and very purposeful. European male travelers entered West African societies with deep convictions that men's sexual desires were important to satisfy. As European men arrived in West Africa, they participated in all of the sexual institutions available to them as visitors: public prostitution, private prostitution, and concubinage. Public prostitutes were disparaged as "whores" by many European men, but in fact they were (at least in Ghana and the Ivory Coast but probably in other parts of West Africa, too) enslaved women who had been assigned sex work. As slaves, they did not choose their work. The women were initiated into their roles in public ceremonies, received small gifts for their services from their clients, kept a portion of their pay (enough "to subsist them in cloathes and necessaries"; the rest went to their masters or mistresses), and received pensions when they retired. They commonly suffered from sexually transmitted diseases as a result of "prostituting themselves to the unsound as well as the sound." In each of the towns that had public prostitutes—not all did—there might be "two or three of these miserable wretches." These victims of "institutionalized rape" (as one historian has called them) were also "conscripted public servants" (as the historian Emmanuel Akyeampong argues) who helped stabilize intergenerational tensions by providing younger, unmarried men with something they demanded. "As long as they are sound, and in flower, they are in very great esteem." Their high value to African men rendered public prostitutes pawns between European and African traders. There was, according to Bosman, no better way for a European trader in a "dispute with his subordinate negroes" to "bring them to reason than by taking one of these whores into custody, and confining her in the fort." Not only would the bachelors quickly be brought into line, so would the married men who worried about "the danger" of the bachelors "lying with men's wives."[30]

Some early modern West African societies also tolerated the existence of private prostitution among free women. There was nothing desirable about the work or the low status it conferred on the prostitute, but it provided a livelihood to poor women and assertive women who had lost the protection of their families. "Handsome" women without other resources were "permitted to earn what money they please with their bodies," Bosman said of the Rice Coast. It also provided the same outlet for male sexuality that public prostitutes did. Some European men hired prostitutes to work for them during their stays or used domestic servants as if they were prostitutes. During a visit to the slave trading center on Bunce Island in Sierra Leone in the early 1720s, the British naval surgeon John Atkins eyeballed the thirty or so "private Traders" who had settled there. "They all keep *Gromettas* (Negro Servants)," he later reported. Female servants, he noted, did more than "keep House" and tend to the traders' slaves. They also were "obedient to any Prostitutions their Masters command." The recognized social place of prostitution in some West African societies suggests, Akyeampong points out, that "male sexual needs, as opposed to female sexual needs, have always been recognized in Akan society."[31] This accommodation of male sexual needs extended to visitors, guests, and trading partners from abroad.

Ordinary European sailors probably hired prostitutes, but elite male travelers (ships' captains, prosperous traders) were, in all likelihood, less inclined to do so—if only because they did not have to. Hospitable West African leaders greeted European traders as hosts. They greeted strangers with cool drinks, snacks, and a moment to rest. They allowed their visitors to rent housing; buy food, water, and firewood; and hire African crew, servants, guides, and interpreters. They ensured the safety of their guests' persons and their property. And they provided female company to the leadership. In return, visitors were expected to pay taxes, give gifts, and trade exclusively with their host and landlord. "When a 'Grandee' is visited by another Grandee," Charles Wheeler told William Smith, one "who comes one or two Days Journey, and perhaps designs to stay there for some time," the local leadership "gives his Visitant the Choice of one of his Concubines to be his Companion, and to lie with him during his Stay." When Wheeler met the woman selected to be his companion, he found her anything but objectionable. She was "a young lady in her Prime, her Stature was tall, and she was well proportion'd." Wheeler admitted that "the Sight of her, produc'd some Emotions in me in her Favour." Wheeler approved the choice and his host sent them to their "house, just by his own Palace" with a few slaves to serve them. Wheeler's host took no chances with his visitor, lodging him close to his own palace and cosseting him with female company and slaves—all to welcome his guest, to present himself as a generous host, and to remind Wheeler of the many gifts he had to give. Many traders learned the wisdom of taking a female companion. Doing so safeguarded their relationships with male leaders; it ensured that they would not, unintentionally or otherwise, have sexual encounters with inappropriate women.[32]

Married African men may have worried about bachelors, European and African, but European men also had to take care. Bosman warned other European men who might go to West Africa: "He who debauches a Negro's wife here, is not only generally entirely ruined, but his relations often suffer with him: for if the injured person be a rich and great man, he is not contented with ruining the malefactor only, but will not be quiet till he hath removed him out of the way." The woman also took her life in her hands. Everyone, except perhaps public prostitutes, was invested in the proper channeling of sexual energy. Prostitution and concubinage ideally protected marriage (and extramarital liaisons): they were intended to preserve the institution from desecration by fallible human beings and to protect husbands, wives, and single men from the shame of adultery. As Wheeler's Black Lady told him, with likely exaggeration: "you will never hear among us, [...] that the Visitant cuckolds the Husband, and debauches the Daughters, and Women-servants," as Wheeler had told her happened in Europe. Concubinage between European men and African women tamed the sexual threat posed by single men.[33]

It also, and probably more importantly, served as an exchange of gifts between men hoping to build mutually beneficial relationships. In concubinage, European and African men secured their alliances to one another through the exchange of women's sexuality. Some African men wished the exchange in women went both ways. The king of Dahomey once requested that William Smith bring him a woman from England. "If there is any Cast-off Whore, either White or Mullattoe, that can be persuaded to come to this Country, either to be his Wife or else practice her old Trade," Smith would "gain his Majesty's heart by" enticing such a woman to Benin.[34] In some ways, then, sex was beside the point. More to the point was the bond between host and visitor that the exchange of women helped to cement.

But sex between English men and African women did so much more than domesticate visiting men's sexuality and provide European men with a way into local markets. In many ways, it changed everyone involved. Like cross-cultural relationships have the potential to do in any context, past or present, the intimacies of sex and companionship could both transform and deepen prejudices. European men in Africa found their assumptions about the nature of female sexuality, gender roles, and beauty all called into question. Charles Wheeler, for one, quickly came to understand that his "Aversion" to "Polygamy" was nothing more than "the Prejudice of a different Education." Sounding every bit the cultural relativist, Wheeler insisted that in time he became "a little habited to this Custom" and appreciated that "Different Nations have different Customs, and consequently different Ideas of one and the same Thing." Chastity in Guinea, he had learned, consisted not of absolute abstinence from sex outside of marriage, but abstinence during pregnancy. In fact, Wheeler was delighted to learn that, unlike proper English ladies, "the Ladies of this Country imagine it no Fault to be free, nor to be fond of a man; their Notion is, that they were made for their Diversion as well as Use, and therefore they say they ought to excite in the Man amorous Thoughts and Desires." Wheeler, who had already been casting "an amorous Eye" on the woman he would come to call his "Black Lady," gave in to desire. "Her Ladyship embrac'd me several times, stroaking me from my Shoulders to my Waste, both behind and before. At Midnight we went to Bed, and in that Situation I soon forgot the Complexion of my Bedfellow, and obey'd the Dictates of all powerful Nature. Greater Pleasure I never found." She became his companion for the duration of his decade in Guinea.[35]

Joseph Hawkins, who worked on a "Guinea Trader" (a slave ship) in the mid-1790s, took a little longer to adapt to his surroundings than Wheeler did, but he, too, found his assumptions about sexuality and heterosexual relationships stretched. Hawkins could not have anticipated that during his trip to Iboland he would take up with not one, but two women, nor that he would consider them his "wives." But that is just what he did. His account of his travels, published in 1797, offers a soft-core rendition of the moment "that for the first time in my life, I was to repose with the dusky daughters of Africa." The coconut oil lamps were running low of oil as he lay himself on a "large kind of mattress made of cotton, thin but not uncomfortable." He turned to face his "Ebo companions," one "a tall slender and comely but sedate girl," the other a "plump, middle sized wench" who giggled much. That night, he had a "pleasant repose" with the "dusky daughters of Africa." The next morning, he reflected on his newfound situation. It was decidedly "odd." It made him homesick for "my own more favoured country-women."

But in time Hawkins came to appreciate his wives. They took him for walks, seeking "every means to divert and please me, [. . .] by plucking flowers, and fruits, or picking up pieces of broken arrows or lances, and at the same time, pointing at places, and speaking as if I understood every word they said." They were trying to teach him their language, of course. And at first, Hawkins resented being in the position of a student, finding it "very loathsome."

> But after some time, I must confess, the pains they took to please me, and the little efforts they made in the house, with their labour to teach and make me understand their language, soon softened my disgust: from laughing at their folly, I came to like it, and to be thankful for their efforts to excite it—and in short, I soon became so habituated to my situation, as not only to be satisfied, but pleased with it. In fact, I felt a fondness for both my wives, although I reluctantly confess it to the ladies of my former acquaintance.[36]

There was nothing timeless about the fixation that Englishmen and white Americans would develop regarding interracial sex and marriage between Africans and whites. Many other English travelers referred to their African companions just as Hawkins did: as "wives" and "ladies"; some considered themselves to be "husbands" and "married."[37]

Not only did some Englishmen learn to esteem the dark and the light in African skin, its softness and its glow, but some also gained the interpretive nimbleness to comprehend, if not respect, the place of cloth and hair in West African self-presentation. African women's dress and hairstyles were understood by admirers and detractors alike to be essential and inseparable elements of women's public identity. Which, in fact, they were: West Africans considered cloth and plaited hair to be woven arts. Hair and string both could be woven into bodily ornamentation, the former done on a human body and therefore possessing a social and sensual aspect.[38] European men could not help noticing these woven arts. In classically male-chauvinist language, Willem Bosman congratulated African men for their sartorial restraint by comparison with African women's "addict[ion] to sumptuous attire." Like "the female sex" the world over, African women, "even" enslaved women, were vain. "Accordingly, the women's dress is richer than the men's." African "Ladies plat their hair very artfully," bedecking it with "their Fetiches, coral and ivory." They adorned their arms, legs, and waists with "gold chains and string or coral" and dressed according "to their fashions." African women's primping was "skilled" and "artful." It was designed, Bosman thought, to "allure" European men, an undertaking at which African women reputedly were highly successful. "Their greatest power is over those who make no difference betwixt white and black, especially where the former color is not to be found."[39] According to John Matthews, a "full drest" African "lady," dressed in layers of cloth and jewelry, cut "no contemptible figure." She wore a petticoat made from "her common country cloth," a dress of a more luxurious cloth, a head wrap to match, and jewelry everywhere—ears, neck, wrists, and fingers. Her hair would be "neatly and curiously plaited"; sometimes it was "shaved in small circular or crescent formed spots."[40]

Not everyone, it must be noted, thought highly of African women's sartorial choices. Francis Moore thought the women who dolled up with blue-and-white head wraps were all right, but those who "let their Hair hang down on each Side of their Heads" in braids reminded him of horses with plaited manes. So did the women who braided their hair and wore bells atop their heads, a combination that "makes 'em look not unlike the Fore-Horse of a Country Farmer's Team."[41] African women's body ornamentation was skillful, elegant, and seductive. But none of that precluded comparison with European farm animals.

While European men wrangled conflicting thoughts and feelings about African bodies, Africans, of course, had no such chore. "Of all the things in the world," the art historian Sylvia Boone wrote of Mende aesthetics, "*people* are the most beautiful." Of people, Boone found that women were thought of as the most beautiful. "Nothing that has a vagina can be called ugly," says a vivid Mende proverb. Indeed, women were "beauty incarnate"; beauty was female, and women were all beautiful, more and less. It was they who possessed what was arguably everyone's favorite attribute: breasts.

During her field research on Mende beauty ideals in the twentieth century, Sylvia Boone found that "no amount of familiarity with the breast seems to diminish its appeal." Infants nursed from them, children toyed with them, girls and women took pride in them, adult men admired and palpated them. Breasts, Boone found, "are desired and worshipped." Yet, for all that, "perfect breasts are rare in the world." Ideally, breasts should be firm, round, close to the chest ("like a saucer") and thick—neither distended nor protruding. They should not "jiggle or shake even when a girl dances or runs." Needless to say, even girls who had such breasts in their youth bid them adieu after nursing a few babies.[42]

Many commentators claimed that West Africans liked dark skin best, the darker the better. Sir John Mandeville wrote, in one of the earliest published texts in English, that Africans considered dark skin to "hold a great beauty, and aye the blacker they are the fairer they think them." Mandeville wrote, with apparent perplexity, "if they think them not black enough when they are both, they use certain medicines for to make them black withal." Mandeville could not believe that such measures were frequently necessary, for "that country is wonder hot, and that makes the folk thereof so black."[43]

But these commentators may have missed what was happening. Scholarship on color preferences in West Africa suggests that, in the twentieth century, Africans admired skin that was neither very light nor very dark, but brown skin. *Balance* was key. "Beauty" in Africa "is a mean," wrote the renowned historian of African art and aesthetics Robert Farris Thompson. That is, beautiful bodies must be, as one of his informants told him, "neither too tall and not too short, not too black and not too yellow." Thompson found the same emphasis on balance throughout West Africa: "the Akan of the Ivory Coast similarly believe that the beautiful woman is moderate in height, neither as tall as a giraffe nor as short as a pygmy." The Bete of Côte d'Ivoire, like the Kongo, disliked reddened eyes (which were associated with violence and cruelty), but the Bete also had an aversion to eyes that were too white, the color of death. Ideal eyes for Bete and Kongo people should be clear, bright and smiling. Bete insisted that noses ought to be "neither too snubby nor too aquiline," ears "neither too large nor too small." Kongo people preferred skin color of a middling tone. As one of Thompson's informants told him, "a very darkly pigmented skin is not considered beautiful, nor is a fair complexion." Very dark skin was compared to scorched, "sooty *mfilu-*

trees, where a prairie fire has passed." Light skin raised the question of illness originating in the spirit realm: "the mother is considered to have come into contact, for example when bathing, with *nkisi Funza* or *simbi*-spirits." But a person with a shining brown complexion, now *that* "is pleasant to look upon." Balance was important throughout the body. From head to toe, beautiful bodies were harmonious, everything fit together easily with no one part jarringly drawing attention to itself. Beautiful women moved gracefully, with straight posture, flexible hands, swaying hips.[44]

When skin was dark as soot or light like sickness, it was seen to be out of balance and lacking life. West Africans shared with Europeans a love of glowing, shining skin. It was a sign of "vital aliveness." Dull skin resembled dust or dirt, ash or illness; bright, shiny skin was beautiful skin. It was achieved by frequent bathing (once or twice a day) and by the consistent application of oil or, in some regions, shea butter. To keep skin glossy and smooth also required keeping it free of bug bites, fungi, and scars—no easy task in tropical regions. Women should be free of most body hair, which dulled skin's appearance. West Africans also believed that vitality arose from the personality. Beautiful women smiled shyly, were sweet, modest, submissive; West Africans prized many of the same characteristics that European men favored in their African lovers.[45]

Blackness in early modern Africa and Europe was neither prized above all other forms of beauty nor consistently understood to be the very antithesis of the beautiful. Unlike the more consistently negative meaning it would gain in eighteenth- and nineteenth-century America, early European ideas about black bodies were deeply unsettled, containing complex and contradictory meanings. The Africans that early modern Englishmen imagined consisted not of headless or one-eyed people of the ancient and medieval past, nor of people who were uniformly hideous to look at. Instead, African bodies were diverse: black and tawny, sinful and hospitable, crooked and symmetrical, scarred and soft, graceful and slavish, foul and clean, loose bodied and hardy, wanton and sweet, naked and well dressed, beastly and beautiful.[46] At points, European men even shared beauty ideals with West Africans: people of both continents adored cheerfulness in women and warmed to their smiles. They esteemed graceful, straight bodies; bright skin; the elegance and status of cloth. They shared, to different degrees, the notion that beauty existed primarily among women. Of course, unlike Africans, European men also thought Africans were suspiciously close to animals, entirely too "naked," and darker than could be pure.

The unsettled attitudes of European male travelers to Africa would not, however, survive their journeys into the slave trade. Over the eighteenth and nineteenth centuries and in America, ambivalence would largely disappear as certainty and scientificity displaced the earlier contradictions. When American scientists invented their own concept of race, they did so by defining black bodies as, among other things, singularly ugly.

NOTES

1. Richard Jobson, *The Discovery of the River Gambra*, edited by David P. Gamble and P. E. H. Hair (1623; London: Hakluyt Society, 1999), 100–104; Arnold Hughes and David Perfect, *The Historical Dictionary of the Gambia* (Lanham, Md.: Scarecrow Press, 2008), 40; David P. Gamble and P. E. H. Hair, introduction, in Gamble and Hair, *Discovery of the River Gambra*, 44, 64.

2. Richard Ligon, *A True and Exact History of the Island of Barbados* (1657, 1673; London: Frank Cass, 1970), 12–13; Jennifer L. Morgan, *Laboring Women: Reproduction and Gender in New World Slavery* (Philadelphia: University of Pennsylvania Press, 2004), 13.

3. Ligon, *True and Exact History*, 15–17.

4. De Marees quoted in Morgan, *Laboring Women*, 31.

5. Wheeler in William Smith, *A New Voyage to Guinea: Describing the Customs, Manners, Soil, Climate, . . .* (London: Printed for John Nourse, 1745), 252, 263–64, 255; Smith, *New Voyage to Guinea*, 211; Willem Bosman, *A New and Accurate Description of the Coast of Guinea, . . .* (London: J. Knapton et al., 1705), 122.

6. Ligon quoted in Stephanie Smallwood, *Saltwater Slavery: A Middle Passage from Africa to American Diaspora* (Cambridge, Mass.: Harvard University Press, 2007), 158; John Atkins, *A Voyage to Guinea, Brasil, and the West-Indies* (London: Printed for Caesar Ward and Richard Chandler, 1735), 179; Joseph Hawkins, *A History of a Voyage to the Coast of Africa* (Troy: Printed for the Author by Luther Pratt, 1797), 86; Smallwood, *Saltwater Slavery*, 160–61. On commodification in American slavery, see Walter Johnson, *Soul by Soul: Inside the Antebellum Slave Market* (Cambridge, Mass.: Harvard University Press, 1999); Edward E. Baptist, "'Cuffy,' 'Fancy Maids,' and 'One-Eyed Men': Rape, Commodification, and the Domestic Slave Trade in the United States," *American Historical Review* 106, no. 5 (2001): 1619–50; Smallwood, *Saltwater Slavery*.

7. On African women's appearance, see Jobson, *Discovery of the River Gambra*, 100–101; John Adams, *Sketches Taken during Ten Voyages to Africa, . . .* (London: Hurst, Robinson, and Co., 1822), 6–8; Charles Wheeler in Smith, *New Voyage to Guinea*, 253.

8. Francis Moore, *Travels into the Inland Parts of Africa* (London: Edward Cave, 1738), 131; Atkins, *Voyage to Guinea*, 49–50.

9. Ligon, *True and Exact History*, 51. See also Richard Bright journal in *Guinea Journals: Journeys into Guinea-Conakry during the Sierra Leone Phase, 1800–1821*, ed. Bruce L. Mouser (Washington, D.C.: University Press of America, 1979), 55.

10. P. E. H. Hair, "Attitudes to Africans in English Primary Sources on Guinea up to 1650," *History in Africa* 26 (1999): 59; Kathleen M. Brown, *Good Wives, Nasty Wenches, and Anxious Patriarchs: Gender, Race, and Power in Colonial Virginia* (Chapel Hill: University of North Carolina Press, 1996); Morgan, *Laboring Women*, 14; Kathleen M.

Brown, *Foul Bodies: Cleanliness in Early America* (New Haven, Conn.: Yale University Press, 2009). Joyce Chaplin found a similar rise in criticism of Indian uses of their bodies after the 1650s. See Joyce E. Chaplin, *Subject Matter: Technology, the Body, and Science on the Anglo-American Frontier, 1500–1676* (Cambridge, Mass.: Harvard University Press, 2001), 243–79.

11. James Bruce cited in Samuel Stanhope Smith, *Essay on the Causes of Variety of Complexion and Figure in the Human Species* (New Brunswick, N.J.: J. Simpson, 1810), 140.

12. Adams, *Sketches*, 7–8, 21–23.

13. Joseph Hawkins, *History of a Voyage*, 86.

14. A. M. Falconbridge, *Narrative of Two Voyages to the River Sierra Leone during the Years 1791–1793* (London: Printed for L. I. Higham, 1802), 40, 44.

15. John Matthews, *A Voyage to the River Sierra Leone* (London: Printed for B. White & Son, 1791), 92–93, 98.

16. Smith, *New Voyage to Guinea*, 213; Bosman, *New and Accurate Description*, 395.

17. François Bernier, "A New Division of the Earth" (1684), reprinted in *History Workshop Journal* 51 (spring 2001): 247–50. On Bernier's standing in the history of racism, see Siep Stuurman, "François Bernier and the Invention of Racial Classification," *History Workshop Journal* 50 (2000): 1–21; and Pierre H. Boulle, "François Bernier and the Origins of the Modern Concept of Race," in *The Color of Liberty: Histories of Race in France*, ed. Sue Peabody and Tyler Stovall (Durham, N.C.: Duke University Press, 2003), 11.

18. Bernier, "New Division of the Earth," 249.

19. Adams, *Sketches*, 41.

20. Hawkins, *History of a Voyage*, 86; William Snelgrave, *A New Account of Some Parts of Guinea and the Slave-Trade* (1734; London: Frank Cass, 1971), 51.

21. Georges Louis Buffon, *Buffon's Natural History* (1749–1804; London: J. S. Barr, 1792), 283–84, 289.

22. Georges Louis Le Clerc (Count de Buffon), *Histoire Naturelle* (1749–1804; London: n.p., 1792), 69; Buffon, *Buffon's Natural History*, 283–84, 289.

23. Charles Wheeler's account is reproduced in Smith, *New Voyage to Guinea*, 253.

24. Matthews, *Voyage to the River*, 92.

25. Buffon, *Buffon's Natural History*, 280.

26. François Leguat quoted in J. F. Blumenbach, "Observations on the Bodily Conformation and Mental Capacity of the Negroes," *Philosophical Magazine* 3 (1799): 141–47, 144.

27. Wheeler quoted in Smith, *New Voyage to Guinea*, 253; Thomas Gray quoted in Chaplin, *Subject Matter*, 190.

28. Wheeler in Smith, *New Voyage to Guinea*, 252–53.

29. "Every man hath his whore" quote in John K. Thornton, *Africa and Africans in the Making of the Atlantic World, 1400–1800*, 2nd ed. (New York: Cambridge University Press, 1998), 66; Jobson, *Discovery of the River Gambra*, 97; Ligon, *True and Exact History*, 9–10; Francis Moore, *Travels into the Inland Parts*, 121; P. E. H. Hair, *The Atlantic Slave Trade and Black Africa* (London: Historical Association, 1978), 14–15;

Gamble and Hair, introduction, 97; Charles Wheeler in Smith, *New Voyage to Guinea*, 253; Charles W. Thomas, *Adventures and Observations on the West Coast of Africa* (New York: Derby & Jackson, 1860), 199, 222.

30. Bosman, *New and Accurate Description*, 424; Emmanuel Akyeampong, "Sexuality and Prostitution among the Akan of the Gold Coast, c. 1650–1950," *Past and Present* 156 (1997): 146–51, 156, 163. "Institutionalized rape" quote attributed to Adam Jones in Akosua Adomako Ampofo, "The Sex Trade, Globalisation and Issues of Survival in Subsaharan Africa," *Research Review of the Institute of African Studies* 17, no. 2 (2001): 30. "Prostituting themselves" and "in flower" quotes from Bosman, *New and Accurate Description*, 424.

31. Atkins, *Voyage to Guinea*, 39–40; Bosman, *New and Accurate Description*, 539; Akyeampong, "Sexuality and Prostitution," 163.

32. George E. Brooks, *Eurafricans in Western Africa: Commerce, Social Status, Gender, and Religious Observance from the Sixteenth to the Eighteenth Century* (Athens: Ohio University Press, 2003), 28, 29, 56, 71, 141; Smith, *New Voyage to Guinea*, 94; Wheeler in Smith, *New Voyage to Guinea*, 251–52. See also Ligon, *True and Exact History*, 9–10; Bruce L. Mouser, introduction, in *Guinea Journals*, 7–8.

33. Bosman, *New and Accurate Description*, 422; Wheeler in Smith, *New Voyage to Guinea*, 252.

34. Smith, *New Voyage to Guinea*, 183–84.

35. Wheeler in ibid., 244–45, 253.

36. Hawkins, *History of a Voyage*, 13, 69–71, 85.

37. Jobson, *Discovery of the River Gambra*, 97; Smith, *New Voyage to Guinea*, 252; Hawkins, *History of a Voyage*, 71, 85, 69–70; Atkins, *Voyage to Guinea*, 94.

38. Mariane C. Ferme, *The Underneath of Things: Violence, History, and the Everyday in Sierra Leone* (Berkeley: University of California Press, 2001), 49–59.

39. Bosman, *New and Accurate Description*, 387–88.

40. Matthews, *Voyage to the River*, 108–9.

41. Moore, *Travels into the Inland Parts*, 75.

42. Sylvia Boone, *Radiance from the Waters: Ideals of Feminine Beauty in Mende Art* (New Haven, Conn.: Yale University Press, 1986), 82, 102–7.

43. Sir John Mandeville quoted in Alden Vaughn and Virginia Mason Vaughn, "Before Othello: Elizabethan Representations of Sub-Saharan Africans," *William and Mary Quarterly* 3rd series, 54, no. 1 (1997): 19–44, 22–23.

44. Robert Farris Thompson, *African Art in Motion: Icon and Act* (Berkeley: University of California Press, 1974), 26, 49–52; Robert Farris Thompson, *Flash of the Spirit: African and Afro-American Art and Philosophy* (New York: Vintage Books, 1984), 5; Boone, *Radiance from the Waters*, 89, 120, 122–29. Also see Lynn M. Thomas, "Chapter One: Cosmetic Practices and Colonial Crucibles," in *A History of Skin Lighteners in South Africa and Beyond*, Duke University Press, forthcoming.

45. Thompson, *African Art in Motion*, 9; Boone, *Radiance from the Waters*, xix, 48, 151 n76, 120, 132; Marlene Elias, "African Shea Butter: A Feminized Subsidy from Nature," *Africa* 77, no. 1 (2007): 37–62. Sylvia Boone's scholarship is based on field re-

search conducted during the 1970s and 1980s. She found that it had historical precedents and that many of her conclusions held true for as far back as the era of the slave trade. See Boone, *Radiance from the Waters*, 23–25, 143.

46. See also Jennifer L. Morgan, "'Some Could Suckle over Their Shoulders': Male Travelers, Female Bodies, and the Gendering of Racial Ideology," in *Laboring Women*; and Brown, *Foul Bodies*.

CHAPTER 2

Toiling in the Fields

Valuing Female Slaves in Jamaica, 1674–1788

TREVOR BURNARD

Affy was born into slavery in 1767, and later baptized by her owners as Sarah Af-fir. She was still alive, age sixty-six, an old woman by Jamaican standards, when emancipation came in 1834. She lived on Mesopotamia Estate in western Jamaica. Mesopotamia produced sugar and rum, which meant that for much of her life, certainly for the period in which she had her six children (a very large number for an enslaved Jamaican woman in the latter half of the eighteenth century), Affy was involved in planting, growing, and harvesting cane. She started work at age seven in the gang of young, largely unskilled slaves who weeded the lawns. Af-ter escaping that work briefly for a few years in her early teens, she graduated to working in the second field gang (each gang involved slaves employed in growing sugar). From age sixteen until age thirty-one, she was assigned to the Great Gang. In this occupation, she shared the fate of 85 percent of adult women on Meso-potamia of doing the most onerous and backbreaking work within the Jamaican plantation economy. During her time as a member of the Great Gang, working from sunrise to sunset, six days a week, she had four black and two mixed-race children. The black children followed her into the field. Her two daughters had lives perhaps more typical of female enslaved women in Jamaica than that of Affy. Both Princess and Hagar died in adulthood—Princess at twenty-six and Hagar at forty-one—and neither had children. By 1798, when Affy was thirty-one, the years of toil had destroyed her health. She was listed as "weakly" in one of the inventories that provide what little information about her life we have. By 1803 she had to be removed from the field to work as a washerwoman and then as a nanny for children and a seamstress. By 1824, age fifty-seven, she was an invalid, afflicted by scrofula. The last mention in the records that we have of her came in 1833 when she was considered "worthless" by her employers, being assigned a value of £0, down from the £85 she would have fetched if she had been sold off the estate when she was a "prime" field hand in her twenties. That value of £0 is a poignant reminder of how slave owners' managerial strategies, which on

Mesopotamia involved concentrating more and more females after 1800 into the demanding tasks of sugar cultivation, wrecked women's lives and their health.[1]

Few groups in human history have been more interested in profit seeking, more interested in developing, measuring, and improving the human capital investments that they had, and less concerned about the morality with which they treated the human capital that they had than Jamaican slave owners in the eighteenth century.[2] As the eighteenth-century historian Charles Leslie declared, "no Country excels them in a barbarous Treatment of Slaves, or in the cruel Methods they put them to death." They also excelled in the infant discipline of human capital evaluation. A study of early accounting methods on British West Indian plantations suggests that the accounting methods used were highly effective in monitoring and evaluating labor. A study of such practices, it is suggested, shows that planters in the West Indies had a greater concern for short-term economic performance than for moral and social considerations.[3]

No other slave society in the Americas, with the possible exception of early nineteenth-century British Guiana, worked their enslaved people so hard and with so little concern about how enslaved people coped.[4] White Jamaicans were not only assiduous in working slaves as hard as they could, they were also increasingly successful in implementing accounting systems that measured their human capital more comprehensively and more effectively than was the case in any industry before well into the nineteenth century. During the eighteenth century, planters worked out means whereby they made use of an increasingly large number of items of agency information in order to make increasingly more accurate and increasingly detailed assessments of the individual characteristics of enslaved people so that they could value them more precisely.[5] By the middle of the eighteenth century, the pricing of slaves was becoming more precise and more detailed. The majority of enslaved people were listed by name in slave lists and were individually priced with relatively little lumping of prices around predetermined values. In other words, when slaves were priced in an inventory, the prices varied considerably within a listing. Thus, in the inventory of Samuel Orr, from 1779, his 132 slaves were listed one after another by price, with the prices of women working the field varying from £40 for the cheapest and thus least valuable to £90 for the most valuable. Consequently, Celia, valued at £85 was followed immediately by Dido, valued at £70, and then by Quasheba (noted as "old") at £45 and Chloe at £90. The three "housewenches" were valued at the end of a list of field women and were valued more highly than other enslaved women. Maria was considered to be worth £100, while Grace and Mulatto Nancy were each valued at £120.

From the 1730s, appraisers of inventoried estates increased the information they presented in inventories about individual slaves so that enslaved people were differentiated by such things as health and occasionally by age and presumed ethnicity. Appraisers almost always differentiated by gender, with lists of slaves customarily dividing men from women and girls from boys. We have no description of how appraisers went about the process of evaluating the values they assigned to individual men, women, and children. The composition of inventories, however, with their monotonous lists of enslaved people, listed by name and price, one after another, in large batches suggests that appraisers followed a common practice of calling enslaved people together, dividing them by gender and then by occupation before inspecting each enslaved person minutely and assigning a value, based on their perception of an individual's age, health, and capacity, to each slave they saw. The order by which groups of enslaved people were assessed reflects white Jamaicans' understanding of hierarchies within slave communities. The standard list of a slave labor force started off with men, headed by drivers and then by tradesmen, before listing field workers and ending usually with the superannuated men, followed by women, usually more undifferentiated than men, given that the vast majority of women were field workers, and ending with boys, girls, and occasionally children. In most cases, women with "suckling" children were listed alongside other women without any notice in price being given to the infant child (who by this definition had no independent value).[6]

One indication of the hard-headedness and calculating business sense of Jamaican slave owners was their determination to get as much value out of enslaved women's labor as they could. Indeed, Jennifer Morgan has argued that one explanation for the introduction of slavery into the West Indies is that African women—who tended to be the primary field workers in Africa—were quickly introduced as field workers on West Indian plantations, inverting a "gender ideology that applied to white women and work" whereby white women did not work in the field and thus entailing "a fundamental restructuring of the notion of women's work."[7] From the start, West Indian planters were innovative, by European standards, in not differentiating between men and women as field workers. Indeed, in early Jamaican listings of slaves in inventories, men and women were listed indiscriminately, suggesting that slave owners saw little difference in the work capacities of men and women.[8] Such lack of gender differentiation in gangs on sugar estates became customary. Planters divided slaves by physical capacity but not by sex: they insisted that the "stoutest and most able slaves ... without any regard being had to their sex" should do the hardest work, such as digging cane holes, doing dunging and cutting, and harvesting cane. David Collins in 1803 insisted that there are "many women who are capable of as much labour as man, and some men, of constitutions so delicate, as to be incapable of toil as the weakest women."[9] By the early eighteenth century, women not only worked in the field doing hard work as much as men, but they also became the majority of field hands on sugar plantations. Women and men were hired at the same rate by plantations needing extra labor, suggesting that there was little differentiation in what they did as ordinary field laborers on estates. Moreover, there was no technical reason women could have not have been trained in high-value occupations such as boilers or carpenters.[10]

The question to ask, given the above information, is why Jamaican slave owners consistently discounted females when pricing slaves when they had few reasons to think of female slaves as less valuable than male slaves. (I use "males" to refer to both adult men and male children. Similarly, I refer to "females" when discussing both adult women and female children. Children were considered adults around the age of sixteen.) Tables 2.1 and 2.2 show that females were worth less than males, both on their arrival on the island on slave ships and also when put to work in occupations in the countryside and in the town.[11] Moreover, the gender differential in favor of males and especially men increased considerably over time, especially as more elaborate accounting systems for valuing slaves developed in the late eighteenth century.[12] In the late seventeenth century, the gender differential between men and women was relatively small—13.8 percent. By the early eighteenth century, this differential had increased to 17 percent. The real increase in gender differentials came in the 1730s and lasted until at least the 1780s. It reached a peak of 36 percent for slave listings made between 1735 and 1744 but remained very high, even if declining until the mid-1780s. The gap in the price of men over women remained stubbornly over 25 percent from the 1730s onward.

Several reasons suggest themselves to answer the question posed above. First, the nature of the work experience and the extent of gender discrimination against women by mostly male planters, especially in agriculture, made it difficult for women to attain positions that were valued highly in the marketplace (which, of course, was a marketplace shaped mostly by what white male planters thought most important and which did not necessarily correspond to the elusive concept of what was actually "valuable," such as the amount of money produced for planters by any worker). The slaves who attracted the highest values in inventories were drivers and tradesmen: virtually no woman became a driver, and the trades were entirely closed off to women. Thus, most women became field workers, with fewer than 15 percent of adult women workers in non–field work occupations. Female slaves working outside of the plantation economy, in places like Kingston, tended to be seamstresses and washerwomen. Urban male slaves found employment on the wharf, within the transport sector, or as tradesmen, all

TABLE 2.1

Prices of Slaves by Gender, Jamaica 1775–1787

Price, £	Slaves, total no.	Males, no.	Males, %	Males, cumulative number by %	Females, no.	Females, %	Females, cumulative number by %
200–50	13	13	1.8	1.8	0	0	0
150–70	29	29	3.9	5.7	0	0	0
130–40	53	51	6.9	12.6	0	0	0
110–20	59	59	8.0	20.6	0	0	0
100	144	81	11.0	31.5	62	9.3	9.3
90–95	143	68	9.2	40.7	77	12.6	20.9
80–85	144	58	7.8	48.6	86	12.9	33.8
70–75	132	65	8.8	57.4	67	10.1	43.9
60–65	99	43	5.8	63.2	56	8.4	52.3
50–55	114	48	6.5	69.7	54	8.1	60.5
40–45	124	66	8.9	78.6	58	8.7	69.2
30–35	78	28	3.8	82.4	46	6.9	76.1
20–25	99	41	5.5	88.0	48	7.2	80.3
10–18	84	34	4.6	92.6	50	7.5	90.8
Under 10	98	43	5.8	98.4	55	8.3	99.1
0	18	12	1.6	100.0	6	0.9	100.0

SOURCE: Slave databases as described in chapter endnote 2. Prices are in Jamaica currency. The conversion to sterling is £1.40:£1.00. John J. McCusker, *How Much Is That in Real Money? A Historical Commodity Price Index for Use as a Deflator of Money Values in the Economy of the United States*, 2nd ed. (Worcester, Mass.: American Antiquarian Society, 2001), 246–54.

TABLE 2.2

Slave Prices and Gender Differentials in the Jamaican Slave Population, 1675–1784

Years	Men, %	Women, %	Boys, %	Girls, %	MVOW, %	BVOG, %	MVOB, %	MVOG, %
1675–1700	17.6	15.14	8.95	7.16	13.8	20.0	49.0	52.7
1700–1724	22.3	18.46	10.96	8.76	17.0	20.1	50.7	52.5
1725–35	18.7	16.12	10.10	8.08	14.0	20.0	46.1	49.9
1735–44	23.0	14.70	9.70	7.84	36.0	19.2	57.8	46.7
1745–54	31.1	21.33	13.52	11.2	31.4	17.4	56.5	47.6
1755–64	37.8	25.28	17.84	14.7	33.2	17.5	52.9	41.8
1765–74	40.8	29.86	20.66	16.9	26.8	18.1	49.4	43.3
1775–84	51.1	37.91	25.28	20.1	25.8	20.5	50.5	47.0

SOURCE: Inventories, 1B11/3/1–65. The columns Men, Women, Boys, and Girls indicate the percentage of enslaved people noted as belonging to each category of person. The figures do not add up to 100 percent since, especially before the second half of the eighteenth century, enslaved people were often not distinguished by age or gender. In general, slaves over the age of fifteen who were in full-time employment were considered adult "men" and "women."
MVOW = Percentage by which men were valued more than women
BVOG = Percentage by which boys were valued more than girls
MVOB = Percentage by which men were valued more than boys
WVOG = Percentage by which women were valued more than girls

of which were relatively highly valued and which also provided means whereby they could augment earnings by private work.[13] The gender differential between males and females in urban environments was particularly high. Second, slave owners demonstrated a clear gender bias toward males and against females, reflecting a wide acceptance of patriarchy as a value that operated not only in white society but also within slave communities as well. Slave owners favored slave men as leaders over women and children and even when there were no obvious advantages for slave owners in having their slaves male rather than female—as in the fields—they tended to value more highly what males did over the value they placed on female labor.

The extremely wealthy planter and attorney Simon Taylor made planters' bias clear when he advised his fellow planter and client Chaloner Arcedeckne that "You want Men infinitely more than Women, for there are many things which Women cannot do, as Cutting Copperwood, Wainmen, Boilers, Distillers, Stokers, Mulemen etc."[14] In part, slave owners' gendered attitudes made it axiomatic that what women did would be devalued. Because more women did field work than men, this activity, even though it often involved quite a lot of skill in certain areas and was physically very demanding, was often denigrated as both unmanly and also unimportant. By contrast, slave owners thought that what men did was automatically more valuable than what women tended to do.[15]

Finally, slave owners valued slaves, at least during the period before abolition when the supply of new slaves from Africa was abundant, almost solely for their productive rather than for their reproductive potential. Until at least the 1770s, children were priced so low for their value to be close to nominal. Indeed, women's reproductive role was close to totally discounted. The evidence suggests strongly that, before the 1780s, slave owners not only preferred to buy rather than breed fresh additions of slaves but also that they considered pregnancy a sickness and the production of children by their enslaved women to detract from their primary value, which was mostly as field hands doing hard manual labor.

But why did slave owners concentrate so much on improving the human capital implicit in men rather than in women? It is true that in the most significant area of the economy—the large, integrated plantation sector—slave owners were able to increase greatly their investment in women as well as their investment in men. The increases in both women's and men's values on large plantations were dramatic. The data in tables 2.3 and 2.4 show that the increase in the value of adult men was 166 percent and that of adult women was 169 percent over the whole period of this study, and 96 and 88 percent, respectively, for the period after 1700. The differential between the price of adult men and the price of adult women on large estates, most of which would have been sugar plantations,

TABLE 2.3

Average Price by Age, Jamaica 1775–88, Healthy Slaves Only

Age	Men, no.	Avg. Price, £	Women, no.	Avg. Price, £	Difference, £
66+	2	26.81	1	28.57	−1.76
45–65	37	53.47	29	46.06	7.41
25–44	245	76.31	174	58.89	17.42
15–24	135	66.48	120	48.69	17.79
5–14	85	34.87	64	31.36	3.51
<5	53	11.71	58	10.78	0.93
15–44	473	64.34	412	50.10	14.24
TOTAL	557	59.76	458	47.76	12.00

SOURCE: Slave databases as described in endnote 2. This table lists the prices given for 557 slaves whose precise age is noted in the records. Very few slaves were listed by age in Jamaican records, hence the small sample size.

TABLE 2.4

Average Price by Occupation and Gender,
Healthy Adults Aged 20–40, Jamaica 1775–88

Gender/Occupation	Number	Avg. Price, £
All men	291	53.86
Tradesmen/drivers	93	71.65
Field men	198	45.52
All women	229	42.96
Domestics	24	45.17
Field women	205	42.71

SOURCE: Slave databases as described in endnote 2.

neither increased nor decreased. Given that productivity in sugar cultivation rose appreciably from midcentury, and given that women were disproportionately numbered among the ganged laborers who were responsible for that remarkable rise in productivity, the differential in prices between adult men and adult women on large estates should have shrunk.

Why it did not shrink is unclear. It is possible that field men were valued more than field women both because they were more usually chosen as work leaders and also because when certain tasks—such as building or construction work— were to be done, men tended to be chosen to do this rather than women.[16] Of course, this is a circular argument: because men did certain kinds of work, that work was then valued more highly just because men did it. Table 2.4 gives the price differentials between men and women, with the main factor influencing prices being the very high values assigned to tradesmen. But the evidence from inventories suggests that such circular thinking indeed applied in the assignment of values placed on individual slaves. Whether planters were right in thinking that men produced more income and thus should be valued more for purposes of resale requires more detailed investigation through examination of productivity and income production on individual estates. The limited evidence available about what income was produced in what kind of work suggests that planters valued field workers too low and tradespeople too highly. David W. Ryden suggests that productivity gains and increases in plantation incomes came mainly through agricultural innovation, mostly in the production of tropical crops, more and more of which were produced by women as men were assigned to other tasks.[17]

In addition, women were more likely to do low-status jobs such as weeding than were men. Outside the large plantation, planters tended to place more importance on increasing the value of men than of women, with the value of enslaved men belonging to planters increasing 185 percent from 1674 to 1784, and 130 percent after 1700, while the value of enslaved women advanced less rapidly, the respective figures being 141 and 103 percent in the same period. Overall, men working in agriculture became more valuable over time in relation to women. Whether this relative increase in the value of men as priced in inventories compared with women reflects real differences in the productivity rates of men is unclear. What is important is that planters thought men more valuable than women and indicated their gender preferences in slave valuations. This gender bias had an impact on how planters went about increasing human capital within slaveholdings, with males the focus of human capital increases rather than females.

Were white Jamaicans correct to value women less than men? Was what women did as workers in fact less valuable than what men did? To an extent it was less valuable because women were not able to move out of the field in order to do skilled work that was either deemed more valuable or was in fact (though this is unproven) more valuable than work in the field. More importantly, planters' devaluation of female work had a self-fulfilling function. Women could have been trained to be masons or boilers or drivers. Instead they were given the worst jobs on the plantation, especially dunging and cane holing. The effect on their health was serious. David W. Ryden shows in analyzing an early nineteenth-century planter's slave force that the values of females declined dramatically after their "prime" in their twenties and early thirties. He argues that the divergence in price among field slaves after slaves reached past the age of thirty can be explained by the harshness of the tasks assigned them. They were never released from the field to less demanding occupations. They continued to work in the occupations that historians have shown were the most physically demanding and the most sapping of health.[18] Planter management strategies ensured that female health would suffer as they got older. Significantly, much of the damage to women's health was done when women were in their prime childbearing years. There were a greater number of older women who were unhealthy than there were older enslaved men who suffered ailments.[19] Applying survival analysis techniques to mortality patterns on Mesopotamia Estate, Simon D. Smith and Mark Forster have shown that the labor regime that women endured exerted a large and quantifiable effect on female mortality that became worse relative to men after 1800, just as the percentage of field workers who were women rose from around 44 percent between 1762 and 1792 to 52 percent female from 1809 to 1834. This increase was most likely caused by women's growing involvement in cane growing. Increased exposure to field labor reduced a woman's likely survival rate by about 30 percent.[20]

But even if slave owners did not value the work that women did as highly as they did the work of men, why did they not put a value on other aspects of female life? Women were not just producers; they were reproducers. They were also sexual objects. That slave women were readily available for sexual exploitation was hugely important to white men, who felt that exploitation of slave women was one of the advantages pertaining to being white and male in Jamaica. Indeed, the raping and sexual exploitation of slave women was endemic in eighteenth-century Jamaica, even if slave owners knew that the fact that they and white underlings could rape slave women with impunity seriously compromised smooth management of estates.[21]

Was there any value placed on reproduction? A body of literature has grown up that assumes that planters placed high values on women's reproductive potential. In the main, this literature bases its arguments on common sense—the common sense that any owner of slaves would appreciate the essentially "free" additions to a slave force that children would bring. Consequently, it has become almost axiomatic not only that slave women actively sought abortifacients to abort children but also that such abortions were a form of resistance against slavery.[22] It might be possible that slave women had abortions as a means of demonstrating some sort of control over their bodies or as a form of self-defiance, although that flies in the face of the high value placed on motherhood within African societies as a mark of defining what becoming a woman meant. It is certainly true that some enslaved women had abortions. If they did so, however, they did so for reasons that were unrelated to what their owners thought of such actions.[23]

If women thought procuring abortions would alarm slave owners, they were wrong, at least before amelioration began in the last two decades of the eighteenth century. Slave owners were at best indifferent and usually hostile to women producing children. They knew that good treatment allowed women to breed more successfully. Edward Long, for example, claimed "that those Negroes breed the best, whose labour is least, or easiest" and lamented that on sugar estates, where reproductive rates were lower than elsewhere, "but few children will be brought up . . . whatever number may be born; for the mothers will not have sufficient time to take due care of them."[24] From long practice, however, women were given little time before the birth to prepare themselves for childbirth; did not receive sufficient nutrition to be able to bear children with ease, especially as male field workers ate most of the animal protein available; and were forced back into the fields before children were weaned.[25] Both Richard Ligon in Barbados in 1647 and Hans Sloane in Jamaica in the late 1680s indicated that women went back to work either one week or at most two weeks after childbirth.[26]

That practice of making nursing women work soon after giving birth continued throughout the eighteenth century. Even in the nineteenth century, the lack of time allowed pregnant women to recover from childbirth and planter resentment at slave women's practices with children, such as lengthy lactation, was a major source of friction between slave owners and women.[27] Planters would have greatly preferred women not to become pregnant. It harmed women's health and sometimes resulted in death for women as well as for their children. It certainly resulted in large numbers of miscarriages. Amanda Thornton has done a detailed study of women's fertility patterns in the well-documented slave force of Thomas Thistlewood. She shows not only that miscarriages were frequent but that infant mortality was probably around 420 infant deaths per 1,000 births, which is extraordinarily high, even by eighteenth-century standards.[28]

Slave owners were probably right, if callous, to discourage women from getting pregnant, at least in the period prior to 1788 before abolitionist pressures made the politics of child-rearing more complicated for slave owners and after which date they had to at least show some concern with managing pregnancies and for trying to increase the number of children born and raised into adulthood.[29] But before 1788, the pregnancies of enslaved women hardly ever resulted in additional inputs of labor into the plantation. We are handicapped by the lack of evidence about children in West Indian slave societies (the lack of evidence in itself says something about slave owners' indifference to children). We do not even know, except in rare circumstances, how many children women had and how many survived past infancy. Moreover, we do not even know how many children were born into slavery in Jamaica and how many were transported to Jamaica through the slave trade. Probably most children were born in Jamaica. The only slave listing that details ethnicity for children under the age of fifteen, for the slaves on the York estate of William Gale, suggests that 113 were born in Jamaica and 6 were born in Africa.[30]

How then do we answer why slave women were valued less highly than men, even when women were worked very hard and were probably very productive? There are three possible answers. It may be that women did less valuable work than men. As already discussed, that seems unlikely, given the value that was provided by women working very hard in cane fields. Also as discussed, it may have been due to unthinking sexist assumptions that saw whatever man did as valuable and whatever women did as less valuable. It also may have been connected to issues of social control. Men were valued more than women because if they were not placated, then they might use physical resistance against enslavement. For that reason, slave owners advocated that privileged slaves, all of whom were men, would be "particularly encouraged, and invested with some authority over the rest of the Negroes."[31]

The nature of the sources used in this chapter does not allow for a definitive answer to this question. But an examination of white attitudes toward gender supports an interpretation that the reason that women were valued less than men revolves around a modified version of social control. White men were frightened by black men, and although they tried to tell themselves that when black men were courageous and unflinching under the worst kinds of torture that this reflected their unfeeling animalistic nature, they were inclined to doubt the efficacy of such an interpretation. Certainly, white Jamaicans' response to Tacky's Revolt (a large slave rebellion, headed by enslaved men, in 1760) indicates that white Jamaicans had very complicated responses to the stoicism that black men exhibited under torture.[32] Moreover, African males' ability to withstand or at least endure torture and violence directed against them made slave owners realize that they could not control slave men solely through violent means. Slave men needed to be bought off with positions of authority. Just as importantly, they needed to be bought off through allowing slave men to exercise in Jamaica the kind of patriarchal authority over women that they had exercised in Africa. A belief in patriarchy united black and white men. But in Jamaica, patriarchy had an unusual valence. The patriarchy of white men was that of unrestrained power and sexual opportunism. A white man was expected to fornicate with black women, drink excessively, gamble, fight, and cow dependents—not least black men— through the constant and arbitrary application of violence and terror.[33] But when white men had sexual relations with black women who were the wives of enslaved men, black men fought back. In particular, black men could draw on shared patriarchal values that made clear to white men that they should not meddle with established enslaved marital relations.[34]

White men believed that authority should be in the hands of men and assumed that slave men would be leaders in the slave community. They gave them the best jobs and allowed them authority over slave women. As long as slave men's authority did not interfere with the ability of white men to do as they pleased on plantations, masters were happy to allow black men to exercise a degree of patriarchal dominance.[35] Planters expected men to be dominant and organized their work forces so that slave men had more power than slave women. What little evidence we have from slaves directly about the proper gender balance of power suggests also that black men expected to be bosses within their own patriarchal kingdoms.[36]

White men's pursuit of black women then was problematic in a society with shared patriarchal assumptions. Slave owners needed to show black men in particular that they were strong, virile men who ruled as they pleased the little kingdoms of white autocracy that were Jamaican plantations. What better way was there for white men to show who was in control than for them to have the pick of black women whenever they chose?[37] But, as white men knew, their violation of slave women breached a common understanding held by both black men and white men that men had a measure of patriarchal dominance over women of their own color. Black men were pushed into rebellion when white men infringed on their patriarchal and sexual rights. John Taylor, an early chronicler of life in Jamaica, argued as early as 1687 that while black men could only be controlled through violence, it was also necessary to ensure them access to black women. He argued that "After a planter hath purchased some twenty, thirty or more Negroa slaves, he first gives to each man a wife, without which they will not be contented, or worke. Then he gives to each man and his wife one half accre of land for them to cleare for themselves."[38]

Masters were convinced that supporting male authority was the way to prevent discord in the slave quarters. They made men heads of household and accepted that slave men had rights over their wives and children, analogous to what they considered to be their own rights over white women and white and colored children. Yet slave patriarchy was a tender fruit, always likely to be stamped out by masters' assertions of authority and by the overwhelming presumption that white Jamaicans made in favor of white men indulging their every desire. In short, when we ask why black women were valued less than black men in the valuations that slave owners made, we can start to understand the apparent contradictions implicit in slave owners not maximizing their investments in slave women through connecting the pricing of women to a larger context of white men maintaining not just white but also black patriarchy.

The consequences of white men affirming some degree of black men's authority over women, conflicted though this was by the constraints placed on any slave exercising authority within a slave system controlled by violence from white men, were significant for black women in the period of African slavery. The most important consequence was that women were increasingly limited in the kinds of work they did. They found it much harder to escape work in the fields than did men, as can be reflected in the price differentials assigned to women rather than men in inventories. They appear to have started work in the fields slightly earlier than men (being assigned to the hardest working field gangs two or three years before men) and seldom escaped such work while they were in their most fertile years. The result was very low fertility, considerable reproductive problems, and little assistance, at least from white managers and overseers, in combining the arduous task of raising children in slavery while doing backbreaking field work.

The sad story of Abba, one of Thomas Thistlewood's slaves, shows just how difficult it was to be a mother and a worker in mid-eighteenth-century Jamaica. Purchased in 1758 as a young girl arriving from Africa, she was Thistlewood's property until he died in 1786. Her thirteen pregnancies resulted in ten live births and six surviving children. The work that she did in the field reduced her health so much that she could not provide for her children through working in her family's provision fields when she wasn't working in the cane field. Thistlewood tried to assist her by having her taught to be a washerwoman and seamstress, but even this was not enough. The system worked against her. Enslaved women could prosper only if they remained healthy, protected their provision grounds from theft by other slaves, worked hard, and had only a small family. When slaves became ill, as Abba often did, and had a large family, they struggled. When Thistlewood died, the effects of field work and the difficulties of finding the necessities of life and a large family meant that Abba was deemed to be "old" and weak—even though she was probably only in her early forties. She was valued at £40, which was £30 to £40 less than women of a similar age who did not have large families. Abba had not quite become "worthless" but was well on her way to being seen as such. Studying how enslaved women in Jamaica were valued shows clearly how rationally effective slave management and ruthless accounting methods made slaves into disposable people.

NOTES

1. Sarah (Affy) Affir's life is covered in Richard S. Dunn, *A Tale of Two Plantations: Slave Life and Labor in Jamaica and Virginia* (Cambridge, Mass.: Harvard University Press, 2014), 75–90.

2. The empirical evidence is from two databases, one being derived from 10,222 inventories. This database lists the prices recorded for 259,617 slaves. Inventories, 1B/11/1–64, Jamaica Archives, Spanishtown, Jamaica. The second database contains 1,405 slaves from five lists of slaves that have detailed agency information on such things as age, ethnicity, health and color. Inventories, 1B1/11/3/56, Records of Prospect Estate, 0627–0019, Barclays Group Archive, London; "List of Slaves on York Estate, Jamaica, 1 Jan. 1778," Gale-Morant Papers, 3/c, University of Exeter Library, Exeter, England.

3. Richard K. Fleischman, David Oldroyd, and Thomas N. Tyson, "Plantation Ac-

counting and Management Practices in the U.S. and the British West Indies at the End of Their Slavery Eras," *Economic History Review* 64 (2011): 786.

4. Richard S. Dunn, "Sugar Production and Slave Women in Jamaica," in *Cultivation and Culture: Labor and the Shaping of Slave Life in the Americas*, ed. Ira Berlin and Philip D. Morgan (Charlottesville: University Press of Virginia, 1993), 49–72; and Kenneth Morgan, "Slave Women and Reproduction in Jamaica, c. 1776–1834," *History* 91 (2006): 231–54.

5. Trevor Burnard, "Collecting and Accounting: Representing Slaves as Commodities in Jamaica, 1674–1784," in *Collecting across Cultures: Material Exchanges in the Early Modern World*, ed. Daniela Bleichmar and Peter C. Mancall (Philadelphia: University of Pennsylvania Press, 2011); and Trevor Burnard, "From Periphery to Periphery: The Pennants' Jamaican Plantations, 1771–1812 and Industrialization in North Wales," in *Wales and Empire, 1607–1820*, ed. H. V. Bowen (Manchester: Manchester University Press, 2011).

6. For how enslaved people viewed this brutalizing and dehumanizing process, see Frederick Douglass, *Narrative of the Life of Frederick Douglass: An American Slave* (1845; rpt., Amawalk, N.Y.: Golden Owl, 1995), 27.

7. Jennifer L. Morgan, *Laboring Women: Reproduction and Gender in New World Slavery* (Philadelphia: University of Pennsylvania Press, 2004), 60, 145, 147; and David Eltis, *The Rise of African Slavery in the Americas* (Cambridge: Cambridge University Press, 2000), 85–113.

8. Burnard, "Collecting and Accounting," 185–86.

9. David Collins, *Management and Medical Treatment of Negro Slaves in the Sugar Colonies* (London: J. Barfield, 1803), 176.

10. Peter Thompson, "Henry Drax's Instructions on the Management of a Seventeenth-Century Barbadian Plantation," *William and Mary Quarterly*, 3rd ser., 86 (2009): 565–604; and Heather Cateau, "The New 'Negro' Business: Hiring in the British West Indies, 1750–1810," in *In the Shadow of the Plantation: Caribbean History and Legacy*, ed. Alvin O. Thompson (Kingston: University of the West Indies Press, 2002), 100–120.

11. David Eltis and Stanley L. Engerman, "Was the Slave Trade Dominated by Men?," *Journal of Interdisciplinary History* 23 (1992): 237–57.

12. Caitlin C. Rosenthal, "Slavery's Scientific Management: Accounting for Mastery," in *Slavery's Capitalism: A New History of American Economic Development*, ed. Sven Beckert and Seth Rockman (Philadelphia: University of Pennsylvania Press, 2012), 62–86.

13. B. W. Higman, "Jamaican Port Towns in the Early Nineteenth Century," in *Atlantic Port Cities: Economy, Culture, and Society in the Atlantic World, 1650–1850*, ed. Franklin W. Knight and Peggy K. Liss (Knoxville: University of Tennessee Press, 1991), 117–48.

14. Simon Taylor to Chaloner Archdeckne, July 23, 1770, in *Travel, Trade, and Power in the Atlantic*, ed. Betty Wood (Cambridge: Cambridge University Press, 2002), 93.

15. Trevor Burnard, "Evaluating Gender in Early Jamaica, 1674–1784," *History of the Family* 12 (2007): 81–91.

16. Justin Roberts, *Slavery and the Enlightenment in the British Atlantic, 1750–1807* (New York: Cambridge University Press, 2013).

17. David W. Ryden, *West Indian Slavery and British Abolition, 1783–1807* (New York: Cambridge University Press, 2009), 84–92.

18. Richard S. Dunn, "'Dreadful Idlers' in the Cane Fields: The Slave Labor Pattern on a Jamaican Sugar Estate, 1762–1831," *Journal of Interdisciplinary History* 17 (1987): 795–822.

19. Amanda Thornton, "Coerced Care: Thomas Thistlewood's Account of Medical Practice on Enslaved Populations in Colonial Jamaica, 1751–1786," *Slavery and Abolition* 32 (2011), 535–59.

20. Martin Forster and S. D. Smith, "Surviving Slavery: Mortality at Mesopotamia, a Jamaican Sugar Estate, 1762–1832," *Journal of the Royal Statistical Society*, ser. A, 174, pt. 4 (2011): 907–29.

21. Sidney Mintz, *Three Ancient Colonies: Caribbean Themes and Variations* (Cambridge, Mass.: Harvard University Press, 2010), 49; Trevor Burnard, *Mastery, Tyranny, and Desire: Thomas Thistlewood and His Slaves in the Anglo-Jamaican World* (Chapel Hill: University of North Carolina Press, 2004), 156–64.

22. Morgan, *Laboring Women*, 114; Barbara Bush, *Slave Women in Caribbean Society, 1650–1838* (Bloomington: Indiana University Press, 1990), 139–49; and Stella Dadzie, "Searching for the Invisible Women: Slavery and Resistance in Jamaica," *Race and Class* 32 (1990), 21–38. But see Morgan, "Slave Women and Reproduction," and Dunn, *Tale of Two Plantations*, 163.

23. Londa Schiebinger, "West Indian Abortifacients and the Making of Ignorance," in *Agnotology: The Making and Unmaking of Ignorance*, ed. Robert N. Proctor and Londa Schiebinger (Stanford, Calif.: Stanford University Press, 2008), 149–62.

24. Edward Long, *The History of Jamaica . . .* , 3 vols. (London: T. Lowndes, 1774), 2:435–36.

25. On slave nutrition, see Kenneth Kiple, *The Caribbean Slave: A Biological History* (New York: Cambridge University Press, 1984), 80–85; Richard Follett, *The Sugar Masters: Planters and Slaves in Louisiana's Cane World, 1820–1860* (Baton Rouge: Louisiana State University Press, 2005).

26. Long, *History of Jamaica*, 2:435–36; Richard Ligon, *A True and Exact History of the Island of Barbadoes . . .* (London: Peter Parker, 1657), 46–48; and Hans Sloane, *A Voyage to the Islands of Madeira, Barbadoes, Nieves, S. Christopher and Jamaica*, 2 vols. (London: By the author, n.p., 1707, 1725), 1:cxlvii, xlviii, lii.

27. For Louisiana, see Richard Follett, "Heat, Sex, and Sugar: Pregnancy and Childbearing in the Slave Quarters," *Journal of Family History* 28 (2003): 510–39.

28. Thornton, "Coerced Care."

29. Katherine Paugh, "The Politics of Childbearing in the British Caribbean and the Atlantic World during the Age of Abolition," *Past & Present* (2013): 119–60; Sasha Turner, "Home-Grown Slaves: Women, Reproduction and the Abolition of the Slave Trade, Jamaica, 1788–1807," *Journal of Women's History* 23 (2011), 39–62.

30. "List of Slaves on York Estate." See also Audra Diptee, "African Children in the British Slave Trade during the Late Eighteenth Century," *Slavery & Abolition* 27 (2006): 183–96.

31. Gordon Turnbull, *Letters to a Young Planter . . .* (London: Stuart and Stevenson, 1785), 43.

32. Trevor Burnard, "Slavery and the Enlightenment in Jamaica, 1760–1772: The Afterlife of Tacky's Rebellion," in *Enlightened Colonialism: Civilization Narratives and Imperial Politics of the Age of Reason*, ed. Damien Tricoire (Basingstoke: Palgrave Macmillan, 2017), 227–46.

33. Ibid., 83–84.

34. Burnard, *Mastery, Tyranny, and Desire*, 53.

35. B. W. Higman, *Slave Population and Economy in Jamaica, 1807–1834* (Cambridge: Cambridge University Press, 1976), 187–211; and Michael Craton, *Searching for the Invisible Man: Slaves and Plantation Life in Jamaica* (Cambridge, Mass.: Harvard University Press, 1978).

36. Burnard, *Mastery, Tyranny, and Desire*, 175–240.

37. Ibid., 156–62.

38. David Buisseret, ed., *Jamaica in 1687: The Taylor Manuscript at the National Library of Jamaica* (Kingston: University of the West Indies Press, 2008), 267.

CHAPTER 3

Reading the Specter of Racialized Gender in Eighteenth-Century Bridgetown, Barbados

MARISA J. FUENTES

One night between October 2 and 4, 1742, an enslaved boy left his owner's house alone. His heart may have pounded loud in his ears from fear, anxiety, and anticipation as he adjusted the concealed sword strapped to his lean waist, beneath the women's clothes he had donned. He may have been sweating and nervous as he passed others in the dark streets on his way to his destination, avoiding eye contact and any gestures that would give him away. He would have walked carefully to avoid stumbling over the cobblestones or stepping hard on rocks with his bare feet. He may have thought about his family or friends, about never seeing them again whether he failed or succeeded in his task. Acquiring the clothes from another enslaved girl or woman was likely the result of a tense plea, filled with despair and desperation. The dress or skirts he wore were perhaps long and cumbersome, but they hid the sword, and his master thought the female clothes would mask his identity as he made his way to another white household in Bridgetown, Barbados. It is likely that his master, Dudley Crofts, ordered the boy to go to the Moore residence dressed in women's clothes to kill Daniel Moore, his romantic rival. Mr. Moore's wife, Agatha Moore, may have urged Crofts to get rid of her husband so that she and Crofts could marry. It is unknown what time the boy arrived at the Moore residence or who he met when he reached the tree in the garden. It might have been a nurse residing with the Moore family or another male slave named Johnny.[1]

We will never know the exact circumstances of his discovery but can surmise that he experienced extreme dread at the prospect of being caught as a slave in disguise and armed with a lethal weapon. Attempts to harm a white person, instigate or participate in a revolt, or otherwise enact one's will as a slave carried at worst a death sentence, and the mode of punishment was usually painful and slow.[2] Soon after his arrival to the Moore house, he was caught by someone and arrested. He would spend at least a few days in the town jail awaiting trial by three freeholders and two justices of the peace: all white men. The common jail would be crowded and dank in the tropical October of Barbados, but he would at least have been in the company of other slaves awaiting similar fates. They would perhaps speak to each other inside the cell, but the intimate conversations of the enslaved never reached the archive, and no records of his trial exist. Although he would be asked to answer for his presence at a household to which he was not bound, his words and name would not be recorded in the archive. He would be surrounded by many white men who would speak on his behalf and against him. His testimony would hold no weight in the decision of his guilt or innocence of attempted murder. He would be acquitted of all charges.[3]

The archive in which this enslaved boy appears is meant to represent the affairs and entanglements of white Barbadians. Descriptions of enslaved women are explicitly absent. Historical methods demand that one adhere to the logics, descriptions, and actions of the actors represented in archival documents. There are no black women mentioned and thus, nothing can be said about them here—no generalizations can be made from even a fragment. However, I argue that reexamining the boy dressed in women's clothes, moving out and alone at night tells us something important about the presence of enslaved women in Bridgetown and the expectations and assumptions of enslaved women's bodies, public sexualities, and the vulnerability of mobility in eighteenth-century urban Barbados. Examining the terms by which white and black women could appear in public, the boy's female gendered performance, and the empowered sexuality of white women enables us to think about the constructions of black female subjection.[4] It is precisely the specter of enslaved women in this case and in Bridgetown that allowed the boy access to darkened streets and the house of white strangers.

Traditional historical methods that rely on empirical evidence can leave scholars of female slavery at an acute disadvantage with an inability to articulate the subjective (sexual) experiences of black women in slave societies beyond the dichotomy of victim or sexual agent. Therefore, new and innovative methodologies must be applied. In the tradition of historians whose subjects by necessity, demand "constructive speculation," because of their subjugated positions, this work takes up the call of radical or critical historians such as E. P. Thompson, who argue that "it is scarcely possible to give a coherent historical account of an incoherent presence, but some attempt must be made."[5] I also employ a feminist (historical) methodology to this court case that is necessary for producing additional knowledge about race, gender, sexuality, and power out of significantly mined and fragmented documents. This is an effort to write a "history of the dominated" and "[reclaim] the archival material for contrary purposes."[6]

The purpose of this work is to persist in seeking new ways to understand enslaved female subjectivity when the colonial archive and empirical methods conspire to erase them. This methodological exercise shows how the specter or "invisible presence" of enslaved women shaped the actions and possibilities for *everyone* in this colonial Caribbean slave society and implicates how we read the archives of slavery in general. This particular case is just one example of how to think about the ways in which the presence of black women in a slave society informed not just the actions and positionalities of whites but also how overrepresentations of white affairs and gazes in the archive created the historical conditions by which black women can disappear. In other words, enslaved women profoundly influenced the production of labor, laws, and social subjectivities in slave societies, for white and black men and women, whether they appear in the archives or not. Critically reading this court case to think about how racial and sexual ideologies about enslaved women played out in the lives of others is an effort to exemplify how they are constituent to the archive and the lives of their contemporaries when they are not explicitly represented. It is also an effort to think about how black female sexualities were produced in a state of captivity. These are difficult questions to address within an archive that did not record the interior and intimate in the lives of the enslaved. But these questions must be pursued or we risk reproducing the very power of the archives of slavery to consign enslaved women's sexual experiences to the unknowable.[7]

My methodological task of reading for enslaved women's captive sexuality is also informed by the caution articulated by Kirsten Fischer and Jennifer L. Morgan. They urge us not to "lose sight of agency and desire [of the enslaved because] the sexual behavior of individuals remains under-theorized compared to the analysis of the impact of sexual rules and sexualized representations of colonized women and colonizing men," and also remind us that "white women also participated in the imperialist production of images that resonated with both sexual and national meanings."[8] Indeed, this chapter seeks to link the sexual subjectivities of white women to enslaved women and men, using, "whatever sources are available . . . to try to include women's perceptions of 'others' and of themselves."[9] In this way, this work relies on the juridical evidence detailing the actions of white men and women, and an enslaved boy, in order to delineate how both white and enslaved black women were subjugated differently by colonial power. In some respects it may seem as if this case cannot offer any empirical material that aids our understanding of enslaved women's subjugation or enslaved sexuality more generally. Yet, white women's access to particular types of power and the enslaved boy's nocturnal public movements expose just how enslaved women were positioned ideologically within eighteenth-century urban Barbados. Pursuing the specter of enslaved women in the shadows of this archive presents a new method for us to historicize their experiences.

PERFORMING ENSLAVED WOMANHOOD:
THE BOY, THE DRESS, AND THE DAGGER

In Bridgetown, Barbados, between July 1740 and the summer of 1742, Mrs. Agatha Moore, wife of Daniel Moore, had a sexual affair with Dudley Crofts, Esquire. In the midst of the affair, Agatha Moore gave birth to a daughter on May 3, 1742, whose paternity was likely not her husband's.[10] Two incidents brought the illicit sexual conduct of these lovers to public attention and subsequently to the Governor's Council, the highest court of appeals in this British colony. The first episode occurred in May 1741, when Crofts and Mrs. Moore were caught together by her husband who had been sleeping upstairs.[11] The second event transpired somewhere between October 2 and 4, 1742, as a young enslaved boy owned by Dudley Crofts, was detained in the vicinity of the Moore household dressed in women's clothes and armed with a concealed sword.[12] What ensued from these circumstances was a multifaceted legal web of petitions, criminal trials, and countersuits as the council tried to sort out what, if any, crimes had been committed by the parties involved and who would ultimately recompense for any damages incurred.

The Honorable Thomas Harrison, a justice of the peace for the precinct of Bridgetown, sat at the heart of this legal chaos. He presided over the investigation against Dudley Crofts for the "crime" of adultery and the separate case against the slave boy for purportedly conspiring to murder. And it was Harrison who was eventually held responsible for his poor handling of these proceedings.[13] Gathering several witnesses to testify against Crofts for both alleged crimes, Harrison presumed Crofts's guilt and imposed on him more than £10,000 in security bonds. In retaliation, Crofts petitioned the council for redress from financial and character damage. On October 4, 1743, the governor and council held a ten-hour session to review all depositions, petitions, and complaints related to Crofts's plea of redress and Harrison's statement defending his own actions.[14] Among the evidence gathered and read during the council meeting was a full deposition by Agatha Moore discussing her role in the sexual affair. In addition, several other witnesses commented on whether Dudley Crofts purposely sent his armed and disguised enslaved boy to his rival's house, or if the boy was summoned by a member of the Moore household. Both the testimonial depictions of the enslaved boy's movements and Agatha Moore's language describing her illicit sexual behavior reveal how discourse, prevailing racial and gendered ideologies about black women, and uses of power produced the violent sexual realties enslaved women (and men) experienced in colonial Caribbean slave societies.

There are only a few references to the boy in the Crofts versus Harrison case, but they provide insight into the power dynamics in eighteenth-century Barbados and the specter of racialized gender. The first mention of the boy dressed in women's clothes appears in Judge Harrison's rebuttal to Dudley Crofts's complaint of financial and personal injury. Harrison, explaining why he imposed such a large bond for security on Crofts, argued that he felt that Crofts was a criminal threat to Daniel Moore:

> The reason which induced [me] to demand such a recognizance was because [of] a complaint made to [me] by the sd Daniel Moore against a Negro of [Crofts]. The negro had taken his Masters Sword which [Crofts] acknowledged to [me] he had directed him to take and went the proceeding night therewith disguised in womens Cloaths to the house of Thomas Withers Esqr where Mr Moore lived and where the Criminal Correspondence between [Crofts] & the wife of the sd Mr Moore was carried on and as from the circumstances I had reason to believe some mischief was intended by [Crofts] against Mr Moore. . . . I thought it my Duty to require proper security from [Crofts].[15]

At issue for Harrison and the slave court was whether Crofts instructed his slave to attempt murder or merely permitted the boy to go to the Withers-Moore household, as he had allegedly been summoned to the Withers-Moore house by a nurse working there.[16] The next few references to this incident relate to witnesses testifying whether they heard Dudley Crofts acknowledge that he directed his enslaved boy to go to the Withers-Moore household in disguise and with a sword. Most of the witnesses present in the initial confrontation between Judge Harrison and Crofts agreed that Crofts acknowledged in public that he merely allowed the boy to go. But no one could confirm if it was by Crofts's intent to murder Daniel Moore or if the boy went responding to a summons from the Moore household. Crofts, his lawyer Thomas Lake, and two other witnesses testified that the boy was summoned to the house by another male slave named Johnny who carried a message from the nurse, beckoning him to come at night and meet her "under a tree." They argue that he took the sword, with Crofts's permission, to defend himself from possible attack by another enslaved male named Johnny belonging to Mr. Withers or Mr. Moore.[17] We do not have testimony in the voice of the enslaved boy, only fleeting moments where white male deponents state what they heard him say.

Samuel Webb, a witness called on behalf of Dudley Croft, deposed, That he did not hear the said Crofts say he delivered his Boy or Directed him to take a sword along with him up to Mr. Wither's where the said Daniel Moore then lived but he heard his Boy say and Acknowledge that a negroe named John belonging to the said Withers having Come to him & told him that the nurse at Mr Withers desired he would come to her under a tree in the Garden. He of his own Accord took a [illegible] [sword or dagger] of his masters in order to Defend himself.[18]

The boy was eventually acquitted of all charges against him, an unusual action given his deceptive disguise and possession of a lethal weapon. According to further testimony by witness Richard Hall, "it did not appear upon the trial of the said negro that he had made any attempts upon the House or Doors of Mr. Withers or that he offered any violence whatever, upon which he was acquitted."[19] However, it is clear that Judge Harrison and the men who tried him did not believe he acted on his own accord. In this instance we might consider how "will" is both recognized and disregarded by the colonial authorities in reference to enslaved criminality.[20] This was both an example of how colonial slave law arbitrarily recognized the boy's humanity in order to try him for his purported criminal actions while at the same time denying he could have enacted his own will apart from the desires of his master. That he was acquitted despite being caught armed and in disguise elucidates how the authorities could ultimately decide when to consider enslaved people as sentient beings and when to deny their humanity and will.

It is also plausible that Crofts's motive for sending the boy was murder, as Agatha Moore stated in her deposition, "for that if her said Husband died, she would perform the Promise or Oath she had made to him, that she would marry the said Dudley Crofts."[21] Did Agatha Moore then, enable the enslaved boy's actions of attempt to murder by suggesting to Crofts that if he would do something to get rid of her husband she would marry him? Is this statement, so easily dismissed by Governor Robinson in later proceedings, evidence that the boy was directed to commit violence against a white man and thus risk death himself?[22]

Since the enslaved could not deny the requests of their owners, we might consider how the boy's actions were an enactment of his owner's will. Through his actions, the boy was caught as an accessory to Crofts's sexual desires, entangled in Crofts's sexual interactions with Agatha Moore and his desire to possess her. Because "the notion of will connotes more than simply the ability to act and to do; rather, it distinguishes the autonomous agent from the enslaved," the boy could not refuse or disobey direction and was forced to participate in his own possible demise by being caught in a white household under questionable circumstances.[23] In other words, the boy became a (sexual) vessel for white men and women's sexual desires. This is the fungibility of the enslaved exemplified. He faced danger in both resisting his master's will and in possibly attempting to murder or bring harm to any white, which carried the sentence of death.[24] Moreover, the absence of testimonial discussion as to why the enslaved boy donned women's clothes points to the ontological condition of enslaved people and how racialized gender functioned in this colonial slave society.[25] In one way, this lack of concern addressed the enslaved boy's nonthreatening gender behavior. In "womens cloaths," he did not elicit a (sexual) threat to white masculinity.[26] But there is more at stake here. In addition to the slave boy's unremarkable attire, we might ask what social expectations allowed a disguised enslaved "woman" to approach a white household at night?

In eighteenth-century Bridgetown, as with many other Caribbean port cities dependent on domestic work, enslaved women were in the demographic majority. Hundreds of ships a year called at Bridgetown, the capital port city in which Agatha Moore and the enslaved boy resided; such ships were laden with material products and captive Africans, who supplied the labor for sugar plantations as well as domestic labor in town. Although demographic sources are rare for the eighteenth century, Jerome Handler estimates that in 1786 approximately 62,115 slaves, 16,167 whites, and 838 free people of color were living in the colony.[27] The gender demographics of Barbados and Bridgetown were also unique for a Caribbean colony. Unlike Jamaica and the Leeward Islands, Barbados attained a slight majority of white women in the population by the early eighteenth century. For example, Hilary Beckles states that "in Jamaica, white women constituted no more than 40 percent of the white community up to 1780, while as early as 1715 white women outnumbered white men in Barbados by one percent, and by seven percent in 1748, leveling off at about fifty-two percent female for the remainder of the slavery period."[28] Understanding this has implications for our analysis of white and black women in the eighteenth-century Caribbean. By the early eighteenth century, white women in Barbados constituted a slight majority of the population of the island at about 51 percent and remained so until the era of emancipation.[29] The lack of a critical mass of white women in Jamaica and the Leewards shaped the economic, social, and sexual opportunities for white women in a distinctly different way than for white women in Barbados.[30] Additionally, women of African descent also constituted a majority of the enslaved population, particularly in towns. In Bridgetown, these female majorities influenced the sexual-cultural character of urban slave society. For example, Beckles's scholarship challenges Caribbean historiography that focuses on the planter "patriarch," showing that "58 per cent of slave owners in [Bridgetown] were female, mostly white . . . [and] women owned 54 per cent of the slaves in town." Furthermore, he points out that "white women also owned more female slaves than male slaves."[31] How then, do we historicize white and enslaved women's sexuality in a slave society where they inhabited the demographic majority?

As urban dwellers, enslaved women served white people in various capacities. They were domestic servants, nursemaids, wet nurses, sex slaves either for personal hire or for service in a brothel, washerwomen, and market women. If the enslaved boy had been instructed to murder Daniel Moore (a likely possibility despite his acquittal), an enslaved woman who was a stranger to a household would have been more easily admitted than an enslaved male. Black women constituted the majority of household servants, and interactions between white men and black women occurred frequently. It would not have been odd for a female slave to arrive at a stranger's house on some errand. In addition, black women's access to public space marked a difference in gendered and sexual expectations for enslaved women and white women.[32] Elite white women were not allowed in public unaccompanied, especially at night. Their sexuality was hidden, protected, and defended in the name of honor and virtue, which were at the very heart of white female identity. The frequency with which black women traversed urban spaces suggests how they were perceived as sexual agents, lascivious, and "unwomanly." As objects of commerce for different types of (sexual) labor, enslaved women were not associated with virtue nor were their sexual identities protected from harm. Indeed, as Edward Long discusses in reference to enslaved wet nurses and domestic slaves, "there is scarcely one of these nurses who is not a common prostitute, or at least who has not had commerce with more than one man."[33] In contrast, Long's observations about the roles white women occupied, equally demonstrate varied perceptions of black and white womanhood and implied sexualities. He states that "the domestic life of [white] women, which prevents them from exercising abroad as much as the other sex, naturally inclines them to love those active amusements which may be followed within doors."[34]

Enslaved women's mobility outside the domestic realm evoked a certain type of freedom that white women could not exercise. Carefully reading the enslaved boy's movements and performance in female dress, through town and at night, exposes the ways in which enslaved and black women's seemingly unfettered mobility was actually a position of vulnerability in this slave society. White women were protected by law and domestic enclosure, whereas enslaved women were required to perform a particular type of public availability resulting in exposure. Dudley Crofts, through his enslaved boy, exploited this understanding of black women's public exposure and position, sending him out to perform the normative embodiment of black womanhood as publicly visible, unchaste, lascivious, sexually wanton, and available to serve.

Another way to consider the circumstances and consequences of the boy's surreptitious movements is to understand the intimacy of whites and the enslaved in the domestic sphere. As the court case makes clear, there was a dispute between two white households, which would cause anxiety for the enslaved laboring in each house. White strife and the breakup of households had profound effects for those bound to their owners in slavery. White unrest might lead to liquidation of assets and in turn lead to slave sales or labor reassignment. Many white families had relatives on country estates and were involved in sugar production. Slaves could be moved around from town to country if households were in flux. A palpable fear would certainly have been felt by the enslaved of Crofts and Moore.[35] Moreover, despite racial rules of conduct, particularly those that regulated the behavior of enslaved and free Afro-Barbadians, household slaves served their owners intimately and would have absolutely been aware of Mrs. Moore's infidelities and sexual transgressions.[36] Perhaps the stress of the situation led the enslaved of each household to threaten each other. Moreover, the boy may have been caught in a trap set by the "white" nurse, who in trying to protect her family charges in the Withers-Moore home was trying to stop the affair between Crofts and Agatha Moore, and used the armed boy to bring the situation to the public.[37]

Most relevant in this discussion are the ways in which enslaved subjectivity (subjugated and criminalized), male and female, enabled particular types of social, racial, sexual, and gendered power for white men and women. Key to understanding this, in the absence of a comparable archive for enslaved men and women, is a discussion of the labor and sexual roles they performed in the context of a colonial port city such as Bridgetown, Barbados. In addition, establishing the singularity and similarities of this site and court case to other Caribbean contexts will further illuminate the specific relations of power deployed through sexuality constituent to such slave societies.[38] In other words, what made Agatha Moore's sexual agency possible? How was her agency predicated on the sexual exploitation of enslaved women and men? What does the performance of black womanhood enable the boy to accomplish in eighteenth-century Bridgetown, and what are the terms by which white and black women could be in public? Exposing the relations of power here—economic, gendered, racial, and sexual— changes the ways in which we historicize white women's relationship to patriarchy in slave societies. And, the movements of a boy dressed as a black female relates directly to white women's sexualities and social power.

Although certainly hindered by patriarchal norms that placed white women in a subordinate economic, social, and political position to white men, there is substantial evidence that white women maintained economic power through slave ownership and certainly shaped what was acceptable and unacceptable sexual behavior in Barbados. In the following deposition, I argue that, aside from the power to subsist economically, Agatha Moore was able to access and deny a type of sexual agency even in her ruin, which enabled a privilege unavailable to enslaved women.

WHITE WOMEN AND DISTRESSED SEXUALITY

The following discussion explores how white women in slave societies, caught behaving counter to normative gender, racial, and sexual expectations could rhetorically deploy what I term *distressed sexuality* in order to challenge the ruin and shame attached to their actions. For the purposes of this discussion, distressed sexuality encompasses two related meanings. The first refers to the actual affliction white women experienced from the public disgrace of their perceived sexual deviance in the context of the eighteenth-century Caribbean. This speaks to how existing gender norms regulated white women's sociosexual behavior in relation to white men, black men, and black women. There were rigid gender and sexual expectations in place for white women.[39] The second part of the concept signifies the agency available to white women in "shame"—that is, their ability to make certain claims about their inviolability despite "consenting" to transgressive sexual acts. This is achieved by claiming to consent to sexually illicit acts "unhappily" or "against better judgment" in order to maintain one's virtue. Sexual inviolability and consent represent agential acts and subjective statuses to which black women in the same society had no access.

Discourses of sexual behavior, either the "virtuous comportment" of white women or the "lasciviousness" of black women dictated the nature of sexual performance publically and privately. I use this case to articulate how more diffuse forms of power—different from overt physical modes—were used to negate enslaved women's sexualities and leave them vulnerable to sexual violence.[40] We know that racial and gendered subjugation of enslaved men and women was maintained through repeated acts of violence and terror.[41] Gender and racial hierarchies in slave societies required constant articulation because these hierarchies were inherently unstable as the enslaved resisted at every turn.[42] These reiterations of power (i.e., the ways in which white patriarchal power reasserted itself in the face of challenge or instability) took place during the commodification process on slave ships, at the auction block, through the force of whip and law, and most importantly for this chapter, within the realm of sexuality, sexual behavior, and sexual violence.[43] One of the ways to pinpoint these instabilities and demarcate the reiteration of patriarchal and white supremacist power in slave societies is to track the moments of identity crisis. As the Crofts versus Harrison court case demonstrates, seemingly "stable" gender and racial identities did falter, and Agatha Moore's deposition and the boy's female apparel and mobility allow us to map the ways in which white female sexual identity might be reaffirmed, especially in a situation of distress. Furthermore, the power of white women to "reaffirm" their "virtuous" identities equated to a kind of sexual agency that enslaved women could never acquire, as they were "property" and could not assert decisions in sexual encounters.

While examining the intricacies of white female distressed sexuality, I refer back to the specter of racialized gender in the experiences of the young boy who was forced to enact his master's (sexual) will through gender disguise, thereby exemplifying the underlying racial and gendered ideologies about black women and their expected presence in the domestic realm of white households. This also examines how both black males and females were forced to surrogate their owners' sexualities, a further subjugation in their enslaved status. In order to make more general comments about how white women's Georgian sexualities were in a dialectical relationship with enslaved women, it is necessary to understand and elucidate the circulation of both types of racialized sexual ideologies to gain a more complete picture of enslaved women's sexualized lives. Closely examining how patriarchy produced a relational subjection of black and white women in eighteenth-century Barbados, and perhaps Caribbean slave societies more generally, allows us to gain new insight into black female subjection in the absence of an archive documenting their powerlessness.[44] My application of theoretical texts to the study of the available archives is an effort to get at the palimpsestic nature of archival sources, the quotidian and complex experiences of sexuality in slave societies, and the archival silences of enslaved women inherent in archives of slavery.[45] Thus, closely reading the deposition of Agatha Moore enables an elaboration of the parameters of sexual culture in eighteenth-century Barbados, thereby implicating the limits and domination of black female sexuality.

AGATHA MOORE: DEPOSED

On October 11, 1742, Judge Harrison took a long statement from Mrs. Moore regarding her role in the sexual liaison with Dudley Crofts. Neither Mrs. Moore's husband, Daniel, nor Crofts seemed to object to this action, and Crofts was invited to cross-examine her but did not show up.[46] In her deposition, related by Harrison in the third person, Agatha Moore explains how Crofts began his seduction of her:

[Deponent] positively says that she never gave the said Dudley Crofts any hints or signs to encourage him to endeavor to seduce her ... the said Dudley Crofts very much importun'd her to commit adultery with him which she then refused declaring she could not consent to his desires as it would be cruelly injuring to her Husband and she could not answer it on any account but he then very much pressing that the next time they had a convenient opportunity she would give him her promise she was prevailed on by him to promise she would.[47]

Her deposition continues to recount the several sexual encounters she had with Crofts:

In the said month of July in the said Year one thousand seven hundred and forty [when] her Husband the said Daniel Moore being gone to Scotland [district][48] the said Dudley Crofts came up to her said Father's house [her father being off the island] ... and after dinner he the said Dudley Crofts claimed the promise which the said Deponent had before made to him and which promise this Deponent then very unhappily complyd with by suffering the sd Dudley Crofts then to commit adultery with this Depont. And which he afterwards from time to time repeated with this depnt as they had convenient opportunities.[49]

Crofts and Mrs. Moore were eventually caught together by her husband in May 1741, and Mrs. Moore was later discovered writing a letter to Crofts. She admitted through carefully crafted language that though she left the island after discovery by her husband, when she returned she continued to correspond with Crofts by letter and she, "having acquainted him of her Husband [soon] being gone, the said Dudley Crofts came up to this ... house & then & there committed adultery with her, which he has never done since."[50] She ends her statement by saying that she asked to Crofts to cease writing to her, "for that if her said Husband died, she would perform the Promise or Oath she had made to him, that she would marry the said Dudley Crofts."[51] In the midst of the affair that began in 1740 and continued until the summer of 1742, Agatha Moore gave birth to a daughter on May 3, 1742, whose paternity remains questionable.[52]

This deposition from a young elite white woman in the 1740s admitting to transgressive sexual behavior is remarkable in its context. It remains the only case of its kind found in the minutes of the Barbados Council from 1700 to 1800. Although there may be cases against bastardy and adultery in the lower courts of common pleas, this case represents an unusual window into the intimate lives of Barbados's white elites.[53] Moreover, Governor Thomas Robinson, who made the final decision in these cases, declared that "it does not appear that any good or Lawful use could be made of so extraordinary [a] Deposition [by Agatha Moore] which his [Excellency] said he belivd was without Example."[54] His remarks might be a way to protect the image of the "virtuous white woman" by claiming that Agatha's deposition and behavior were the exception — an aberration to the societal norm.

One could easily argue that Agatha Moore was a victim of patriarchy in this case. Mrs. Moore's centrality to the events and her testimony were relegated to supportive evidence, and the case was essentially about deciding which white male involved was dishonored. All the white men involved in the proceedings, as plaintiffs or defendants, more or less reclaimed their lives, and their reputations were redeemed in the course of the case.[55] Judge Harrison was censured by the council and forced to resign all public positions except his elected seat of vestryman of St. Michael's Parish. Crofts paid a £200 fine for adultery but was vindicated of any alleged criminal behavior, and Daniel Moore resumed his business as a merchant.[56] In contrast, Agatha Moore disappears from the Barbados archive, though she may appear in British documents abroad. The deposition is awkward and disempowers Mrs. Moore on multiple levels, most strikingly in the way it states what she the "deponent" said, but never in her own words or through direct quotes. This legal format conspires to distort her testimony in significant ways most obviously by substituting what she actually said with Judge Harrison's interpretation of her testimony in third person. Additionally, her absence at the council meeting, a space for propertied white men only, left her without the ability to clarify and defend herself against the language of "whoredom" that permeates this historical record. Mrs. Moore would likely have been socially ruined, despite her "honesty," and leaving the island was probably her only recourse. Yet, on further examination of her language and position, I argue that Mrs. Moore was not necessarily destitute. And, recognizing the resources she accessed even in her sexual distress, demonstrates her ability to harness a type of power to which enslaved, freed, and free black women did not have access.[57]

When Mrs. Moore came of age, she inherited residential properties in Bridgetown.[58] We know from the laws of the time that white women surrendered their property upon marriage, yet many wills left by widows demonstrate both a retention of property through their marriages but also their attempts to circumvent the laws by giving property in trust to a male friend so as not to have their property seized by marriage.[59] If she was forced to flee Barbados, she took with her material resources to support herself. More important for understanding the various types of power within this slave society is how Agatha Moore in her deposition utilized rhetorical strategies that appealed to the patriarchal system in place, denying her agency in order to recoup her gendered and racial power, while at the same time subtly pronouncing her free will.

Claiming "seduction" by Crofts, Agatha Moore disputes her consent (and will) in the affair. She states that "she never gave the said Dudley Crofts any hints or signs to encourage him to endeavor to seduce her" and that "[she] unhappily complyd . . . by suffering the sd Dudley Crofts then to commit adultery with this Depont."[60] This language was meant to elicit sympathy from the prospective audience in arguing that she unwillingly participated in "immoral" behavior. Putting on record that she did not initiate the affair or the advances from Crofts allowed her the discursive room to claim innocence and a certain type of victimization through the discourses of seduction. In Saidiya Hartman's scholarship, "discourses of seduction" refers to the ways in which enslaved women were presumably always willing in sexual encounters despite the fact that their status as enslaved prevented their refusal. Hartman argues that "seduction makes recourse to the idea of reciprocal and collusive relations and engenders a precipitating construction of black female sexuality in which rape is unimaginable."[61] Hartman is speaking specifically about the consequences of sexual renditions of enslaved women as sexual agents. In Agatha Moore's discursive strategy, discourses of seduction become the means through which Agatha Moore can claim victimization.[62] These divergent meanings of seduction enacted on white and black female bodies mark precisely the relational or dialectical sexual configurations of white and black female sexualities. The fact that Agatha Moore could speak about her "unwillingness" to engage in transgressive sexual acts and blame her "seduction" on Crofts delimits the significant schism between the sexual subjectivities of white women and enslaved women. White women could defend their honor, even in sexual distress, whereas enslaved women, as property, a status that implied their sexual availability to men, could not even give consent.

Confounding her denial of sexual agency (white women certainly were not allowed to claim sexual agency in the traditional sense), Agatha Moore then admitted to informing Crofts of "convenient" moments when they might have sex undisturbed and promised Crofts that she would marry him if anything happened to her husband.[63] This latter point lends evidence to the possibility that Crofts sent his slave boy to murder her husband to hasten the process by which he might fully and legally possess Mrs. Moore. She may have unwittingly encouraged the murder of her husband by Crofts's enslaved boy. Equally important are the ways in which Mrs. Moore inhabited a status of privilege, allowing her a range of discursive options to defend herself in the face of sexual distress. These options spoke to a specific type of subjection that both oppressed her as a woman and empowered her as a white woman.

Michel Foucault has raised questions about the relationship between discourses of sex and power relations that can be used to further analyze this case: "In a specific type of discourse on sex, in a specific form of exhortation of the truth, appearing historically and in specific places . . . what were the most immediate, the most local power relations at work? And, how were these discourses used to support power relations?"[64] Ideology and discourse shaped the life conditions, experiences of freedom and enslavement, for everyone in slave societies. Combined, the discursive power of racial ideology worked in force to subjugate, mark as deviant, and make sexually accessible black women's bodies for public consumption at the same time and in relation to the ways in which white women were figured through law, gender, race, and sexual norms. As stated earlier, discourses of sexual behavior, either the virtuous comportment of white women or the lasciviousness of black women, dictated the nature of sexual performance publically and privately. Agatha Moore's deposition and her language within it represent the rhetorical space that white women could exploit to feign innocence. Beyond mere rhetoric, Agatha Moore's (sexual) subjectivity was made clear in this moment. The concept of "seduction is a meditation on liberty and slavery; and will and subjection in the arena of sexuality."[65] Mrs. Moore's ability to claim seduction and disempowerment ironically spoke to her empowerment within this system of racial hierarchy. Contrary to the ways in which the concept of agency is utilized in historical scholarship on slavery as resistance to domination, Mrs. Moore denied her agency, appealing to patriarchal norms (of white female submission and honor) in an attempt to rescue her innocence and sexual virtue. Moore thus reproduced the "discourses used to support power relations" in Barbados slave society; her innocence or guilt and her ability to speak at all on her own behalf expose the perhaps more subtle forms of power available to white women. Moreover, Agatha Moore's "shame" in her sexual distress meant that she inhabited a position of status from which to fall. This status, although tenuous, gave her a position of power over enslaved, freed, and free black women in the same society. Of course, if Agatha Moore had been caught having sex with a black man, free or enslaved, her power to evoke "unwilling consent" would be greatly reduced. In all likelihood, her ruin would have been unrecoverable unless she claimed rape. Yet, however limiting the double standard of interracial sex was for white men and women in Caribbean slave societies, Agatha Moore's recourse to exclaiming rape not only elaborates her power but also highlights the disempowered enslaved male whose imminent execution followed any such encounter by the eighteenth century. All of these strategies—these avenues that bespoke her status, subjectivity, and placement in the racial and gendered hierarchy— were possible because of the subjugation of black women.

It is nearly impossible to track enslaved women's sexual desire in the archive beyond their strategies seeking material comfort. The project of recovering black women's sexual desire in slavery pushes us against a troubling dichotomy of sexual victim and sexual agent. Other scholarship about similar cases involving white men and women, in both Jamaica and the Leeward Islands prove useful in understanding the sociosexual world of the eighteenth-century Caribbean, but I argue more might be elucidated on this topic. Trevor Burnard's "'A Matron in Rank, a Prostitute in Manners': The Manning Divorce of 1741 and Class, Gender, Race, and the Law in Eighteenth-Century Jamaica," exposes through an analysis of Mrs. Manning's alleged adultery that white women "were seriously disadvantaged in [Jamaica]." Burnard argues that "[the] aftermath of the case illustrates the handicaps White women faced in a society designed almost solely for White men."[66] A white woman accused of both adultery with a white man who was a political rival to her husband and of having sex with male slaves was shamed by the norms of Jamaican society, suffering a public divorce and moral ruin while the white men in the case essentially escaped such public dishonor. One could argue that Agatha Moore, like Mrs. Manning, fell victim to similar ruin and her disappearance from the archives traces her forced flight from Barbados's society and a level of "historical invisibility."[67] Yet, Agatha Moore's substantial deposition given in her own defense reveals how the particularities of Barbados demographics and the recourse she had to voice her position shows striking differences in the lives of these two women and in these two Caribbean slave societies.

Similarly, by examining several cases of adultery and sexual transgressions in the Leeward Islands among white men and women, Natalie Zacek contends that "the idea that early modern English society was sexually restrained and that of the West Indian colonies promiscuous and unfettered is a false dichotomy that has been continuously reified by scholars."[68] Interrogating several cases in which white men and women engaged in extramarital affairs and were punished and shunned and a case in which a brother and sister implicated in an incestuous relationship were protected by nonfamily members, Zacek concludes that "white society in the Leewards proved itself willing, if not always pleased, to accommodate certain forms of sexual license, but it fervently resisted those which it saw as directly assaulting or mocking the patriarchal ideals upon which colonial British American society was based."[69] At stake for both Burnard and Zacek is an examination of the transgressive sexual behaviors between whites in Caribbean slave societies, the relationship between carnal regulation in the metropole and British colonies, and perhaps the degree to which sexual culture changed and adapted from Europe across the Atlantic.[70]

Comparatively, in the historical scholarship on enslaved women, our desire to search for agential acts has led to conversations about their limited "choices" within the system and the material and economic benefit they gained through their relationships with white men. This may have come in the form of eventual freedom for themselves or their children or both, and other "privileges" they may have acquired through concubine relationships. The limits to these analyses of freedom and material accumulation, especially contrasted with white women such as Agatha Moore, are that these gains did not result in arresting the lingering hypersexualized ideologies of black women, as this type of sexual distress did not disappear in freedom. Black women's bodies were not afforded the same protections as those of white women, and the Crofts court case makes clear that, even in sexual distress, white women had avenues of physical and material if not emotional escape and cultural capital with which their reputations could be at least marginally repaired in instances of "fornication" and even in cases of rape that were adjudicated through colonial law.[71] This is to point out how white and black women experienced sexuality in vastly distinct ways.

In conclusion, how do we write histories of sexuality and domination that do not merely reproduce the colonial masculine gaze? Kathleen Brown and Sharon Block share these concerns by asking "in connecting sexuality to broader systems of power, how do we best avoid replicating the dynamics of colonial society in our own histories?"[72] To avoid this, we must remain attentive to the multivalent power relations that impacted enslaved women in the eighteenth-century Caribbean and continue to develop new methods for historicizing the specter of racialized gender in the archives of slavery.

NOTES

1. For another account of this scene or this case and the genealogies of the white families involved, see Karl Watson, "Obsession, Betrayal and Sex in Eighteenth-Century Bridgetown," *Journal of the Barbados Museum and Historical Society* 51 (2005): 242–62.

2. See John Baskett, ed., *Acts of Assembly, Passed in the Island of Barbadoes from 1648 to 1718* (London: By Order of the Lords Commissioners of Trade and Plantations, 1732), 118–26. "If any Negro or Slave whatsoever shall offer any Violence to any Christian, by Striking, or the like, such Negro or other Slave shall, for his or her first Offence, by Information given up on Oath . . . shall be severely whipped by the Constable . . . for his second Offence of that nature, he shall be severely whipped, his Nose slit, and be burned in some part of his Face with a hot Iron."

3. Barbados Minutes of Council CO31/21/D1: 43–90, National Archives London (hereafter NAL).

4. I use *subjection* here in the Foucauldian sense, as Judith Butler explains, "Foucault refers to subjection in *Discipline and Punish*, and this word, as is well known, carries a double meaning: *assujetissement* means both subjection (in the sense of subordination)

and becoming a subject." Judith Butler, "Bodies and Power, Revisited," *Radical Philosophy: A Journal of Socialist and Feminist Philosophy* 114 (2002): 16.

5. E. P. Thompson, *The Making of the English Working Class* (London: Victor Gollancz, 1966), 451.

6. Saidiya Hartman, *Scenes of Subjection: Terror, Slavery, and Self-Making in Nineteenth-Century America* (New York: Oxford University Press, 1997), 10.

7. See Camilla Townsend, introduction, in *Malitzin's Choices: An Indian Woman in the Conquest of Mexico* (Albuquerque: University of New Mexico Press, 2006), 1–10. In her introduction, Townsend discusses the risk of leaving undocumented historical subjects to historical obscurity.

8. Kirsten Fischer and Jennifer L. Morgan, "Race and the Colonial Project," *William and Mary Quarterly*, 3rd ser., 60, no. 1 (2003): 197.

9. Ibid., 198.

10. Watson, "Obsession, Betrayal and Sex in Eighteenth-Century Bridgetown," 347. I am indebted to Dr. Watson for bringing this case to my attention when I was a graduate student in Barbados. Through dumb luck, as sometimes happens with archival research, I stumbled across the original documents in the National Archives in Kew (London) shortly thereafter. Watson has since published an important analysis of the many details of this case, including a thorough genealogy of the Withers/Moore, Crofts, and Harrison families. See Watson, "Obsession, Betrayal and Sex."

11. Barbados Minutes of Council CO31/21/D1: 66, NAL.

12. Ibid., 51.

13. Ibid., 76–90.

14. Ibid., 43–90.

15. Ibid., 51.

16. The name Withers refers to Mr. Withers, Agatha Moore's father. Mrs. Moore's maiden name was Withers; she and her husband lived in her father's house on High Street in Bridgetown at the time of this case. See Watson, "Obsession, Betrayal and Sex," 243.

17. Barbados Minutes of Council CO31/21/D1: 68, NAL.

18. Ibid., 58.

19. Ibid., 69.

20. Hartman, *Scenes of Subjection*, 85–86.

21. Ibid.

22. The Barbados Slave Act of 1661, which was modified in 1676, 1682, and 1688, made it a capital offence for a slave to murder or attempt to murder a white person. For the text of these laws, see Baskett, *Acts of Assembly*.

23. Hartman, *Scenes of Subjection*, 81.

24. Baskett, *Acts of Assembly*, 118–26.

25. See Kathleen M. Brown, *Good Wives, Nasty Wenches, and Anxious Patriarchs: Gender, Race, and Power in Colonial Virginia* (Chapel Hill: University of North Carolina Press, 1996), wherein she discusses the case of Thomas Hall, a white indentured servant who was likely an hermaphrodite, esp. pp. 75–80.

26. It is also presumed that the boy was not dressed in white women's clothes, which would have certainly brought a significant amount of censure, as clothing and material culture also reinforced status in slave societies.

27. Jerome S. Handler, *The Unappropriated People: Freedmen in the Slave Society of Barbados* (Kingston, Jamaica: University of the West Indies Press, 2009), 18–19.

28. Hilary McD. Beckles, *Centering Woman: Gender Discourses in Caribbean Slave Society* (Kingston: Ian Randle Publishers, 1998), 64.

29. Hilary McD. Beckles, *Natural Rebels: A Social History of Enslaved Women in Barbados* (New Brunswick, N.J.: Rutgers University Press, 1989), 14–15.

30. See Trevor Burnard, "'A Matron in Rank, a Prostitute in Manners . . .': The Manning Divorce of 1741 and Class, Race, Gender, and the Law in Eighteenth-Century Jamaica," in *Working Slavery, Pricing Freedom: Perspectives from the Caribbean, Africa and the African Diaspora*, ed. Verene Shepherd (London: St Martin's Press, 2002), 133–52; and Natalie Zacek, "Sex, Sexuality, and Social Control in the Eighteenth-Century Leeward Islands," in *Sex and Sexuality in Early America*, ed. Merril D. Smith (New York: New York University Press, 1998).

31. Hilary McD. Beckles, "White Women and Slavery in the Caribbean," *History Workshop Journal* 36 (1993): 69–70.

32. See, for example, the discussion of the denigrating sexual images and sexual exploitation of enslaved women in the Caribbean in Barbara Bush, *Slave Women in Caribbean Society, 1650–1838* (Bloomington: Indiana University Press, 1990), esp. pp. 110–18.

33. Edward Long, *The History of Jamaica*, 3 vols. (London: T. Lowndes, 1774), 2:276–77.

34. Ibid., 2:541.

35. Watson, "Obsession, Betrayal and Sex," 254.

36. Ibid.

37. Ibid.

38. The concept of "relations of power" is borrowed from Foucault, who argues that "we need a new economy (read theory) of power relations" that tracks how power relations are acted out—or more specifically, how power relations (which connote a *relationship* between entities) can be understood as struggles or a series of strategies employed to achieve submission of the other. See Michel Foucault, "The Subject and Power," *Critical Inquiry* 8, no. 4 (1982): 777–95.

39. For a partial list of scholarship on white women in plantation societies, see Anne Firor Scott, *The Southern Lady: From Pedestal to Politics, 1830–1930* (Chicago: University of Chicago Press, 1970); Catherine Clinton, *The Plantation Mistress: Woman's World in the Old South* (New York: Pantheon Books, 1982); Elizabeth Fox-Genovese, *Within the Plantation Household: Black and White Women of the Old South* (Chapel Hill: University of North Carolina Press, 1988); Brenda E. Stevenson, *Life in Black and White: Family and Community in the Slave South* (New York: Oxford University Press, 1997); Kirsten Fischer, *Suspect Relations: Sex, Race, and Resistance in Colonial North Carolina* (Ithaca, N.Y.: Cornell University Press, 2001); Burnard, "A Matron in Rank"; Sharon Block, *Rape and Sexual Power in Early America* (Chapel Hill: University of North Carolina Press, 2006); and Thavolia Glymph, *Out of the House of Bondage: The*

Transformation of the Plantation Household (Cambridge: Cambridge University Press, 2008). I am also aware of Brooke Newman's "Gender, Sexuality, and the Formation of Racial Identities in the Eighteenth-Century Anglo Caribbean World," *Gender and History* 22, no. 3 (2010): 585–602.

40. This work in the United States began with Deborah Gray White's text, *Ar'n't I a Woman? Female Slaves in the Plantation South* (New York: W. W. Norton, 1985). Other scholarship to which this chapter is indebted includes Beckles, *Natural Rebels*; Bush, *Slave Women in Caribbean Society*; Betty Wood, *Women's Work, Men's Work: The Informal Slave Economies of Lowcountry Georgia* (Athens: University of Georgia Press, 1995); Jacqueline Jones, *Labor of Love, Labor of Sorrow: Black Women, Work, and the Family from Slavery to the Present* (New York: Vintage Books, 1985); Kathleen Brown, *Good Wives*; David Barry Gaspar and Darlene Clark Hine, eds., *More than Chattel: Black Women and Slavery in the Americas* (Bloomington: Indiana University Press, 1996); Hartman, *Scenes of Subjection*; Leslie Schwalm, *A Hard Fight for We: Women's Transition from Slavery to Freedom in South Carolina* (Urbana: University of Illinois Press, 1997); Beckles, *Centering Woman*; Leslie M. Harris, *In the Shadow of Slavery: African Americans in New York City, 1626–1863* (Chicago: University of Chicago Press, 2003); Trevor Burnard, *Mastery, Tyranny, and Desire: Thomas Thistlewood and His Slaves in the Anglo-Jamaican World* (Chapel Hill: University of North Carolina Press, 2003); Jennifer L. Morgan, *Laboring Women: Gender and Reproduction in New World Slavery* (Philadelphia: University of Pennsylvania Press, 2004); Stephanie M. H. Camp, *Closer to Freedom: Enslaved Women and Everyday Resistance in the Plantation South* (Chapel Hill: University of North Carolina Press, 2004); Daina Ramey Berry, *Swing the Sickle for the Harvest Is Ripe: Gender and Slavery in Antebellum Georgia* (Urbana: University of Illinois Press, 2007); Cecily Jones, *Engendering Whiteness: White Women and Colonialism in Barbados and North Carolina, 1627–1865* (Manchester: Manchester University Press, 2007); Glymph, *Out of the House*; and Saidiya Hartman, *Lose Your Mother: A Journey along the Atlantic Slave Route* (New York: Farrar, Straus and Giroux, 2008).

41. For an example of terrorizing techniques employed by colonial authorities in Jamaica that went beyond the living, see Vincent Brown, *The Reaper's Garden: Death and Power in the World of Atlantic Slavery* (Cambridge, Mass.: Harvard University Press, 2010). See also Diana Paton, *No Bond but the Law: Punishment, Race, and Gender in Jamaican State Formation, 1780–1870* (Durham, N.C.: Duke University Press, 2004).

42. For the text from which I draw on the concept of unstable identities, see Judith Butler, *Gender Trouble: Feminism and the Subversion of Identity* (New York: Routledge, 1990), 178, wherein she explains that gender is performed and therefore produced and these repeated performances result in the effect of a norm or static state of being: or a "true gender." Gender (and other social identities) is maintained, argues Butler, by "the tacit collective agreement to perform, produce, and sustain discrete and polar genders as cultural fictions is obscured by the credibility of those productions—and the punishments that attend not agreeing to believe in them."

43. For a discussion about the solidification of racial categories through the policing

of sex, see Fischer, *Suspect Relations*. This chapter applies much of Fischer's argument to the context of eighteenth-century Barbados. My argument differs, however, in my focus on an elite white woman due to the lack of a substantial population of lower-class white women in the colony and a large gap in the archives concerning lower court cases. Moreover, I am interested in how elite discourses and sexual distress of white women shaped the limits for enslaved women in this Caribbean society.

44. On relational subjection, see Butler, "Bodies and Power, Revisited," 16.

45. For a discussion of archival silence and enslaved women, see Marisa J. Fuentes, "Power and Historical Figuring: Rachael Pringle Polgreen's Troubled Archive," *Gender and History* 22, no. 3 (2010): 565–84.

46. Watson, "Obsession, Betrayal and Sex," 253.

47. Barbados Minutes of Council, CO31/21/D1: 65, NAL, 65.

48. The northern part of the island of Barbados. See Watson, "Obsession, Betrayal and Sex," 255.

49. Barbados Minutes of Council CO31/21/D1: 65, NAL.

50. Ibid.

51. Ibid.

52. Watson, "Obsession, Betrayal and Sex," 347.

53. For a discussion of legal cases dealing with sexual transgressions in the colonial period, see Fischer, *Suspect Relations* and Natalie Zacek, *Settler Society in the English Leeward Islands, 1670–1776* (New York: Cambridge University Press, 2010). I thank anonymous reviewer 2 for providing this important point.

54. Barbados Minutes of Council CO31/21/D1: 76, NAL.

55. See Watson, "Obsession, Betrayal and Sex"; and Burnard, "Matron in Rank" for discussion of the subjugation of white women in this time period.

56. Watson, "Obsession, Betrayal and Sex," 262.

57. Agatha Moore inherited property in Cheapside, Bridgetown, from her grandmother Mary Thomsome while still an infant. Although this property would transfer to her husband upon marriage, it is possible, since this case did not end in divorce, that Mrs. Moore retained some economic resources after her "ruin." See Watson, "Obsession, Betrayal and Sex," 247.

58. Watson, "Obsession, Betrayal and Sex," 247.

59. See Barbados Deeds 1775–1778, no. 182, and Recopied Wills (RB6/29–30), Barbados Department of Archives, Black Rock, for examples of white women managing their property in slaves and land. In many cases, white women circumvented colonial laws that transferred their property to their husbands by leaving their property "in trust" to a third party for the duration of their marriage. These trusts were also formed by white women in order to ensure that their daughters and nieces would retain inheritance, despite their marriages.

60. Barbados Minutes of Council CO31/21/D1: 65, NAL.

61. Hartman, *Scenes of Subjection*, 81.

62. For a discussion on the rhetoric and use of the language of seduction in similar cases in the colonial context, see Fischer, *Suspect Relations*.

63. Barbados Minutes of Council CO31/21/D1: 65, NAL.

64. Michel Foucault, *The History of Sexuality*, vol. 1, *An Introduction*, trans. Robert Hurley (New York: Vintage Books, 1990), 97.

65. Hartman, *Scenes of Subjection*, 81.

66. Burnard, "Matron in Rank," 145.

67. See Watson, "Obsession, Betrayal and Sex," 254, and Burnard, "Matron in Rank."

68. Zacek, "Sex, Sexuality, and Social Control," 191.

69. Ibid., 207.

70. Burnard also ponders the implications and accusations of Mrs. Manning allegedly having sex with black male slaves.

71. See Block, *Rape and Sexual Power*.

72. Sharon Block and Kathleen M. Brown, "Clio in Search of Eros: Redefining Sexualities in Early America," *William and Mary Quarterly* 60, no. 1 (2003): 11.

CHAPTER 4

As if She Were My Own

*Love and Law in the Slave Society
of Eighteenth-Century Peru*

BIANCA PREMO

This chapter is intended to both evoke and provoke emotion.

The eighteenth-century Lima slave owner Petronila Vásquez deeply loved her slave María Antonia. Indeed, she said she loved her with "a tenderness more than if she were [her] daughter." Here we might pause and gauge our reaction to this proclamation of maternal, masterly love. Perhaps like me, you regard this statement with discomfort. Certainly suspicion. Maybe even disgust. But let's continue with the slave owner's description of her relationship to María Antonia. Petronila recounted how she "raised and educated her from her earliest years as if she were my own daughter, feeding her and giving her whatever gifts she wants, dressing her in more than a luxurious manner, committing all my faculties, with no other aim than that she serve me by hand and accompany me through the discomforts of the many illnesses that I suffered, [and] in all this her correspondence [with me] was reciprocal."[1] Perhaps now some of our initial discomfort has subsided. It appears that Petronila might not be talking about "love" as we understand it today. Rather, it seems more akin to "interest" or "investment" in a material sense. Or, perhaps, it is something more like the resigned estimation or fealty that historians such as Lawrence Stone argued belong to a premodern history, before we loved each other, ourselves, and our property like we do today.[2] Indeed, even though the scholarly fathers of theories of master paternalism such as U.S. historian Eugene Genovese and Brazilian sociologist Gilberto Freyre took for granted the sincerity of master-slave affection, they also suggested that such feelings were distinct from (and more desirable than) modern (capitalist) emotions and race relations.[3]

Petronila's proclamation of love seems even more distant from us because her affective exchange with María Antonia was part of a swap also involving work and commodities. Consider, too, that her statements were produced in a civil lawsuit initiated by María Antonia's uncle, who was attempting to force Petronila to accept 150 pesos for the woman's freedom. Knowing this, we might feel safe in dismissing altogether the owner's claims to love as the self-serving protestations of a person who held another human in bondage and who was motivated, above all, by an interest removed in both space and time from our own emotional universe.

In this chapter, I would like to think about feelings in slave history. Or, better put, I would like for us to feel about our thinking about slavery. I do so by working with evidence culled from an examination of over five hundred civil disputes involving slaves, and particularly slave children, in eighteenth-century Peru.[4] At the most general level, I use these lawsuits to consider the legal history of slavery within the history of emotion.

Doing so involves, first, outlining the structures of our own contemporary emotional responses to questions of affection in bondage, placing them in historical and historiographical perspective. Next, the chapter explores a particular kind of emotion: the paternal/filial or familial feelings expressed in court cases brought by urban slaves against masters. Arguing that emotion was long part of the legal lexicon available to Spanish American litigants involved in contestations over slavery and freedom, I then explore various articulations of reciprocal emotion between master and slave and consider where, within these discourses, we can fit the desire for freedom. I want to encourage closer study of master-slave emotions not only to enrich our understanding of the history of law and bondage, not only to deepen our knowledge of the emotional lives of slaveholders and the enslaved themselves, but also to make us aware of our own interests in thinking and feeling about slavery.

This is a timely endeavor, for some argue that we historians are in the midst of an "emotional turn," propelled in no small part by historian William Reddy, whose *Navigation of Feeling* has become a fast classic in the decade since its appearance.[5] Reddy is perhaps best known for his formulation of "emotives," a concept that permits scholars to sidestep the vexing question of whether language about emotion actually reflects some true inner state by reversing the order and proposing that the utterance of an emotion leads to its historical realization.[6] Such a rendering releases the constraints imposed by the modern separation of "feelings" from "interests."[7]

Reddy advances something else useful in the *Navigation of Feeling*: the concept of the "emotional regime," or the normative order of emotions that facilitates the stability of a political structure.[8] It might be, as Erin Dwyer points out in her foray into the history of emotions in the U.S. antebellum South, that "emotional regime" is too top-down a concept to capture the complexity of emotions in a slave system. But I propose that it is useful not so much to understand historical actors' emotions toward slavery as much as our own feelings about slave history.[9] Our impulse to dismiss the legal proclamations of love within Atlantic slavery as inauthentic, outdated, or corrupted—our discomfort, disgust, and suspicion—is part of our own contemporary emotional regime. This regime is founded on liberal notions of agency, history, and humanity itself. Under its power, we assume that slave history was founded first and last on the repugnance of bondage, and that enslaved people directed all of their actions and feelings at being liberated from it, either through actual manumission or by means of psychological or sociological autonomy.[10]

This, I admit, is a conceptual regime difficult to rebel against. In my two decades of research into slave lawsuits in the courts of the Spanish American colonies, I consistently have been astonished by the perseverance and creativity of enslaved litigants who used the legal system to keep their family members from being sold away, to seek new, more benevolent owners, to resist mistreatment, and, in some very moving cases to be explored here, to be freed.

Yet embedded in the appreciation, even admiration, for slaves' legal perseverance is recognition or identification. *Recognition* is used here in a post-Enlightenment sense in which, in order to align oneself with a contemporary human rights regime, we must empathize with others and assume in them attributes that accord with modern notions of self. I return to this thought at the end of the chapter, but here I wish to remind us that the empathy, the recognition, and the identification that the modern observer feels for slaves have their own history.

After centuries of wrestling with the role of passion in moral understanding (more frequently than not, passion was something to be governed), seventeenth-century Europeans were moved to a philosophical interest in emotion as an amoral, autonomous state.[11] From this, we get the rise of Enlightened sentiment in the eighteenth century, first as externalized sentimentalism, then as an internalized notion of self and a conceptualization of feeling as substance. Bound up in these last shifts in sentiment—in both their externalized and internalized varieties—was empathy. Empathy became constitutive of modern notions of humanity and rights, and in turn it was implicated in concepts of history and historical agency.[12]

As scholars such as Susan Buck-Morss have pointed out, "history" has not always known what to do with slaves. "Free" and "slave" were key categories for historicist philosophies of the type Georg Wilhelm Hegel advanced, but they also were abstracted from the experiences of actual, living, breathing slaves.[13] Contemporary slave historiography certainly has struggled against history's abstracting impulse and the depersonification and decontextualization of the slave.[14] Yet it remains true that, in our present emotional regime, our sympathies in history are predicated on veneration for individuals as agents and self as property. And they pivot centrally on a particular modern notion of liberty.

Modern freedom, so important to our present understanding of historical agency, is, according to Elizabeth Povelli, construed as "a state of social nondetermination." Movement in time, we imagine, should be toward greater individual autonomy from the relationships and institutions that constrain. One can see the traces of this thinking in contemporary slave historiography, where there is a tendency to read the past as a progressive march to the triumph of the emancipated sovereign subject.[15] This can make thinking of the relationships of enslaved people outside of the quest for liberty almost unnecessary.[16]

Yet if we were to inventory the legal discourses employed in the hundreds of lawsuits involving enslaved litigants in Spanish America, we would find that in the overwhelming majority emotive language referred to relationships that did not necessarily strain toward freedom as non-determination.[17] Actually, emotive language often did the opposite by supporting the larger social status quo of slavery. Many of the cases enslaved litigants brought before the end of the eighteenth century were not suits for freedom but rather what, borrowing from historian Frank Proctor, we might call "autonomy suits"—suits aimed at improving slaves' lives by permitting them to find new owners or remain with family members, but not necessarily suits seeking freedom and certainly not overt challenges to the system of slavery itself.[18] And even after Spanish American slaves began to very actively use the civil courts in individual freedom cases in the latter half of the eighteenth century, their legal arguments reveal a complicated but nonetheless connected emotional history with owners.

Slavery could be nourished with love in the legal system because written law in the Spanish American colonies ensnared slave, slaveholder, and judge alike in a tangle of affective ties. Some of those ties abetted slaves' attempts to elevate their own chosen relationships over their obligations to their owners. In ecclesiastical lawsuits in Spanish America, love reigned as a legal discourse because slaves could sue masters on canonical grounds to prevent being separated from their spouses.[19] In civil courts, love reigned as rhetoric because of the high frequency with which Latin American masters manumitted slaves based on slaves' integration into family relationships. The result was to legally make freedom and slavery part of the same system of affective relationships rather than to set them in opposition.

Put differently, social determination served as the plot line for legal narratives for both master and slave, even in slaves' struggles to better control their own fate. Thus Petronila's claims to have loved her slave were far from unique, and they were accompanied by slaves' own statements—though often more brief and formulaic in character—of having served their masters with "love" in turn.

Of course, as this volume shows, relationships between slaveholding men and enslaved women were often violently sexualized and some, more controversially, might be labeled as "romantic." I wish to set aside those particular relations for now, in part because there are excellent works on Lima that detail the labor-love-sex-violence nexus among adult slaves and explore the ramifications for the offspring of such unions.[20] But I also want to shift attention away from those relationships because, in eighteenth-century Spanish American lawsuits, affection between slave owners and slaves was more frequently cast as paternal and filial rather than as romantic or sexual.

To be clear, these expressions are typically found in cases of urban slavery, where domestic rather than plantation work predominated, and where slaves and masters lived cheek by jowl. Thus the language corresponded to the lived experience of residential intimacy between master and slave, making it doubtful that it was "just talk" devoid of any content at all. In particular, freedom lawsuits frequently involved slaves raised in the "house and power" of their masters—a position of intimacy that at once socialized slaves and masters emotionally and, as we see later, simultaneously raised some slaves' expectations concerning their own value and ability to determine how and where they or their family members lived and worked.[21]

Conflicts within such households provide historians of Peru an opportunity to rethink the place of law in Peruvian slavery. Slaves developed a kind of customary law of slavery based in the intimacies of the slaveholding household. They countered masters' property rights by exposing private matters, including extralegal manumission arrangements, to judges.[22] As we follow these scholars in seeking to understand love and law in slaves' lives, we might note that even as slaves began to contrast the unwritten promises that made slavery work with owners' formal property rights, it was not necessarily slaves' membership in the household and access to family secrets that was extralegal or beyond the law. In fact, these were fundamental to Spanish American slave law.

The language of affection and intimacy between slaves and masters drew on medieval codes in which slaves were considered as part of the "family" or the "private" domain. During the Middle Ages in Europe, legal formulations of familial reverence and debt to caregivers created what one medievalist refers to as an "economy of care."[23] Medieval Castilian law, which remained in force even as Spanish kings amassed an increasing body of law specifically for the New World, followed suit. As a legal construct, slavery relied precisely on the creation of quasi-familial bonds between owners and slaves, particularly if slaves were children.[24] If, as Povelli tells us, modern ideas of subjectivity turn on freedom as nondetermination, early modern Spanish law advanced a hyper socially determined notion of legal subjects, including slaves.

The laws that governed the American colonies codified the notion that master authority derived from naturalized patriarchal authority. The slave was envisaged as a man with a family and so, too, was his master. For example, a slave owed both his master and the master's family "obedience" and was even beholden to give his life in their defense. In turn, masters were prohibited from killing or seriously injuring not only his slave but also the slave's wife and children.[25]

As laws represented enslavement as a family in bondage to another family, it created a nested situation in which the power and obligations of elders and masters coexisted with the power and obligations of servants to the children they reared. Every child was said to be subordinate to his or her parents by nature, termed as owing a "natural debt." Yet children also owed the "natural debt" of obedience to anyone who raised them, presumably even servants.[26] In turn, servants owed a special filial debt to masters who cared for them from birth, a debt described as "the honor and reverence that they should have toward their father."[27]

The enslavement of Africans in the New World only intensified these medieval legal discourses of affective exchange within the Spanish slaveholding family.[28] The idea that familial relationships bound masters as well as slaves never faded, even as the scale and brutality of human bondage became almost inconceivable. For example, in 1563 one of the earliest individual laws concerning the increasing enslavement of Africans issued for the Spanish American colonies gave the fathers of slave children a kind of right of first refusal to buy children when owners wished to sell them.[29]

Legal emphasis on master paternalism accelerated just as slaves were making increased use of the civil courts to challenge masters at the end of the eighteenth century. Carlos IV's 1789 *Instruction on the Education, Treatment and Employment of Slaves* essentially emphasized the responsibilities of masters rather than the obligations of slaves.[30] The single reference to the debt that slaves owed to their masters presented their obligation as filial. Slaves were to "obey and respect the Owners and Overseers, carrying out the tasks and labors that they are given according to their ability, and venerating [their masters] as *Padres de familia* [*paterfamilias*]." Some interpretations of slave owners' obligations had become so legally exacting that one lawyer could argue in a 1797 freedom suit that any owner who did not protect and care for slaves violated slaves' fundamental "natural rights." "Those Masters who do not fulfill their obligation should not, in a rigorous sense, be considered true Lords of their servants . . . for the inhumanity with which they treat them reaches the extremes of annihilating and destroying the sacred Rights of Nature."[31]

Thus late eighteenth-century discourses of inhumanity and natural rights served slaves well. But rather than use this language to counter notions of affective obligation outright, Peru's enslaved litigants frequently extended these obligations to judges, drawing on similarly codified language about justice as paternal. Take, as one of many examples, the words of Francisca Suazo, a freed *morena*, who litigated against the owner of her daughter, Jacinta, by claiming that "Humanity has an interest in the patronage of the indigent slave, and in providing the means [for him] to improve his lot[.] Your highness, in his pious love, cannot be indifferent to the delay of this benefit, not even for an instant."[32] Thus both the letter and practice of law could reinforce love language, building affective obligation into both master-slave relations and the very practice of slave law.

Even if some slaves were ready to spill household secrets in court to improve their condition, in many instances it was owners who discussed the emotional intimacies of the household in court. Love language was especially pronounced among female owners of female slaves.[33] The gendered and generational transference of affection forces us to take seriously, if not at face value, the ubiquitous claims of affection in slave cases. The mixed-gender labor practices that urban slavery inspired, which often involved slaves rearing masters' children as well as female masters overseeing the rearing of enslaved children, was a rich medium for the growth of affective reciprocity. (I found at least one case of a female slave master who suckled a newborn slave baby.)[34]

As was obvious in the opening quotation in which Petronila quickly elided caring as affection and caring as labor—first for her own "rearing and educations" of María Antonia as a child and then her expectation that María Antonia would, in turn, care for her in her illness—labor and emotional companionship were part of the same complex. Slave owner Doña María Antonia Collasos imagined a chain of affective and labor reciprocities between women and children in households with slaves. She freed both the enslaved Victoria and Victoria's child, Baltazar, in "attention to the good service and the love the cited Victoria has professed to me, and for having raised for me various children at her breast."[35]

I do not want to suggest that this love talk precluded discussions of property rights and the occasional insistence by a master that slaves were not legal persons but mere possessions. The owner who in 1790 likened the enslaved Juana Portocarrero to a possession like "furniture" should confirm our modern suspicion that material interest could be dehumanizing.[36] And some owners could be openly cynical even when discussing their love for or benevolence toward slaves. Consider a master's reaction to the charges of excessive cruelty (*sevicia*) that the enslaved Antonio brought against him. Antonio complained not only of physical abuse and onerous work assignments but also that Don Pedro Escandón refused to sell him at the price his former owner had stipulated in his will (since Antonio had served his dead master "with love"). Don Pedro countered by pointing out that he had always treated all of his slaves well, not only out of "Christian charity, but also in consideration of the fact that they are personal capital [*caudal*]." Cruel treatment, he explained, would only "dissipate them."[37]

Nonetheless, the argument that master kindness was an economic imperative was not slave owners' only, or even most successful, legal tactic. Instead, owners defended themselves by likening slaves to their own children. Far more typical than Don Pedro's raw reference to the value of his slaves were masters' claims of emotional attachment as the basis for claims to legitimate ownership. Doña Agustina Sotomayor put it plainly in court when she said of a slave child whose mother was attempting to remove her, "this is a girl born in my house whom I have loved with distinction."[38]

Indeed, it is striking how often masters rejected slaves' cases against them not with arguments about absolute rights as property owners or denials of slaves' judicial personalities but rather by explaining, in detail, their feelings for them, with both affective and material referents. "I have given my slave a Christian owner and dressed her in noble garments" one master retorted when his slave sought a new owner, in a far more subtle reference to the economy of care than Pedro Escandón's.[39]

The obvious question is what slaves thought about this affective exchange. Their frequent, but often rote, references to having served their owners "con amor" (with love) do not offer us much deep insight into their feelings about the owners who claimed to love them as their own children. In part, this is to be expected since, to be in civil court in the first place, enslaved litigants often needed to convince judges of masters' cruelty, tyranny, and special hatred. But in one common kind of suit—those in which they claimed that dead owners had freed them in their testaments—love almost always makes an appearance. For example, Toribio Sosa of Trujillo, Peru, claimed that he served his former owner with "love and loyalty" and, as a result, was promised eventual freedom in a will.[40]

The arguments enslaved litigants advanced in their lawsuits sometimes contain even more expansive discussions of affective reciprocity, indicating that the master-slave relationship could endure past freedom. In 1738 María Josefa Balcazar's lover indicated that she stayed on with her mistress, Doña Juana Balcazar, for years after she was manumitted because of "much love and favor and for having raised her."[41] As a father and a former owner battled over custody of a freed nine-year-old girl in Trujillo in the 1720s, both emphasized that if awarded guardianship, they would ensure that doting Spanish women who loved her would raise her. The father even claimed that the nuns he had selected to care for his daughter were so affectionate toward her that the girl slept nightly in the same bed as one of them.[42]

Increasingly, however, freedom began to rest at the literal heart of enslaved litigants' references in court to affective exchanges. Lorenzo de Aguilar interpreted the intimacy he shared with his owner as an implicit promise of liberty. In 1755 he brought a suit for his freedom, claiming that he had been lovingly reared "from his earliest years" by his master. "Such was the love and the relaxed atmosphere [*distensión*] that I earned from him (although I am of this sphere)," Lorenzo explained, that it was clear his owner intended to free him. For Lorenzo, love was not merely a feeling but a state of social privilege. Lorenzo's master, for his part, admitted a deep "love" for the slave and acknowledged having reared him with special care. But he denied ever signing papers to free Lorenzo and repeatedly expressed his disappointment at his slave's "ingratitude" in suing for freedom.[43]

As in Lorenzo's suit, masters' sense of betrayal when slaves sued them abound in the increasing number of civil cases slaves brought before royal magistrates in the second half of the eighteenth century. Their disappointment reveals that, while the emotional regime in which slavery functioned facilitated a shared vocabulary of love, the interpretation of love diverged sharply.[44] For Lorenzo, as for us today, love should lead to liberty. But unlike for us, his legal rendering of liberty was earned, not inherent, and thus was embedded in the socially determined roles of master and slave.

Masters, for their part, saw love as a guarantee. They believed in something like a twisted version of a saying popular today: "if you love someone," they thought, "you won't have to set them free (at least not right away)." They conceived of exchanged affection as a preventive against freedom, and while they might have held out manumission as a reward for good service, they often were surprised that their slaves refused to be patient. Like Lorenzo's owner, they openly marveled at what they perceived as betrayal when their slaves made legal moves against them. In at least two cases, masters in Lima in fact sued their own slaves in efforts to renege on grants of freedom because they felt that the slaves had not shown sufficient gratefulness for their love or benevolence.[45]

It is important to note that Lorenzo, who saw himself as earning his freedom as he earned his master's favor, in many ways was a harbinger of things to come, not a representative of "slavery" as an unchanging legal or social institution. In fact, as slaves increasingly brought civil lawsuits against owners at the end of the eighteenth century, they began to make owners second-guess longstanding principles of affective reciprocity. Doña Ventura Alzamora recounted in court how she had taken pity on her slave, Francisco, who "convinced her" to purchase him from the bakery where he was incarcerated, telling her he would "punctually give me daily wages." It was because of this that "I left him free to work wherever he wanted."[46] She recounted the details of her treatment of him: giving him money to go out with his wife and celebrate the day of San Francisco (the slave's namesake), even providing him a cape and Castilian hat, which were sartorial signs of free status. Yet it was clear that she was beginning to regret these actions since they only made Francisco more desirous of liberty.

Still, even as they increasingly sued for freedom, slaves' justification for lawsuits rested on laws and principles of notions of familiarity within slavery rather than notions of individual rights and non-determination, as we might today imagine. One woman seeking liberty for herself and her daughter based a civil case against her owner on her disapproval of her owner's choice of caregiver for her four-year-old. When she could no longer maintain her daughter on her own, the enslaved woman turned her child over to her master but was disappointed to find that the white woman he found to care for the girl was not part of a larger family network but instead someone the slave mother labeled an "outsider" (*agena*).[47] This freedom suit, like many other cases, drew not from the proposition that a freed slave would be launched alone into the world, possessed of her own individual liberty, but rather on the implication that there were other, more suitable family networks awaiting the slave after manumission.

Slaves also referred to the affective arrangements of rearing in freedom cases to expose masters' blatant double standards of loyalty. Antonina Guillén had taken her master's wife to court over her liberty in 1797, and when confronted with a request to find someone to guarantee that her owner would receive daily wages in compensation for the loss of Antonina's labor while the suit made its way through court, her lawsuit creatively threw the charge of ingratitude back onto her owners: "Scandal and amazement would be caused in any tribunal upon hearing that a slave suing for liberty who is nursing a child would have to guarantee her daily wages—not nursing a slave child but the child of the Master himself."[48]

As eighteenth-century slaves mined the veins of affective reciprocity rather than "rights" alone to enrich their cases for freedom, they established ever more direct legal connections between a wide array of legal kinships and the master-slave relationship. One enslaved woman, in explaining her flight from a mistress whom she accused of constant cruelty, invoked canon law on the separation of spouses, claiming it was a model for the union between master and slave. Because of her mistreatment, "this union," her argument went, "is separated and broken, for there is [no union] in slavery when the Master cannot contain his temper."[49]

Keeping in mind these references to "unions" and affective ties both binding and broken, we might revisit our feelings about Petronila Vásquez and María Antonia, with whom we began. In particular, we might consider how the owner Petronila conceived of their arrangement as one that involved "committing all her faculties to the aim" of acquiring something from her slave, "giving her whatever gifts she wants." There is nothing in Petronila's statement that should lead us to believe that her emotional claims to love María Antonia were insincere or false because they accompanied a material exchange. Instead, I wish to suggest that the brutal context in which masters expressed love, betrayal, and sacrifice makes these emotions no less worthy of historical consideration than is slaves' desire for freedom.

Indeed, if we reflect long enough on our discomfort with these emotions, and if we interrogate closely our own tendency to empathize with slaves' quest for freedom while recoiling from slave owners' materially interested emotional attachments to the humans they held in bondage, a more disturbing underside of our own, modern emotional regime might be exposed. A slave owner in 1790s Lima understood that there was more to the emotional world of slavery than the desire for freedom. Clinging doggedly to his dominion over another human being, he argued that "if the principle of liberty consisted only . . . in the desire [*gana*] of slaves to be free, then slavery would already be extinguished."[50] Beyond desire there were the emotional and material exchanges, or the "gifts," as Petronila put it, that made slavery work.[51]

In a book dedicated to the iconography of slave emancipation, Marcus Wood has reflected, *pace* Fanon and Hegel twice removed, that freedom can be viewed as a "horrible gift" bestowed by whites. His point is that the "gift" of freedom turns slaves into empty vessels to be filled with the magnanimity of their liberators.[52] While still acknowledging the leading role that the desire for freedom began to take in slaves' legal constructions of their emotional relationships with masters over time, while still recognizing that slaves had a hand in the production of modern historical notions of agency, we should also be wary of reducing these relationships to no more than an impulse or automatic urge to liberation. To do so, in the end, is to do the history of slavery no favors.

The denial, disgust, and discomfort that characterize our reaction to claims of affection in bondage can too easily conceal a smug comfort in our own identification with slaves rather than owners. What is more, it risks turning slaves into cyphers for our modern imaginings of the self—a being whose historical value is only realized in a relentless searching for totalized, individual autonomy. In the end, the title of this chapter, "as if she were my own," can be read not only in reference to Petronila's claim to a love that drew her slave María Antonia close enough to transform her into something like her own daughter. It also can be read as our

own insistence on recognizing the emotional history of slavery only if it is evacuated of any feelings and attachments that are not compatible with our modern
desire for liberty and our own sense of ourselves.

NOTES

1. "Autos seguidos por Juan Manuel Belasunce contra doña Petronila Vásquez, sobre
que venda su sobrina, María Antonia," Archivo General de la Nación, Perú (hereafter AGN-P), Real Audiencia (RA), Civil (Civ.), Legajo (Leg.) 323, Cuaderno (C.) 2938,
1794, folio (f.) 8.

2. Lawrence Stone, *The Family, Sex and Marriage in England, 1500–1800* (London:
Weidenfeld and Nicolson, 1977).

3. Eugene Genovese, *Roll, Jordan, Roll: The World the Slaves Made* (New York:
Random House, 1974); Gilberto Freyre, *Casa grande e senzala: Formacão da família
brasileira sob o regime de economia patriarcal* (Rio de Janeiro: Maia and Schmidt, 1933).
On Genovese and his insistence on the less self-interested nature of the planter class
compared to the avaricious, self-interested capitalistic U.S. northerner, see Diane Miller
Sommerville, "Moonlight, Magnolias, and Brigadoon; or, 'Almost Like Being in Love':
Mastery and Sexual Exploitation in Eugene D. Genovese's Plantation South," *Radical History Review* 88 (2004): 68–82. The claim that Freyre literally romanticized the
slaveholding past is obviously not my own, but historians of comparative race might do
more to consider the parallels between Genovese and Freyre in terms of nostalgia as a
critique of modernity. For more about the politicization of Brazilian slave historiography and the tendency to omit explicit consideration of the contradictions of intimacy
and slavery, pleasure and profit when drawing from Freyre, see Jane-Marie Collins,
"Intimacy, Inequality, and *Democracia Racial*: Theorizing Race, Gender and Sex in
the History of Brazilian Race Relations," *Journal of Romance Studies* 7, no. 2 (2007):
19–34. Also see Okezi Otovo, "From *Mãe Preta* to *Mãe Desamparada*: Maternity
and Public Health in Post-Abolition Bahia," *Luso-Brazilian Review* 48, no. 2 (2011):
164–91.

4. For a broader study of the civil litigiousness of enslaved subjects in Peru during
the period 1700–1799, I examined 209 cases from Lima in which slaves featured prominently as property and 17 in Trujillo, Peru; and 225 cases brought by enslaved litigants in disputes in Lima, and 94 in Trujillo, Peru. I also looked closely at 169 disputes
involving slaves as both objects and litigants heard in Church jurisdiction in Lima.
The language of intimacy varied little between jurisdictions, but the quest for freedom
as the legal end result was more pronounced over the course of the century in civil
disputes.

5. Jan Plamper, "The History of Emotions: An Interview with William Reddy,
Barbara Rosenwein, and Peter Stearns," *History and Theory* 49 (2010): 237–65, 237;
William M. Reddy, *The Navigation of Feeling: A Framework for the History of Emotion*
(New York: Cambridge University Press, 2001). In Latin American history, the turn is

exemplified in several recent studies featuring emotion, especially where fear of slave uprising figures centrally, including Claudia Rosa Lauro, *El miedo en el Perú, siglo XVI al XX* (Lima: Pontificia Universidad Católica del Perú, 2005); Sonya Lipsett Rivera and Javier Villa Flores, eds., *Emotions and Everyday Life in Colonial Mexico* (Albuquerque: University of New Mexico Press, 2014); Ada Ferrer, *Freedom's Mirror: Cuba and Haiti in the Age of Revolution* (New York: Cambridge University Press, 2014).

6. Also see Monique Scheer, "Are Emotions a Kind of Practice (and Is That What Makes Them Have a History)? A Bordieuian Approach to Understanding Emotion," *History and Theory* 51, no. 2 (2012): 193–220.

7. For more on "interest," see Reddy's interview in Plamper, "The History of Emotions," *History and Theory* 49 (2010): 237–65, 238.

8. Reddy, *Navigation of Feeling*, 125–26.

9. Erin Dwyer, "Mastering Emotions: The Emotional Politics of Slavery," PhD diss., Harvard University, 2012, 4.

10. On the liberal notions of selfhood embedded in the historiography of slave agency, see Walter Johnson, "On Agency," *Journal of Social History* 37, no. 1 (2003): 113–24, 115.

11. David Thorley, "Towards a History of Emotion, 1562–1660," *Seventeenth Century* 28, no. 1 (2013): 3–19.

12. On sympathy and spectatorship as fundamental components of modern notions of self, see Michel Foucault, "What Is Enlightenment?," in *The Foucault Reader*, ed. Paul Rabinow (New York: Pantheon Books, 1984), 44. Note that Lynn Hunt views empathy, à la Rousseau, as the touchstone of modern human rights, *Inventing Human Rights: A History* (New York: Norton, 2008), 20; whereas Dror Wahrman emphasizes empathy's outward orientation, in *The Making of the Modern Self: Identity and Culture in Eighteenth-Century England* (New Haven, Conn.: Yale University Press, 2004). Charles Taylor, in *Sources of the Self: The Making of Modern Identity* (Cambridge, Mass.: Harvard University Press, 1989), shifts the attention to the recognition of human "dignity" in others, 12–13, 185–86.

13. Susan Buck-Morss, "Hegel and Haiti," *Critical Inquiry* 26, no. 4 (2000): 821–65.

14. Notable in this regard is Michel Rolph-Trouillot's work, particularly *Silencing the Past: Power and the Production of History* (Boston: Beacon, 1995).

15. Elizabeth Povelli, "A Flight from Freedom," in *Postcolonial Studies and Beyond*, ed. Ania Loomba, Suvir Kaul, Matti Bunzl, Antoinette Burton, and Jed Esty (Durham, N.C.: Duke University Press, 2005), 143–65, esp. 144. It might be noted that here I eschew engaging Berlin's famous division of "positive and negative" freedoms in favor of recognizing that freedom has endless historical permutations. The one of interest here is our own imagining of freedom as self-determination and the state of not being a slave; Isaiah Berlin, "Two Concepts of Liberty," in *Four Essays on Liberty* (1969; rpt., New York: Oxford University Press, 1979). Also see Jerome Schneewind, *The Invention of Autonomy: A History of Modern Moral Philosophy* (New York: Cambridge University Press, 1989); David Schmidtz and Jason Brennan, *A Brief History of Liberty* (Malden, Mass.: Wiley-Blackwell, 2010). In many ways, the battle of human conservation over

property conservation can be traced back to the differences between Hugo Grotius and John Locke in natural rights theory. See Hunt, *Inventing Human Rights*, 119. I examine in more detail the issue of rights in slave suits—and particularly natural rights discourses of conservation—in *The Enlightenment on Trial: Ordinary Litigants and Colonialism in the Eighteenth-Century Spanish Empire* (New York: Oxford University Press, 2017). Also see Frank T. Proctor, "An 'Imponderable Servitude': Slave versus Master Litigation for Cruelty (*Maltratamiento or Sevicia*) in the Eighteenth Century," *Journal of Social History* 48, no. 3 (2015): 662–84.

16. A good example of an older kind of work that presents all interactions between enslaved people and masters as composed of artifice is Bertram Wyatt-Brown, "The Mask of Obedience: Slave Psychology in the Old South," *American Historical Review* 93, no. 5 (1988): 1228–52. The piece concludes: "An essential self remained inviolable. Behind the mask of docility the slave was still himself and gave the lie to southern claims for 'knowing' their blacks . . . all the problems of betrayal and personal anguish that bondage created, strength and hope were only to be found in the love of family and friends"—family and friends who presumably were also slaves or freed people of color. For a reappraisal of Orlando Patterson's famous pronouncement about the sociological cost of slavery, see Vincent Brown, "Social Death and Political Life in the Study of Slavery: Between Resistance and Oblivion," *American Historical Review* 114, no. 5 (2009): 1231–49.

17. On the importance of intimacy in the law in enslaved people's ecclesiastical suits in the seventeenth century, see Michelle A. McKinley, *Fractional Freedoms: Slavery, Intimacy, and Legal Mobilization in Colonial Lima, 1600–1700* (New York: Cambridge University Press, 2016).

18. Frank T. Proctor III, *"Damned Notions of Liberty": Slavery, Culture, and Power in Colonial Mexico, 1640–1769* (Albuquerque: University of New Mexico Press, 2011), 184–85; "Slavery Rebellion and Liberty in Colonial Mexico," in *Black Mexico: Race and Society from Colonial to Modern Times*, ed. Ben Vinson and Matthew Restall (Albuquerque: University of New Mexico Press, 2009), 21–50. I am less certain than is Proctor of the absence of modern notions of freedom in slave cases prior to the end of the eighteenth century, but I do regard his general chronology, in which autonomy plays a much larger role than does freedom in seventeenth-century cases, as useful in understanding the legal history of slave litigation.

19. Herman Bennett, *Africans in Colonial Mexico: Absolutism, Christianity, and Afro-Creole Consciousness* (Bloomington: Indiana University Press, 2003).

20. Christine Hünefeldt, *Paying the Price of Freedom: Family and Labor among Lima's Slaves, 1800–1854* (Berkeley: University of California Press, 1994). It is worth noting here that many historians have presumed that the offspring of slave-master sexual relations or rape might count on good treatment or manumission, but at least one colonial lawyer argued that animosity and hatred—"a greater captivity" was the more likely outcome. "Autos seguidos por María Gertrudis Montero contra doña Rosa Pérez su ama sobre su libertad por haber tenido 'ilícito comercio' con su marido [*sic*: padre] por el tiempo de tres años," AGN P RA Civ., Leg. 251, C. 2188, 1785, f. 49 v.

21. Being "born" into the "house and power" of slavery was a critical, if today still not completely understood, dividing line in experiences of both master and slave. U.S. southerners viewed masters not "born" in the system but rather newcomers as slave-holders as overly cruel and lacking in the emotional nuance necessary. Dwyer, "Master-ing Emotions," 17–19.

22. Rachel Sarah O'Toole, "Freedom's Modernity in Colonial Spanish America," paper given at the Latin American Studies Association 30th Annual Meeting, May 2013. On "commensality" outside of sexual relations, see Michelle McKinley, "Fractional Freedoms: Slavery, Legal Activism, and Ecclesiastical Courts in Colonial Lima, 1593–1689," *Law and History Review* 29, no. 3 (2010): 749–90, 773–74; and her *Fractional Freedoms*, 185.

23. See Susan Alice McDonough, *Witnesses, Neighbors, and Communities in Late Medieval Marseilles* (New York: Palgrave Macmillan, 2013).

24. Bianca Premo, *Children of the Father King: Youth, Authority, and Legal Minority in Colonial Lima* (Chapel Hill: University of North Carolina Press, 2005); McKinley, *Fractional Freedoms*, 147.

25. Samuel Parsons Scott, trans., *Las Siete Partidas*, ed. Robert I. Burns (Philadel-phia: University of Pennsylvania Press, 2000), 4:22.

26. Ibid., 4:24:3.

27. Ibid., 4:20:3 and 8. For slaves, the natural debt was particularly binding if they were freed by their masters, 4:24:2.

28. Bianca Premo, "Familiar: Thinking beyond Lineage and across Race in the Span-ish Atlantic," *William and Mary Quarterly* 70, no. 2 (2013): 295–316.

29. The law was intended for Spanish fathers and reads "some *españoles* have children with black women, and want to buy them to give them liberty: We order that, if they are to be sold, the fathers who wish to purchase them shall be preferred." *Recopilación de leyes del reynado de las Indias*, 7:5:8 (1687; rpt., Madrid: Antonio Pérez de Soto, 1774): 7:5:6. But by the late colonial period, nonwhite fathers often themselves freed slaves, interpreted the law as applying to them as well. See "Autos seguidos por José Lla-nos, padre de María del Carmen Marín, esclava de Doña María de la Daga, sobre que no la venda," AGN, Cab., C. Civ., Leg. 16, C. 242, 1809.

30. The code is reprinted as "Instrucción sobre la educación, trato y ocupación de los esclavos," in *Colección de documentos*, ed. Richard Koentzke (Madrid: Consejo Superior de Investigaciones Científicas, 1962), 3:643–52.

31. "Autos seguidos por don Antonio Arburúa con su esclava, Andrea Escalante [*sic*: Arburúa], sobre la libertad de ésta [*sic*: su hija]," AGN-P RA Civ., Leg. 203, C. 2616, 1791, f. 28.

32. "Autos seguidos pro Francisca Suazo, morena liberta, contra don Juan José Alz-amora, sobre la libertad de su hija Jacinta," AGN-P, RA Civ, Leg. 70, C. 720, 1807.

33. Note that Frank Proctor III followed up on the assumption that many man-umitted children were the offspring of slaveholding fathers, finding instead that, in colonial Mexico, women frequently manumitted children who had been born into their households. See Frank Proctor III, "Gender and the Manumission of Slaves in New

Spain," *Hispanic American Historical Review* 86, no. 2 (2006): 309–36. Also see Premo, *Children of the Father King*, 219–20.

34. "Autos seguidos por Marta del Carmen Breña contra Don Francisco Iturrino, sobre se le ortogue el instrumento de libertad y se le permita lactar a su hija en su propia casa," AGN, RA, C. Civ., Leg. 132, C. 1345, f. 14, 1815. Also see Hünefeldt, *Paying the Price*, 119.

35. "Autos seguidos por Julian Cabeduzo en nombre de su hermana Victoria y su menor hijo sobre la libertad de ambos, ortogado por su anterior ama, María Antonia Collasos," AGN, RA, Civ. Leg. 57, C. 582, 1805.

36. "Autos seguidos por Juana Portocarrero contra su ama, doña Juliana Portocarrero sobre sevicia," AGN-P, RA, Civ., Leg. 292, C. 2608, 9 v.

37. "Autos seguidos por Antonio Zavala, negro esclavo de D. Pedro Escandón, sobre su libertad y sevicia," AGN-P, RA, Civ., Leg. 103, C. 867, 1746, 46v.

38. "Autos seguidos por María Antonia Oyague contra da. Agustina Sotomayor sobre sevicia que practica contra la esclava María Ignacia, hija de la demandante," AGN, RA, Civ., Leg. 36, C. 3366, 1798.

39. "Expediente seguido por Vicenta Conde y Marín esclava, contra Doña Rafaela Moreno, mujer legítima de don Felix José de Xaramillo, sobre moderación del precio en que ha de pasa a servir a otro dueño," Archivo Regional de la Libertad (ARL) Intendente, Causas Ordinarias (CO), Leg. 299, C. 115, 1788, 12v.

40. "Autos que sigue Thoribio de Sosa contra su Amo Dn. Juan de Sosa sobre sebicia," AGN, Cab., C. Crim., Leg. 6, C. 9, 1776. For the importance of such cases in the seventeenth and early eighteenth centuries, see Michelle McKinley, "Till Death Do Us Part: Testamentary Manumission in Seventeenth-Century Lima, Peru," *Slavery and Abolition* 33, no. 3 (2012): 381–401; Proctor, *"Damned Notions of Liberty,"* 174.

41. "Autos seguidos por doña [*sic*] María Josefa Balcazar contra doña Juana de Balcazar sobre su libertad," AGN, Real Audiencia, Causas Civiles, Leg. 70, C. 549, 1738, f. 1.

42. "Expediente seguido por Juan Lorenzo Rizo, vezino de Trujillo, contra Bartolomé de Zamudio, oficial carpintero, sobre pago de alimentos a una hija natural Petrona Zamudio, libertina," ARL, Corr. CO, Leg. 220, c. 1777, 1728, 5v.

43. "Autos seguidos por Lorenzo de Aguilar contra Don Manuel de Orejuela sobre su libertad," 1755, AGN-P, Cabildo (Cab.), Civ., Leg. 37, C. 663, f. 1.

44. See, for example, "Autos seguidos por Lorenzo de Aguilar contra Don Manuel de Orejuela sobre su libertad," AGN-P, Cab., Civ., Leg. 37, C. 663, 1755; and "Autos seguidos por doña [*sic*] María Josefa Balcazar contra doña Juana de Balcazar sobre su libertad."

45. "Autos seguidos por D. Juan de Prado, contra su esclava Agustina, sobre su libertad," AGN-P, Cab. Civ., Leg. 31, C. 527, 1774; "Autos seguidos por D. Nicolás López Molero contra José Inosciente, sobre la revocatoria de su libertad," AGN-P, Cab. Civ., eg. 37, C. 665, 1777; "Autos seguidos por D. Baltazar de Laya y Llano sobre la revocatoria de la libertad concedida a su esclavo Agustín," AGN-P, Cab. Civ., Leg. 82, C. 1556, 1797.

46. "Autos seguidos por Francisco Castillo contra da. Ventura Alzamora, su ama, sobre que la venda," AGN-P, Cab. Civ., eg. 37, C. 664, 1777, 3v.

47. "Autos seguidos por don Antonio Arburúa con su esclava, Andrea Escalante."

48. "Autos seguidos por Antonina Guillén contra D. Joaquín Barandiarán, su amo, sobre su libertad," AGN-P, Cab. Civ., Leg. 83, C. 1566, 1797, f. 26 v.

49. "Expediente seguido por Michaela Mina, esclava de doña Luisa Luxán Alfaro contra don Joseph Pesantes, marido de esta última sobre que se le venda a otro amo por padecer de abuso excesivo e intolerable sevicia," ARL, Cab., CO, Leg. 44, C. 791, 1741, f. 16. This was not the only parallel drawn in the courts between slave and divorce cases. See "Autos seguidos por Rosa Montenegro," Archivo Arzobispal de Lima (hereafter AAL), Causas de Negros, Leg. 33, exp. 29, 1791–96, f. 2; and "Autos seguidos por María del Rosario Vega, mulata, esclava contra su amo, Don Juan Rodamonte, sobre sevicia y relaciones ilícitas a la que la obligó," AGN-P, RA, Civ., Leg. 292, C. 2607, 1790, f. 3.

50. "Autos seguidos por María Mercedes Olávide," AAL, Causas de Negros, Leg. 33, no. 9, 1792–1797.

51. The emotional regime of U.S. slavery also involved the master class giving "gifts and kind words" to their slaves, just as it turned slave children into "gifts" for white children. See Dwyer, "Mastering Emotions," 94.

52. Marcus Wood, *The Horrible Gift of Freedom: Atlantic Slavery and the Representation of Emancipation* (Athens: University of Georgia Press, 2010).

CHAPTER 5

Wombs of Liberation

Petitions, Law, and the Black Woman's
Body in Maryland, 1780–1858

JESSICA MILLWARD

In September 1810, Letty Ogleton and her five children—Henry, Michael, Lucy, Lucky, and Charles—filed a petition of freedom with the Prince George's County Court of Maryland.[1] According to the petition, the enslaved family was "entitled to their freedom having lineally descended from a free woman."[2] Letty understood that her familial line included a free woman, and she petitioned for her own freedom accordingly. She also understood that she could not leave her children enslaved. In fact, Letty was part of a complex familial circle that included kin scattered across Prince George's County—family members who, like Letty, were equally concerned with freedom. From September to December 1810, fourteen enslaved Ogletons filed freedom petitions with the Prince George's County Court.[3] Much like the freedom suits of the Brown family examined recently by Loren Schweninger, the Ogletons offer a window into the crucial narratives of how freedom was constructed, pursued, and maintained by families of African descent in Maryland.[4]

Despite the fact that the Ogletons were enslaved by seven different owners and lived a distance from one another, they each advanced the same claim: they were descended from a free woman named Maria Ogleton. The Ogletons' attorney, Enoch M. Lowe, testified in a freedom affidavit that the petitioners believed themselves to be "descended from Maria Ogleton, a free East Indian woman in the maternal line."[5] Late eighteenth-century petitions such as those advanced by the Ogletons thus reveal the way that freedom was rooted in reproduction and how the Black woman's body constructed slavery and freedom.

Freedom petitions from the late 1700s reveal the complexities of race and gender in an age marked by revolution. According to the testimony of her descendants, Maria Ogleton did not "look Black." Rather, with her glossy dark hair and red skin she closely resembled indigenous people; they argued that her origins were rooted, at least in part, among the eastern Caribbean Arawaks. This argument by her descendants—that Maria was not "Black" or "African"—was a strategic navigation of the racial landscape. The more notable freedom cases in Maryland reveal that manumission was more likely to be granted if one could prove one's mother was a White, Indian, or woman of African descent born somewhere other than the United States.[6] If proximity to Whiteness aided a freedom suit, then it is fair to assume that a distancing from "Blackness"—perhaps, more specifically, a distancing from what would later be considered "African Americanness"—aided those seeking freedom as well.[7] As exemplified with the Ogleton suits, petitions delineated the intersectionalities of race, gender, reproduction, and motherhood manifested in Black women's lives and that of their descendants. *Blackness* and *womanhood* were malleable concepts and open to interpretation; biology was not. Proximity to Whiteness aided in winning one's freedom just as the proximity to the "monstrous" Black woman, as discussed by Jennifer L. Morgan, could limit one's chances for manumission.[8] Therefore, in the eyes of the court, *Blackness* remained synonymous with *slavery*, and notions of the Black woman's body as evidence and as spectacle replayed themselves throughout courtrooms in the Early Republic; Maryland was no exception.

Slaveholders generally paid little attention to the biological connections among the people they owned unless it suited their interests, but the same could not be said of the enslaved. Testimony grounded in African American oral culture demonstrates that enslaved people not only scrupulously recounted the intricate interrelationships among their forebears but that they also used that knowledge as grounds for their emancipation.[9] In this way, enslaved women in Maryland paralleled other African American women who petitioned for freedom in Revolutionary-era New England. Researchers Catherine Adams and Elizabeth Pleck, for example, demonstrate that legal consciousness was embedded in family ties and that the struggles of African American women in New England courtrooms was an extension of the families efforts to live together and secure freedom for those still in bondage.[10] In the decades following the American Revolution, families such as the Ogletons hoped that by tracing their lineage to a free woman, they could avoid a life in bondage.

Unfortunately, the outcome of the Ogletons' quest for freedom is unknown. The Ogleton family's utilization of the legal system reveals much about the standing of enslaved people and the evolution of their designation as legal property to personhood, not only in the United States but also elsewhere in the African diaspora and exemplified by the situation in Cuba. Alejandro de la Fuente suggests that by making claims upon the legal system, enslaved people enter the archive as architects of their own liberation.[11] Similarly, Laura Edwards argues that the actions of enslaved women, and more importantly their reactions to enslavement, shaped the law in South Carolina.[12] Camillia Cowling's research on

Cuba suggests that enslaved women's deployment of motherhood rights helped define freedom in Spanish slave societies.[13] Enslaved women in Maryland, such as Letty Ogleton, entered the court record as litigants petitioning for their freedom or that of their children. Black women, more specifically their bodies, entered the legal archive as evidence, such as in the case of Maria Ogleton. Regardless of courts' rulings, cases citing a mother's free status opened questions regarding the woman's complexion, hair, and physical features. Indeed, both in Maryland and elsewhere from the late eighteenth to the first half of the nineteenth century, Black women's very bodies held the potential to determine one's claim to freedom.

I argue that enslaved women were keenly aware that freedom, like slavery, was necessarily tied to their womb. Specifically, this chapter is concerned with the ways enslaved women and their descendants transformed their status from property/possession to legal actor by focusing on the relationship between maternity and freedom. Building on Janell Hobson's recasting of Frantz Fanon's argument that the body is indeed evidence, it is through the Black woman's body, then, that freedom can be mapped both for what it includes as well as for what it excludes.[14] Maternity shaped concepts of liberation for enslaved women just as their biological capacities shaped access to that freedom in Maryland. By examining the case of Letty Ogleton and her family, I show that enslaved people used their knowledge of local kinship ties and assessments of anti-Black sentiment to challenge the legal notion of Black people as property and to gain their freedom.

African women were brought into the port of Annapolis during the Atlantic slave trade and through Baltimore as part of the domestic slave trade. Both the slave trade and African Americans' quest for freedom linked the mobility of the Black woman's body to the larger Atlantic world. Maryland's location (and in particular that of Baltimore and Annapolis) on the Atlantic meant that Black women's physicality and the spaces they inhabited and traveled to held implications for freedom. Indeed, enslaved women's very positionality shaped discussions of slavery and freedom during the Revolutionary era.

Enslaved Africans and African Americans in the newly formed United States borrowed the language of the American Revolution to advance their claims to freedom. In New England, Elizabeth Freeman, a midwife and domestic, became the first African American to petition for her freedom in what became the United States. At first called Bett by those who owned her, and later Mum Bett as she is more commonly known, Elizabeth took the name *Freeman* to signify her new status.[15] Elizabeth Freeman was one of countless African Americans who shed a surname their owners gave them, if they had a last name at all. In the post-Revolutionary period, many free Blacks adopted the prefix *free* in names such as *Freeman*, *Freedman*, or *Freedmen* to signify their transition from enslaved to free.

Other Revolutionary-era Blacks used the courts to test the limits of their freedom. In 1781, New England resident Quok Walker sued Nathaniel Jennison for assault.[16] Born to slavery in Massachusetts in the 1750s, Quok had been promised his freedom at age twenty-one by the Caldwell family. After the death of her husband, Isabell Caldwell remarried Nathaniel Jennison but she died when Quok was nineteen. Jennison refused to free Quok, who eventually ran away. When Jennison found him, he and a group of Whites beat him severely. Because Quok believed "freedom" to be his natural right, he did not feel the need to sue for it. Rather, he sued Jennison for assault.[17] Douglas Egerton suggests that "Black Americans [such as Quok] immediately expected the Revolution to offer not merely new opportunities for freedom but also full participation in the new political order."[18] Thus, the courts provided a place to sue for freedom, maintain preexisting free status, and exercise one's new rights once emancipated.[19]

The process of filing a petition for freedom was long and expensive. Bringing freedom suits in Maryland, as elsewhere in the recently formed United States, meant that the enslaved possessed enough social capital for someone to believe their case was worth advancing. Many plaintiffs benefited from their relationships with Quakers or other antislavery religions and organizations, which often filed and paid for suits on the petitioners' behalf. Schweninger notes that fines and court costs could amount to hundreds and sometimes even thousands of dollars.[20] Lawyers had to be hired in order to file the suits and the many motions that were necessary to ensure the appearance of the plaintiffs and defendants in court. The Ogletons' lawyer, Enoch Lowe, followed up each Ogleton freedom petition with a summons to the respective owner. Moreover, Lowe filed a motion forbidding the various owners from selling any of the Ogletons or removing them from the state. The process was long, expensive, and potentially dangerous.

Enslaved Africans who brought freedom suits had to weigh the consequences of their actions. When Jean Baptiste, an émigré from Saint-Domingue (now Haiti), filed a freedom petition in Baltimore in 1818, he faced violent retaliation in his owner's home.[21] Schweninger notes that the "court assume[d] responsibility; the court usually made arrangements for the protection of the plaintiff[s] during the period of litigation. If they were returned to their owners, the court often required the owner to post a bond; if they feared retribution, the plaintiffs could be turned over to the sheriff for protection and hired out for payment of fees; very few ran away; [very few] were severely punished for bringing suit. Some slaves suing for freedom asked for injunctions prohibiting owners or others (slave traders) from taking them beyond the court's jurisdiction."[22] Some of these cases were appealed and went on for years, which led to the enslaved people working as hirelings under court supervision.[23] In some cases, the courts upheld the filed motions and ordered the owners not to sell the petitioner while the case was being heard. Other times, the courts went even further, adding that the owner could be punished if the enslaved person was harmed during the court proceedings. And in some cases the courts assumed legal responsibility for the enslaved person.[24] Despite the fact that the court possessed the power to keep enslaved people safe, they did not fully trust the legal system to protect them. After all, it was the law of *Partus Sequitur Ventrem* (the status of the child follows that of the mother) that kept them enslaved.

Freedom petitions from Maryland provide evidence that the enslaved negotiated their claims to freedom through knowledge of their parentage. If the case made it to court, depositions could provide their lineage; defining this lineage was important to Whites and Blacks alike. Petitions highlighted the tensions involved when "property" sued for rights to their personhood. And petitions, particularly in the state of Maryland, represented the ebb and flow of egalitarianism as antislavery advocates championed the cases of the enslaved. In the decade after the American Revolution, the Maryland General Court of the Western Shore, for example, heard eleven petitions from enslaved people. This highest court in Maryland was the only place one could bring a freedom suit during the eighteenth century. Although the overall number of petitions is low in that period, the power of petitions is found not in the volume of cases heard by the General Court—the cases were heard at the rate of only one or two a year, typically included one or more petitioners in a single case, and were heard over successive sessions of the court. Rather, the power lies in the fact that the number of petitioners remained consistent even in the face of laws designed to keep them in bondage. Their efforts certainly fostered solidarity with others filing suits in other states.

In colonial times, the relationship that African Americans had with the law fluctuated. In 1664 the colony issued a directive that children born to a White woman and Black man (slave or free) would be reduced to the condition of a slave. A law passed in 1681 then repealed the previous ruling. However, that law restricted preexisting legal recourse because Black testimony was no longer allowed in court cases. The contradictory history of Africans and African Americans meant that, as the arbiter of justice, courts contributed to the oppression of Black men and women—but, at the same time, and perhaps more significantly, the courts *also* influenced the notion that freedom was biological.

The 1681 law left open a slim opportunity for enslaved people: they could sue for their freedom provided they were descended from a White woman. For that reason, the majority of the freedom suits in Maryland following the American Revolution did not invoke the revolutionary language such as *equality* and *liberty* that appeared in suits from other locales. Rather, petitioners cited their mothers' free status as the supporting evidence in their suits, the only legal recourse available to them. In some cases the petition included a single plaintiff; in others, petitions were filed on behalf of several people. When Eleanor Toogood sued prominent Annapolis doctor Upton Scott, for example, she testified that she was descended from "a free white woman and well entitled to her freedom."[25] From October 1782 to May 1783, the court heard Toogood's complex case, a story that was well known around the small state capital. Toogood presented evidence that she was the daughter of Ann Fisher, the granddaughter of a white indentured woman and a man of color man named Dick.[26] The court found that Toogood's claim to freedom was valid. Doctor Scott appealed the case to no avail; the court honored Toogood's claim, and she remained free.

In 1782, a petition from Mary Butler, an enslaved washerwoman from St. Mary's County, changed access to freedom for African Americans. Mary Butler could trace back her lineage one hundred years to an Irish immigrant named Eleanor Butler and "Negro Charles," an enslaved man. Eleanor and Charles were married in 1681. This is probably not a coincidence, given that this is the very year that the earlier law condemning the offspring of such a marriage as theirs to slavery for life was repealed. This earlier law in turn had followed the precedent set by Virginia two years prior, in 1662, which ruled that the condition of the child followed that of the mother. With the repeal of the 1664 law, Eleanor and Charles could marry without punishment; Eleanor would remain "free," and their children would not be doomed to lives of servitude. Nevertheless, Eleanor's progeny and future descendants found themselves enslaved.[27]

Oral tradition was important to the descendants of Eleanor and Charles—Mary Butler was raised knowing their story, one passed down to her from older members of her family. Her parents, William and Mary, both declared descent from Eleanor and Charles. William was Eleanor's grandson, and Mary was a great-granddaughter. There is debate as to how close the family lines were between the two parents. Martha Hodes suggests that Mary and William were cousins; Stephen Whitman suggests that they were husband and wife.[28] According to court affidavits, both are true. That they are closely related is not surprising given the many ways that slavery blurred family lines.

In 1770, Mary's parents unsuccessfully filed a petition for freedom. Despite this, their example stayed with her and ultimately influenced Mary to file her own petition sixteen years later. Mary Butler won her suit. Why did her suit work when it did not work for her parents, particularly when both suits were based on descent from the same woman? Stephen Whitman suggests that Butler won her case due to the lack of definitive evidence proving Eleanor married Charles. Thus, her descendants could not be enslaved under any laws.[29] Martha Hodes, however, provides evidence of witnesses testifying that a wedding took place.[30] Ultimately, Mary Butler's successful outcome was based not on whether a wedding took place but rather on hearsay evidence that by the time of her case was permitted in courts.[31]

There is scholarly consensus that the admission of hearsay evidence changed the trajectory of freedom suits in Maryland.[32] The transformative power of hearsay evidence resonates in the cultural realm as well. The orality of African and African American cultures proved valuable when narrating a family's history with detailed testimonies documenting their family lines. And, as Schweninger proves, the majority of court testimonies demonstrate that it is women who were charged with preserving the family genealogy through oral tradition.[33] Hearsay evidence, once inadmissible, presented a new opportunity for seeking freedom, and the Butler case in particular presented a new precedent for admitting evidence. Following the Butler ruling, freedom petitions based on descent from a free White woman were later presented by several enslaved families in Maryland: the Bostons, the Browns, the Queens, and the Shorters.[34]

The admission of hearsay evidence effectively allowed for a Black woman's words, actions, and body to be entered as evidence in court cases. When brothers Charles and Patrick Mahoney sued for their freedom in 1791, they relied on the importance of their ancestor's body and the places she traveled to advance their claims for freedom. The Mahoneys petitioned for their freedom from John Ashton, one of the highest-ranking Roman Catholic officials in Maryland and one of the founders of Georgetown University. The Mahoneys based their case on the fact that they descended from Ann Joice, a free woman. Joice was brought from Barbados to England sometime in the late 1670s, prior to arriving in Maryland. The Mahoneys' lawyers argued that Joice was taken to England during her period of service and resided there for nearly three years. On the basis of having lived in England, they argued that neither she nor her descendants could be held as slaves. There was good precedent for this assumption: In 1772, Lord Mansfield of the English Court of the High Bench ruled in *James Somerset v. Charles Stewart* that slavery was "unsupported" in English common law. Further, Lord Mansfield determined that it was unlawful to forcibly bring a slave into England. *Somerset* contributed to the abolition of slavery in England and the emancipation of bond people throughout the British Empire as the nineteenth century progressed.[35]

While it has been widely understood that *Somerset* reverberated in the British

Atlantic, its use by a Maryland plaintiff expands our understanding of its implications. As Eric Papenfuse notes, the Mahoneys' case drew Maryland into a larger transatlantic debate about lineage, liberty, and the abolition of the slave trade.[36] Certainly the use of *Somerset* signals that Maryland's legal culture was in tandem with the Atlantic world. It also signaled that the Mahoneys themselves understood the implications of their ancestor traveling to England. Hoping to benefit from the *Somerset* precedent, the Mahoneys' defense maintained that traveling to England effectively rendered Ann Joice "free." It took seven years for the case to be decided, and when it was, the decision was not exactly the outcome that the Mahoneys had hoped. In 1798 the court granted Charles Mahoney his freedom, but reversed its ruling when John Ashton appealed the case.[37] Frustrated to be so close to freedom and then to have it taken away, the Mahoneys felt they had little option but to run away. They were caught, however, and returned to Ashton.

Despite losing their case in court, in 1806 the Mahoneys received their freedom from Ashton. The following year, Ashton freed one of their siblings. By 1808, at least six of the seven Mahoney brothers were freed by John Ashton or by fellow Catholic Charles Carroll of Carrollton. What accounts for the manumission of the brothers? Ashton, like the Mahoneys, may have grown weary of the decadelong case; he knew full well the lengths enslaved people would go to achieve freedom. Also, the Mahoneys were not the only family held in bondage by Ashton who were suing him. In 1791, the same year the Mahoneys filed suit, Edward Queen also sued, citing assault and battery by his owner. Edward Queen and his family cited lineage from a free Black woman and argued that they were falsely enslaved. The court agreed and granted Queen his freedom. Following the ruling in 1795, twelve members of the Queen family left the Ashton property.[38] What with the suits and the missing workers, the Queens and the Mahoneys took up a considerable amount of Ashton's time. Ashton's practice of owning slaves also began to attract criticism from other Jesuits. Whatever the reason, the Queens' recalcitrant behavior paid off; eventually, Ashton officially freed ten of the twelve people who ran away.

The cases filed by the Mahoneys and the Queens exemplify how events not only in England but also in the larger Atlantic—Saint-Domingue—influenced the legal culture of Maryland.[39] As French slave owners fled the island with their human chattel, they produced waves of retaliatory rulings on the part of American and West Indian courts. Eric Papenfuse argues that the rebellion in Saint-Domingue influenced the Maryland court's decision to deny the Mahoneys their freedom.[40] Indeed, events in Saint-Domingue triggered responses from Whites and Blacks throughout the Atlantic.[41] For Whites, the uprising was the culmination of their worst fear: as succinctly stated by Leon Litwack, the so-called loyal slave picked up the gun and, in the case of Haiti, the machete.[42] For Blacks in the United States, Haiti promised a world of new possibilities. Haiti connected slave-holders and the enslaved to a larger circle of rebellion in the Atlantic world. Rather than an isolated incident, the events in Haiti represented a new social order.

Haiti had a complicated relationship with property, power, and place. In 1792, Maryland lawmakers advocated for the relocation of White slaveholders fleeing Saint-Domingue. White refugees were welcome but free Black émigrés were not, and lawmakers even forbade slaveholders from Saint-Domingue from freeing their slaves while in Maryland, forcing them to wait three years before releasing anyone from bondage. Clearly, lawmakers had determined that Black rebellion was contagious and they would do what they could to discourage the manumission of Saint-Domingue Blacks.[43]

Freedom suits like those filed by the Mahoneys and the Queens allow us to assess the importance of place within the Atlantic world. But for other plaintiffs, the place that they occupied was as corporeal as it was geographical. In November 1797, Margaret Creek and her lawyer filed a freedom petition in the Baltimore County Court.[44] According to the petition, Creek "had been entitled to her freedom from birth." Creek claimed that she had been held illegally by William Wilkins and maintained that she was "the daughter of Rachel who was the daughter of an Indian woman named Moll or Mary." According to the petition, Mary was "a free native of America who lived and died [as such]."[45] Creek's case took three years to travel through the courts, but ultimately, in March 1800, the court affirmed Creek's freedom. Creek's case bears resemblance to others of the era: she cited lineage from a free woman and was awarded her freedom. She filed the claim as the sole petitioner, so it is not clear whether she had an extensive kin network such as the Mahoneys and Queens. Nonetheless, Creek hired an attorney and utilized the courts and eventually laid claim to her freedom. Although little is known about her save the sparse details of the petition, Creek nonetheless entered the legal space as a woman sure of her heritage being both African and Native American. And if necessary, Creek would exploit one aspect of her heritage over the other if it meant living freely. In this way, Creek was similar to enslaved women in Cuba discussed by Camillia Cowling, who, by asserting their rights, reminded the court that they were not property but women.[46] Cowling suggests that the nature of Black women making legal claims forced the court and, by extension, lawmakers to view the enslaved as people and, by further extension, to view Black women as women. There were gendered values assigned to freedom, but for Black women in particular, entering the legal record—the space of a courtroom—called into question the very same practices of law that placed them outside discussions of liberty, independence, and freedom in the first place.[47] This was particularly important when considering the difference between Creek, who embodied the complexities of race, gender, and status, and Black women in Maryland, whose bodies entered the court record as evidence.

Consider the discussions about the appearance of Catherine Booth. Booth enters the court record via testimony presented in the freedom suit of her descendant, Richard Booth. In 1792, Booth petitioned the Maryland General Court claiming that he "was descended from a free woman and is unjustly deprived of his Liberty by David Weems."[48] Booth maintained that his great-grandmother, Catherine Booth, was freed by her owner, King Harrison.[49] Richard Booth's petition was initially denied and later appealed; the result of that appeal is unknown. But the records of the appeal provide a compelling window into the ways in which physical appearance and racial logic were appended to freedom claims.

Scattered throughout approximately seventy pages of court testimony are the outlines of a second trial—that of Catherine Booth. Deponents on both sides were asked a series of questions: Were they related to either David Weems or Richard Booth? Did they know the great-grandmother Catherine (Kate) Booth? Did they know her daughter Sally? Did they know Sally's daughter Esther, the mother of Richard Booth? What did deponents know about Kate's status as free or slave? What did Kate look like? How did her hair look? Witnesses gave conflicting accounts of Catherine's status, of whether she was a slave or was free; accounts were also given about her heritage, the color of her skin, and the grade of her hair. This line of questioning was standard for petitions based on descent from a "free" woman who was also Black. As with the case of Ann Joice, if it could be determined that the woman did not "look Black," then the chances for freedom were often greater. Certainly litigants identified as Black; however, they did not envision a life of slavery for themselves. They used whatever was in their limited arsenal to plot a course for liberation.

Black women's bodies were used as evidence, and, ironically, it was precisely the distancing from Blackness that provided a loophole for the enslaved to win their cases. If it entered the courtroom as evidence, a Black woman's body connected her descendants to the revolutionary Atlantic, where the questions of slavery and freedom were quite literally being mapped as one traveled between metropoles, colonies, and former colonies. If she had been free, or if she had traveled to someplace and her status had changed, or if it was determined that she had not possessed traits that were distinctly African, her descendants had a claim to freedom. It is both painful and ironic that African Americans renounced their racial identity (at least on paper) in their quest for freedom. The nature of these questions conveys that there was something fundamentally integral about the value of Black women in Revolutionary society. For her descendants, a Black woman's positionality was marked by geography, physicality, and physiology; in addition, as discussed below, freedom was marked biologically.

Petitioners in the late eighteenth century counted on genealogy to bolster their freedom claims, but by the beginning of the nineteenth century, the courts responded by essentially refusing to hear genealogical claims to freedom even as they reinscribed the relationship between reproduction and racial slavery. During the early part of the nineteenth century, county courts throughout Maryland were authorized to hear freedom suits. This allowed enslaved men and women to present cases in local courts, thus avoiding the obstacles to obtaining access to the highest court in Maryland. The provincial courts continued to hear cases, but these were limited to appeals rather than entire suits; the power to hear petition suits was transferred to the lesser courts. In addition to the shift in the location of freedom suit hearings, a much more important transformation was also under way. In November 1809, the Maryland State Legislature introduced a law that they believed solved persistent petitions from bond people who cited their mothers' free or manumitted status as justification for their own release from bondage. The "Act to Ascertain and Declare the Condition of Such Issue as May Hereafter Be Born of Negro or Mulatto Female Slaves" enabled planters to determine the status of any living or future child born to bondwomen to whom they had promised freedom. If declarations of the status of future children were not made at the time the manumission document was presented in court, "then the state and condition of such issue shall be that of a slave."[50]

Presented one year after the U.S. Constitution outlawed participation in the international slave trade, the 1809 law reconciled two opposing yet interrelated facts. The first is that the existence and expansion of the southern slave system depended on the reproductive labor of bondwomen.[51] Slave owners were keenly aware that enslaved women might conceive children after they were promised freedom but before they were released from bondage. The decision to free an enslaved woman involved measuring the potential value of her future labor against the loss of the physical and reproductive labor of both mother and child. Indeed, Stephen Whitman suggests that the majority of young girls who were promised freedom remained in slavery well past their childbearing years.[52] The second is that the propensity of Maryland owners to manumit slaves had the potential to dismantle the slave state. By passing the 1809 law, legislators attempted to obstruct the ability of manumitted women to produce "free" people by closing avenues to freedom based on the mother's status. In doing so, legislators, many of whom owned bond people, reaffirmed the power of slaveholders to assert dominion over their property. Moreover, the 1809 law represented what lawmakers, slaveholders, and bond people already knew: that freedom, like enslavement, was tied to a bondwoman's womb.

By the time the 1809 law was passed, planters had realized that the only legal way they could obtain new slaves was through the reproductive work of their enslaved female population; thus, the decision to manumit a bondwoman involved even more economic disincentives. The 1809 law's emphasis on the slave status of the children of manumitted women effectively prolonged enslavement for another generation of African Americans and ensured that owners would continue to profit from enslaved labor.[53] The law was similar to the precedent set in New Amsterdam (now New York) during the seventeenth century, whereby the enslaved were given "half-freedom": In exchange for their freedom, enslaved men and women agreed that existing or future children would be enslaved and work for the Dutch West India Company. In this way in Maryland, the gradual emancipation of children often meant that enslaved children remained under the control of their mother's master until they reached adulthood.[54] In this system of postnati service, owners promised freedom to children but waited until a time when either they profited little from a child's labor or the child had reached an age of self-sufficiency. A substantial proportion of antebellum Baltimore's free Black population was born as slaves and gained their freedom as young or middle-aged adults.[55] Perhaps provisions for postnati service stemmed from planters' reluctance to lose the potential revenue from sales of children. If that were the case, then the goal of the 1809 law was not to expand freedom through the manumission of bondwomen; rather, as Whitman argues, it was to constrict freedom by allowing planters to determine the postnati status of slave children.[56]

Although the 1809 law restricted access to freedom for future generations, it did not diminish the efforts of African American women and their descendants to use legal and extralegal measures to access freedom. In the ten years before the law was passed, six African Americans filed freedom petitions in Maryland's higher courts.[57] From 1810 to 1820, ten did so. Schweninger's research at the county court level reveals a similar trend.[58] From 1799 to 1809, twelve freedom petitions were presented in Maryland county courts; between 1810 and 1820, seventeen petitions were filed.[59]

Petitioners had to prove that their status as enslaved, free, or gradually manumitted was delineated prior to their mother's manumission. Such was the case of bondwoman Lurena and her daughter Ellen. In 1810, Lurena was promised freedom in the last will and testament of her owner, Rezin Hammond, when she reached the age of thirty.[60] Additionally, it stated that any children born to her were to be freed at age twenty-nine. Hammond's heirs failed to honor the wishes of the deceased and not only kept the mother and her child in bondage but sold them as well. In 1812, two years after the sale, Lurena petitioned for and gained her freedom on the grounds that she was thirty years old at the time of Rezin Hammond's death. Ellen was awarded freedom because she was born after the date of her mother's promised emancipation.[61] Thus, Ellen was illegally enslaved from birth. This case illustrates the complicated legal process of manumission, which often stretched across generations and frequently folded maternity into freedom petitions.

The 1809 law held three significant consequences for understanding how the Black woman's reproductive body was deployed within the law. First, because the law was framed entirely in terms of "women and their issue," the families of manumitted women were not understood to include the fathers of the children. This framing altered the definitions of *household* and *family* for manumitted women. Second, the terms of the law often staggered the dates of manumission for women and their children. As a consequence, responsibility for the upbringing of children was often extended through the mother's extended kinship networks. Third, this shift in legal responsibility laid the foundation for future dialogues about gender, race, and poverty. African American women responded to all three consequences by drawing from the same support systems that had aided them in slavery, namely their extended kin networks.[62]

While the 1809 law had particular importance for African American women and their families, it also provided a mechanism for the planters to keep the children of manumitted women as insurance, in case the economy called for enslaved labor in the future. On one hand, the law could provide an opportunity to escape the system of slavery. On the other hand, the 1809 law could prolong the enslavement of children. Yet interventions by enslaved women and their children challenged the intention of the 1809 law to guarantee the future of slavery through natural reproduction.

With successive generations of African Americans gaining freedom, it is not surprising that African American women went from being perceived as pieces of evidence used by their descendants to obtain freedom to litigants petitioning for the freedom of their children. In this regard, African American women in Maryland were not unique. Following her emancipation in 1827, Isabella Baumfree (later Isabella Van Wagenen, who eventually became known as Sojourner Truth) sued Solomon Gedney for selling her son Peter to an owner in Alabama. Baumfree won her suit, and Peter was recovered and returned to her.[63]

Working within the system meant that for better or worse, enslaved people were subject to the law. Nat Turner's rebellion in Southampton, Virginia, while a victory in the eyes of the enslaved, resulted in tighter restrictions on the lives of manumitted women and their kin. Across the South, laws quickly developed that demanded African Americans relocate outside a state once they were freed, and Maryland was no exception. These laws proved particularly painful for manumitted women whose children were enslaved. In 1833, recently manumitted Sophia Tydings petitioned the judges of the Anne Arundel County Orphans' Court to be allowed to stay in the state of Maryland so that she could be close to her husband, who was free, and her ten children, who were still enslaved.[64] Tydings's request was based on her role as a mother; her petition noted that she "still had an infant at her breast."[65] Tydings was permitted to stay in the state another twelve months. Although the court records do not indicate whether she obeyed the order to leave her children behind the following year, the temporary reprieve must have been excruciating. Facing reenslavement for failing to follow a court order on the one hand and the loss of her children on the other, Tydings's fate was similar to Solomon Northup's—but in the extreme. She faced possible reenslavement should she stay in the state after the expiration date on her freedom permit. Tydings served as an example that, as mothers, manumitted women reminded planters and lawmakers that their familial responsibilities did not end when their freedom began. The court's tendency to grant requests such as these revealed the court's innate notions about biology and the health and care of the slaveholder's property. After all, it benefited the state for Tydings to remain in Maryland to nurse her child, thus providing essential nutrients to an individual destined to spend their life as someone's human property.

Tydings's vulnerability to the court indicates the larger systemic violence of enslavement—the absence of a private life even in freedom. When Robert Williams purchased his wife, Susannah, he did so with the intention of freeing her. A great deal of time passed without Susannah being manumitted. Robert Williams, it seemed, was "deprived of his understanding." The court labeled Williams a "lunatic."[66] Susannah petitioned on behalf of herself and her children to be freed rather than sold to another owner, as Robert seemed ill equipped to provide for his enslaved property—whether or not they were his kin was beside the point. In 1806, the General Assembly of Maryland passed a law transferring Susannah and her children to the chancellor, who would then free them in six months' time.[67] At the end of six months, Susannah and her children were to be manumitted and finally experience the liberation promised years ago. For Susannah, freedom meant that she was not entitled to the private space normally allowed families, for her husband's health necessitated that the court intervene several times during her journey from bondage.

For enslaved people bringing suits, the experience of freedom was just as important its legality. In 1832, a man known only as "Negro Joe" sued for his freedom. He claimed that he was entitled to his freedom based on the fact that his grandmother, Lavinia, and his mother, Dinah, lived "free and undisturbed in possession of their liberty and freedom." According to court testimony, Lavinia and Dinah lived like free women following the 1797 death of their owner, William Machubin. One witness noted that Lavinia and Dinah "were going at large as free women living acting and passing [as free] in all respects," indicating that, over the course of thirty-plus years, the women and their descendants lived as if they were free. According to Joe, the two women continued in the "free and undisturbed possession of their liberty and until the death of Machubin's wife." In 1824, court testimony offered that Elizabeth Machubin "never set up any claim to them." For descendants of Lavinia and Dinah, the experience with freedom nearly came to an end in 1832: Elizabeth Machubin's husband, John M. Burke, inherited her property. At that time, Burke also laid claim to Joe and several relatives. The Anne Arundel County Court agreed with Joe and awarded him his freedom in 1832. The following year, Burke initiated an appeal with the Court of Appeals for the Western Shore, which upheld the lower court's ruling and "Negro Joe" remained free. He had traded the experience of freedom enjoyed by his female predecessors for a legal document stating what he already knew to be true—that he was not property.[68]

As the example of "Negro Joe," indicates, freedom as an experience was not lost on free or enslaved Blacks. Writing about free Black women in South Carolina, Amrita Myers notes that glimpsing and experiencing freedom were precursors to being formally emancipated.[69] What makes the case of this family different is that neither the women nor their descendants were legally emancipated. For "Negro Joe" and other descendants, the experience of freedom preceded their actual status as free Blacks, and many Whites and Blacks in the surrounding area considered them to be free people.

Freedom came with consequences. Whereas the descendants of Lavinia and Dinah were successful in maintaining their freedom, others obtained freedom as long as they enjoyed it outside the United States, epitomized by the case of Betsey and John, an enslaved couple in Frederick County, Maryland. John and Betsey were granted freedom by their owner's will and testament in 1828. Additionally, "any issue of her body" was to be freed as well—provided that the family "leave the United States."[70] The decision to free the couple on the condition that they emigrate was undoubtedly directed in part by the fact that many of the Maryland elite were active in campaigns to resettle Blacks in Liberia.[71] The example of this family underscores how even the promise of freedom had the potential to break up extended families; they would have had to leave familiar surroundings in order to enjoy their freedom. In this instance, where the family enjoyed their freedom was as crucial to lawmakers as how they enjoyed that freedom was to the enslaved.

Place mattered in the lives of Black women and their ability to live freely—whether it was where they could live freely, where they moved to enjoy it, or, in this case, how they used their power to prevent the moving of their children. In neighboring Washington, D.C., Sally Henry, a free woman of color, petitioned the court to prevent an owner from selling her daughter outside of the district. Henry based her request on the fact that her daughter was awaiting a decision from a higher District of Columbia court regarding emancipation.[72] Henry's request was granted and her daughter remained in the city. It is not known if the younger Henry was manumitted at some point later.

The transition of African American women from bodies to agents represents the growing presence and power of free Black women as mothers. Patricia Reid, in her work on Margaret Morgan, reminds us that the experience of freedom was not limited to how Black women and their families perceived it.[73] Morgan was enslaved by John Ashmore. She was promised her freedom by Ashmore in Maryland, but the deed was never executed. Since the promise of freedom, she had traveled to Pennsylvania (a free state) and lived there. Ashmore's heirs decided to reclaim Morgan and the children she bore since leaving Maryland. Having tried unsuccessfully to bring Morgan back to Maryland, Edward Prigg, a slave catcher, brought the case to court in Pennsylvania, the commonwealth where Morgan resided. Though slavery was not legal in Pennsylvania, it was ruled that states held no power in obstructing slave owners from recovering their property. As exhibited in *Prigg v. Pennsylvania* (1842), the attempts of Black women and their kin had national implications as well. These questions of personhood, place, positionality, and traversing slavery and freedom were not resolved in *Prigg v. Pennsylvania*. It would take a suit filed by Dred Scott to force the courts to decide whether African Americans were people or property. For African Americans, the answer was simple; for the nation, the question, the answer, and the responses to the question hastened the country to civil war.

Despite the relatively small number of petitions presented in the wake of the American Revolution, Black women's presence in Maryland courts shifted dramatically from the late eighteenth century to the middle of the nineteenth century. During the revolutionary era, African Americans used their descent from a White woman or free Black woman as a justification for freedom until the mid-nineteenth century, when Black women could enter the court as litigants on behalf of their children. The small absolute number of petitions should not minimize their importance—these successful petitions gave hope and encouragement to others who were enslaved.

Access to freedom in Maryland reaffirmed the central role of women's reproductive labor just as the ability to petition for freedom based on the mother's status revealed the centrality of Black women's bodies in the law. Even when petitioners cited descent from a White or Indian woman, an implicit statement was made regarding the law: Blackness equated to enslavement, and a distancing from Blackness equaled freedom in the eyes of the court. The descendants of White, Indian, and Black women demonstrated that manumission continued to be linked to women's reproductive capacities. The nature of this right to petition changed over time; as it did, so too did Black women's ability to use the law to their advantage. They transitioned from being dissected as evidence to plaintiffs citing their role as mothers in order to enhance their legal rights. Although the nature of how Black women used and were used in court changed from the late eighteenth to the mid-nineteenth centuries, the efforts of African Americans challenged the intent of slavery through natural reproduction by demonstrating that freedom was also inheritable.

NOTES

The author thanks the University of Georgia Press for permission to reprint portions of this chapter from Jessica Millward, *Finding Charity's Folk: Enslaved and Free Black Women in Maryland* (Athens: University of Georgia Press, 2015).

1. Letty Ogleton and her five children, Petition for Freedom, September 10, 1810, Black Papers, Prince George's County Court, Maryland State Archives, Annapolis, Md. (hereafter MDSA). See also accession no. 008967-002-1034, Race, Slavery, and Free Blacks, ser. 2: Petitions to Southern County Courts, part B: Maryland (1775–1866), Delaware (1779–1857), District of Columbia (1803–1865), Slavery and the Law, Proquest History Vault, 2012 (hereafter PHV 2012).

2. Letty Ogleton and her five children, Petition for Freedom, September 10, 1810, MDSA.

3. Anthony [Ogleton], Petition for Freedom, September 10, 1810, MDSA; Amy Ogleton, Petition for Freedom, September 10, 1810, MDSA; Eliza Ogleton and her three children, Petition for Freedom, September 10, 1810, MDSA; Letty Ogleton and her five children, Petition for Freedom, September 10, 1810, MDSA; Amy and Daniel Ogleton, Petition for Freedom, September 10, 1810, MDSA; Milly Ogleton, Petition for Freedom, September 10, 1810, MDSA; Harry, Joan, Mary, Sukey and Nelly, Petition for Freedom, September 10, 1810, MDSA; Charles and Francis Ogleton, Petition for Freedom, September 10, 1810, MDSA.

4. Loren Schweninger, "Freedom Suits, African American Women, and the Genealogy of Slavery," *William and Mary Quarterly* 71, no. 1 (January 2014): 33–62.

5. Rezin Ogleton, Freedom Affidavit, September 1810, Prince George's County, 1810–1850, Maryland State Archives, Archives of Maryland Online, accessed May 6, 2014, http://aomol.msa.maryland.gov/000001/000763/html/am763-1.html.

6. See, for example, Eric Robert Papenfuse, "From Recompense to Revolution: *Mahoney v. Ashton* and the Transfiguration of Maryland Culture, 1791–1802," *Slavery and Abolition* 15, no. 3 (1994): 38–62; and Martha Hodes, *White Women, Black Men: Illicit Sex in the Nineteenth-Century South* (New Haven, Conn.: Yale University Press, 1999).

7. Jessica Millward, "'That All Her Increase Shall Be Free': Enslaved Women's Bodies and the Maryland 1809 Law of Manumission," *Women's History Review* 21, no. 3 (2012): 363–78. See also Cheryl Harris, "Whiteness as Property," *Harvard Law Review* 106, no. 8 (1993): 1709–91.

8. Jennifer L. Morgan, "Gender and Family Life," in *The Routledge History of Slavery*, ed. Gad Heuman and Trevor Burnard (New York: Routledge, 2011), 138–52, esp. 139.

9. Schweninger, "Freedom Suits," 40.

10. Catherine Adams and Elizabeth H. Pleck, *Love of Freedom: Black Women in Colonial and Revolutionary New England* (New York: Oxford University Press, 2010), 132.

11. Alejandro de la Fuente, "Slave Law and Claims-Making in Cuba: The Tannenbaum Debate Revisited," *Law and History Review* 22, no. 2 (2004): 339–69, esp. 346.

12. Laura F. Edwards, "Enslaved Women and the Law: Paradoxes of Subordination in the Post-Revolutionary Carolinas," *Slavery and Abolition* 26, no. 2 (2005): 305–23, esp. 305–6.

13. Camillia Cowling, "Debating Womanhood, Defining Freedom: The Abolition of Slavery in 1880s Rio de Janeiro," *Gender and History* 22, no. 2 (2010): 284–301.

14. Janell Hobson, *Body as Evidence: Mediating Race, Globalizing Gender* (Albany: State University of New York, 2012), 5.

15. Adams and Pleck, *Love of Freedom*.

16. Douglas Egerton, *Death or Liberty: African Americans and Revolutionary America* (New York: Oxford University Press, 2009), 95. See also James Oliver and Lois E. Horton, *In Hope of Liberty: Culture, Community, and Protest among Northern Free Blacks, 1700–1860* (New York: Oxford University Press, 1997).

17. Egerton, *Death or Liberty*, 93–95.

18. Ibid., 95.

19. See Adams and Pleck, *Love of Freedom*, 127.

20. Schweninger, "Freedom Suits," 55.

21. Martha S. Jones, "The Case of *Jean Baptiste, un Créole de Saint-Domingue*: Narrating Slavery, Freedom, and the Haitian Revolution in Baltimore City," in *The American South and the Atlantic World*, ed. B. Ward, M. Bone, and W. A. Link (Gainesville: University Press of Florida, 2013), 119.

22. Loren Schweninger, e-mail exchange with author, April 2, 2014.

23. Ibid.

24. Ibid.

25. *Eleanor Toogood v. Upton Scott*, August term, 1782, Maryland General Court of the Western Shore, Appeals and Judgments, MDSA. See also accession no. 20978201, PHV 2012.

26. *Eleanor Toogood v. Upton Scott.*

27. *Mary Butler v. Adam Craig*, October 1783 Term, Maryland General Court of the Western Shore, Appeals and Judgments, Maryland State Archives (Annapolis, Md.). This case is also discussed in Martha Hodes, *White Women, Black Men: Illicit Sex in the Nineteenth-Century South* (New Haven, Conn.: Yale University Press, 1997), 19–38; and T. Stephen Whitman, *Challenging Slavery in the Chesapeake: Black and White Resistance to Human Bondage, 1775–1865* (Baltimore: Maryland Historical Society, 2007), 62–65.

28. Hodes, *White Women, Black Men*, 19–38; see also Whitman, *Challenging Slavery in the Chesapeake*, 62–65.

29. Whitman, *Challenging Slavery in the Chesapeake*, 64.

30. Hodes, *White Women, Black Men*, 20.

31. As noted in the work of Loren Schweninger, by the mid-1780s, "hearsay" stories—that is, oral history from free and formerly enslaved Blacks—were allowed as evidence in Maryland courts. See Loren Schweninger, "Freedom Suits, African American Women, and the Genealogy of Slavery, *William and Mary Quarterly* 71, no. 1 (2014): 35–62, 41.

32. Ira Berlin, *Slaves without Masters: The Free Negro in the Antebellum South* (New York: Pantheon Books, 1977); Schweninger, "Freedom Suits"; and Whitman, *Challenging Slavery in the Chesapeake*, 95.

33. Schweninger, "Freedom Suits," 39–40; see also Loren Schweninger, *The Southern Debate over Slavery: Petitions to Southern County Courts, 1775–1867* (Urbana: University of Illinois Press, 2008), 2:165.

34. For details of these cases, see Schweninger, "Freedom Suits," 35–62.

35. Dana Rabin, "'In a Country of Liberty'? Slavery, Villeinage and the Making of Whiteness in the Somerset Case (1772)," *History Workshop Journal* 72 (Autumn 2011): 5–29.

36. Papenfuse, "Recompense to Revolution."

37. Archives of Maryland Biography Series, Reverend John Ashton, http://msa .maryland.gov/megafile/msa/speccol/sc5400/sc5496/041700/041715/html /041715bio.html, accessed April 28, 2014.

38. Ibid.

39. Ada Ferrer, *Freedom's Mirror: Cuba and Haiti in the Age of Revolution* (New York: Cambridge University Press, 2014); and Rebecca J. Scott, *Degrees of Freedom: Louisiana and Cuba after Slavery* (Cambridge, Mass.: Harvard University Press, 2005).

40. Papenfuse, "Recompense to Revolution," 62.

41. James Sweet, *Recreating Africa: Culture, Kinship, and Religion in the African-Portuguese World, 1441–1770* (Chapel Hill: University of North Carolina Press, 2003); James Sidbury, *Becoming African in America: Race and Nation in the Early Black Atlantic* (New York: Oxford University Press, 2007); Laurent DuBois, *Avengers of the New World: The Story of the Haitian Revolution* (Cambridge, Mass.: Belknap Press of Harvard University Press, 2004).

42. For discussion of slavery and resistance, see Leon Litwack, *Been in the Storm So Long: The Aftermath of Slavery* (New York: Vintage Press, 1979), esp. chap. 1, "The Faithful Slave," 1–53; and David P. Geggus, ed., *The Impact of the Haitian Revolution* (Columbia: University of South Carolina Press, 2001).

43. Jones, "Case of *Jean Baptiste*," 106.

44. *Margaret Creek v. William Wilkins*, Petition for Freedom, November 1797, General Court of the Western Shore, accession no. 20979704, PHV 2012.

45. Ibid.

46. Camillia Cowling, *Conceiving Freedom: Women of Color, Gender, and the Abolition of Slavery in Havana and Rio de Janeiro* (Chapel Hill: University of North Carolina Press, 2013).

47. Ibid., 378.

48. *Richard Booth v. David Weems*, General Court of the Western Shore, accession no. 20978908, PHV.

49. Ibid.

50. "1809 Law of Maryland," in *Index to the Laws of Maryland*, ed. William Kilty (Annapolis, Md.: Jeremiah Hughes Printing, 1820), 192.

51. For the most recent literature on bondwomen and reproduction, see Daina Ramey Berry, *"Swing the Sickle for the Harvest Is Ripe": Gender and Slavery in Antebellum Georgia* (Urbana: University of Illinois Press, 2007), 77–84; and Jennifer L. Morgan, *Laboring Women: Gender and Reproduction in New World Slavery* (Philadelphia: University of Pennsylvania Press, 2004). For discussion of slave law, see Joseph C. Dorsey, "Women without History: Slavery and the International Politics of *Partus Sequitur Ventrem* in the Spanish Caribbean," *Journal of Caribbean History* 28, no. 2 (1994): 165–207. For classic studies, see Deborah Gray White, *Ar'n't I a Woman? Female Slaves in the Plantation South* (New York: W. W. Norton, 1985); and Barbara Bush, *Slave Women in Caribbean Society, 1650–1838* (Bloomington: Indiana University Press, 1990).

52. Whitman, *The Price of Freedom*, 23.

53. Ibid., 123.

54. Leslie M. Harris, *In the Shadow of Slavery: African Americans in New York City, 1626–1863* (Chicago: University of Chicago Press, 2003), 23–25. See also Morgan, "Gender and Family Life," 146; and Ruth Wallis Herndon, *Unwelcome Americans: Living on the Margin in Early New England* (Philadelphia: University of Pennsylvania Press, 2001).

55. Whitman, *Price of Freedom*, 27.

56. Ibid., 123.

57. See Helen T. Catterall, *Judicial Cases Concerning American Slavery and the Negro* (1926), Digital Library on American Slavery, http://library.uncg.edu/slavery_petitions, accessed June 27, 2017; Jennifer Hull Dorsey, "Documentary History of African-American Freedom: An Introduction to the *Race, Slavery and Free Blacks* Microfilm Collection," *Slavery and Abolition* 30, no. 4 (2009): 545–63; and Schweninger, *Southern Debate over Slavery*.

58. Maryland General Court of the Western Shore, Appeals and Judgments, MDSA 1810–1820; Schweninger, *Southern Debate over Slavery*; and Schweninger Collection, MDSA.

59. Maryland General Court of the Western Shore, Appeals and Judgments, MDSA, 1780–1820; see also Schweninger, *Southern Debate over Slavery*.

60. Lurena and Ellen, Petition for Freedom, 1818, accession no. 20981604, PHV 2012.

61. Ibid.

62. African American networks included abroad marriages and were nuclear, matrifocal, matrilocal, fictive, and extended in scope. See Brenda E. Stevenson, "Black Family Structure in Colonial and Antebellum Virginia: Amending the Revisionist Perspective," in *The Decline in Marriage among African Americans*, ed. M. Belinda Tucker and Claudia Mitchell-Kernan (New York: Russell Sage Foundation, 1995), 27–56; and Dylan Penningroth, *The Claims of Kinfolk: African American Property and Community in the Nineteenth-Century South* (Chapel Hill: University of North Carolina Press, 2003). For the relationship between African cultural survivals and Christianity, see Walter Rucker, *The River Flows On: Black Resistance, Culture, and Identity Formation in Early America* (Baton Rouge: Louisiana State University Press, 2005); and Sylvia Frey and Betty Wood, *Come Shouting to Zion: African American Protestantism in the Americas* (Chapel Hill: University of North Carolina Press, 1998).

63. Margaret Washington, *Sojourner Truth's America* (Urbana: University of Illinois Press, 2009).

64. Schweninger, *Southern Debate over Slavery*, 165.

65. Ibid.

66. Susannah Williams, Petition, February 1806, Schweninger Collection, MDSA. See also accession no. 20980604, PHV 2012.

67. Susannah Williams, Deed of Manumission, 1805, Anne Arundel County Court, Manumission Record, 1797–1807, vol. 825, p. 259. See also Archives of Maryland Online, http://aomol.msa.maryland.gov/000001/000825/html/am825-259.html, accessed June 27, 2017.

68. Negro Joe, Petition for Freedom, 1832, accession no. 20983202, PHV 2012.

69. Amrita Chakrabarti Myers, *Forging Freedom: Black Women and the Pursuit of Liberty in Antebellum Charleston* (Chapel Hill: University of North Carolina Press, 2011).

70. Chester Coleman to John and Betsey, 1828, Frederick County Court Petitions, 1783–1847, MDSA.

71. Eric Burin, *The Peculiar Solution: A History of the American Colonization Society* (Gainesville: University Press of Florida, 2005); Claude Clegg, *The Price of Liberty: African Americans and the Making of Liberia* (Chapel Hill: University of North Carolina Press, 2004); R. J. M. Blackett, *Beating against the Barriers: Biographical Essays in Nineteenth-Century Afro-American History* (Baton Rouge: Louisiana State University Press, 1986); Michele Mitchell, *Righteous Propagation: African Americans and the Politics of Racial Destiny after Reconstruction* (Chapel Hill: University of North Carolina Press, 2004); and Penelope Campbell, *Maryland in Africa: The Maryland State Colonization Society, 1831–1857* (Urbana: University of Illinois Press, 1971).

72. Sally Henry Petition, 1814, accession no. 20481403, PHV 2012.

73. Patricia A. Reid, "Margaret Morgan's Story: A Threshold between Slavery and Freedom, 1820–1842," *Slavery and Abolition* 33, no. 3 (2012): 359–80.

CHAPTER 6

Rethinking Sexual Violence and the Marketplace of Slavery

White Women, the Slave Market, and Enslaved People's Sexualized Bodies in the Nineteenth-Century South

STEPHANIE JONES-ROGERS

Damn old missis was mean as hell. . . . She made me have a baby by one of dem mens on de plantation. De old devil! I gets mad every time I think about it. . . . De baby died, den I had to let dat old devil's baby suck dese same tiddies hanging right here. She was always knocking me around. I worked in the house nursin'.

—HENRIETTA BUTLER

Henrietta Butler was a victim of sexual violence, and a white woman was responsible for her violation.[1] Her owner, Emily Haidee, sanctioned an enslaved man to have sex with Henrietta against her will, and when she remembered her life as a slave many decades later, she bitterly recalled the bodily violations she suffered at the behest of her mistress. Emily Haidee not only authorized Henrietta's sexual assault, which brought forth a child who died shortly after birth, she forced Henrietta to provide maternal and nutritive care to her baby while Henrietta likely mourned the loss of her own. Henrietta's remembrances do not include a cruel and lascivious master who took advantage of his access to her sexualized body: just a white woman who enacted a litany of cruelties on her, including sexual violence.

Scholars have long discussed white southern men's sexual exploitation of enslaved females. They have similarly described white men's commodification of enslaved females' capacity to reproduce and the increased value they placed on fecund women. They have talked about instances of forced breeding, and white men's purchase and sale of particular groups of enslaved women—namely light-skinned, typically racially mixed females, also known as "fancy girls"—for sexual purposes. In much of this literature, scholars describe all of the sexual perpetrators as white men with unfettered access to enslaved female bodies. Conversely, historians describe white women as either a victimized group that had no choice but to endure their male kinfolks' adulterous interracial liaisons with enslaved women, or as vengeful, brutal, and even murderous perpetrators of physical violence against these men's enslaved objects of affection. Sometimes, white women do not figure at all into studies of sexual violence during slavery.[2]

In spite of the new directions taken by ambitious and nuanced historical studies of gender, sexuality, and slavery, many scholars continue to see sexual and sexualized violence as the province of men. By extension, white women's access to enslaved people's bodies appears to be anything but sexual. Few if any scholars discuss women like Emily Haidee, who forced enslaved women like Henrietta Butler to have sex with men who were not of their choosing, and to give life to children born of rape. But Emily Haidee was not alone.

This chapter attends to some of the ways that white southern women committed acts of sexual violence in the nineteenth century. It begins by contemplating how gender biases in nineteenth-century law and in custom, as well as ideologies about racial difference, shape our understanding of sexual violence in this period. It also elucidates how our reliance on these laws in our studies forecloses the possibility of recognizing female perpetrators and uncovering their victims' experiences. The chapter explores how enslaved African Americans defined sexual violence beyond nineteenth-century legal discourse and outside the halls of southern courtrooms, and in doing so, challenges the masculinization of sexual exploitation and human commodification. It contends that enslaved people characterized white slaveholding women's complicity in white men's sexual violation of their bodies, which manifested in both passive and violent modes, their involvement in possibly coercive relationships with enslaved men, and their participation in forced breeding practices, as acts of sexual violence. It shows how some women sought to profit from acts of sexual exploitation and reveals how their choices allowed them to benefit from the slave market economy and contribute to the perpetuation of slavery. In all of these ways, this chapter offers a new conceptualization of the complex relationship between gender, power, sexual violence, and the slave market in the nineteenth-century South.

White women who were involved in acts of sexual violence against enslaved people have remained largely invisible in historical scholarship. This is due in part to our reliance on early English and U.S. lawmakers' circumscribed definition of rape. For them, rape was "the unlawful carnal knowledge of a woman by a man forcibly and against her will."[3] This definition precludes many acts of sexual and sexualized violence that could be committed on the bodies of females and males, and while English common law acknowledged that women could be responsible for aiding and abetting sexual assaults, it nevertheless rendered female perpetrators invisible.[4] Using this conceptualization as a starting point, many scholars describe sexual or sexualized violence as a kind of brutality that only men were capable of committing, and this gendered understanding has profoundly shaped how we have thought about sexually violent acts committed in the plantation South.

What is less apparent from this definition is that race played a decisive factor in determining who could or could not be recognized as a victim of sexual violence in the eyes of the law. Nineteenth-century southern courts and legislative bodies routinely refused to acknowledge black female victims of sexual violence, and virtually all male victims as well.[5] In light of this, historians lack the discursive tools to even begin to study white women who were involved in sexually violent acts against enslaved people. But if we initiate this line of inquiry by looking closely at how we have defined white men's sexual and sexualized violence against enslaved people, we find a framework within which to understand these women and their behavior.

When discussing the sexually violent acts that white men committed within the context of American slavery, historians recognize a spectrum of actions that fall outside of the scope of nineteenth-century rape law. Scholars include acts of nonconsensual sex with and fondling of female slaves by male masters, overseers, or community members. They classify instances of forced breeding as acts of sexual violence too. The eroticized acts of stripping and then whipping enslaved women's naked, bleeding, writhing bodies—or the sanctioning of someone else to do so—have also been included in historians' discussions of sexually violent events.[6] And the psychosexual violence brought about by white men's incessant harassment of enslaved females has not gone unnoticed by historians either. From prevailing vantage points, male perpetrators are responsible for all of these acts, and our emphasis on the sexual dimensions of this violence has contributed to our tendency to focus on men.

Nevertheless, a more expansive understanding of sexual violence as it operated in the context of U.S. slavery makes it possible to see that women could perpetrate acts of sexual and sexualized violence against enslaved people. According to Kirsten Fischer, "violence was a social practice, another performance of race, that transformed official categories of race into a physical relationship: some people had rights to freedom from violence while others did not. . . . As violence inscribed a racial identity onto the body, it also contributed to the racialized understandings of masculinity and femininity." Furthermore, Walter Johnson contends that "the landscape of slavery and labor was a matrix of sexual vulnerability" that shaped the lives of enslaved children and adults, and that "being enslaved . . . was always already a condition of sexual violation."[7] There were slave owners who used their power to compel enslaved people to perform labor in and around their homes with their bodies partially exposed. While enslaved people were completely or partially nude, white southerners disciplined and publicly examined them within southern slave markets. In the case of enslaved women, their breasts might also be exposed to nurse white children. In a variety of ways then, white southerners sexualized the bodies of enslaved people, and although Johnson never writes this in his book, white women were not shielded from any of this. These sexualized dimensions of captivity are not only critical to understanding the dynamic environment within which white men perpetrated acts of sexual coercion and sexualized violence against enslaved people, even men: they help contextualize the sexual violence white women committed against enslaved people as well. White women's complicity in acts committed by others also needs to be understood within this more expansive framework.[8]

How did enslaved people, especially victims, define sexual violence, and whom did they identify as the perpetrators of sexually violent acts? Contrary to what many historians have presumed, enslaved people defined sexual violence in ways that moved well beyond the male perpetrator/female victim paradigm. When they talked about these acts, they very deliberately included white women in their remembrances. Enslaved people focused on white women's complicity in and acceptance of white men's sexual violation of their bodies. They spoke of white women's physical violence against them for refusing to relent to white men's sexual violations. And on rare occasions, they described white women's potentially coercive sexual relations with enslaved men and their initiation of and involvement in incidents of forced breeding.

Harriet Jacobs provided one of the most well-known cases involving a white slaveholding woman's complicity in her husband's sexual violence. From a very young age, Harriet's master, Dr. Flint, verbally harassed her and propositioned her for sex. She tried to ignore and avoid him but eventually neither of these options was possible. At her wit's end, she appealed to his wife for help and protection. Instead of being Harriet's ally, Mrs. Flint misplaced her anger, pain, jealousy, and sense of betrayal on her husband's young and helpless victim. When Harriet's mistress refused to shield her from Dr. Flint, Harriet learned an important lesson about sexual violence in the context of slavery: the law did not protect enslaved females from bodily violation, and neither did scores of white women.[9]

Harriet understood that what was happening to her would remain invisible, unacknowledged, and unnamed in southern courts. Yet, in Harriet's rendering of this injustice, her mistress's inaction and eventual response constituted more than mere complicity, helplessness, jealousy, or rage; her mistress's conduct was an extension of the southern judicial system's failure to shield her from this violence. Harriet cast her mistress as a coconspirator in Dr. Flint's sexual harassment and abuse. In Harriet's mind, her mistress was just as guilty as her master for the wrong being done to her.

While enslaved people frequently cited jealousy as the reason behind white women's inaction, others maintained that their mistresses simply accepted the sexual violence that took place around them. These women were not overtly jealous or vengeful toward enslaved women. They did not complain to the men who engaged in these behaviors either. Nor did they acquiesce because they feared white men's reprisals for protecting enslaved people from their abuse. Exposed to a spectrum of violence enacted on enslaved people since girlhood, white women likely saw sexual exploitation as part of that continuum. They also knew that such acts could augment their families' slaveholdings and their wealth. Chris Franklin said as much when he claimed that mistresses "didn't 'ject [object], 'cause dat mean[t] more slaves."[10] Other formerly enslaved people thought the same, but there were other reasons too.

Some white women did not object to sexual violation because they believed that intervening would endanger enslaved people's lives even further. Annie Young's aunt repeatedly resisted her master's sexual advances. After one attempt too many, she ran away. Her master unleashed bloodhounds on her and when he tracked her down, he beat her about the head until she "bled like a hog." Out of options, she asked her mistress for protection. To her dismay, her mistress instructed her to give in to his sexual advances because otherwise he would likely kill the enslaved woman for refusing him.[11]

Another slave-owning woman refused to intervene because of her belief that her husband's power over the people they owned included the right to sexually violate them. Jacob Manson recalled how "one of de slave girls on a plantation near us went to her missus a tole her 'bout her marster forcing her to let him have sumthin to do wid her an her missus tole her, 'Well go on you belong to him.'"[12] Her mistress did not refuse to help her because she feared her husband's power as patriarch, or because she thought that the enslaved woman had somehow seduced him or welcomed his advances. Her refusal to intervene was grounded in her obscene respect for his property rights that, as she saw it, granted him unfettered sexual access to the human beings he owned.

White women went beyond merely turning their backs on the enslaved women who appealed to them for help. Some of these women physically beat enslaved females into submission, or commanded others to do so, when they refused white men's sexual advances. One enslaved woman repeatedly fended off her master's attempts to sexually violate her, and each time she did so, he concocted reasons to punish her in retaliation. She began to physically fight him, and when her master's mother learned of these altercations, she asked the enslaved woman why she was doing so. The enslaved woman told her about the sexual abuse and asked for protection. Rather than chastising her son for his misdeeds, she sent the enslaved woman to the local courthouse to be beaten for resisting him, and her decision to do so led to further sexual exploitation. The men responsible for this enslaved woman's punishment stripped her naked and whipped her in front of an audience.[13] As this enslaved woman understood it, the punishment she received was also a kind of sexual violence, doled out by male hands, but ordered by a woman.

When enslaved women resisted white men's sexual advances, some white women personally punished them for their refusals. Fannie Moore grew up on a plantation where the overseer repeatedly attempted to sexually assault an enslaved woman named Aunt Cheney. When Aunt Cheney refused to have sex with him, he told her mistress. Instead of reprimanding him, Aunt Cheney's mistress ordered her to the kitchen, stripped her naked, and beat her until she was "jest black an' blue." After that, Aunt Cheney knew the price she would have to pay for resisting him. She relented and eventually gave birth to two of his children. Aunt Cheney suffered multiple acts of sexual violence, some committed in their crudest form by a white man, and another sexually sadistic one inflicted by her mistress.[14]

The work of historians such as Martha Hodes and Loren Schweninger has documented white women's consensual sexual relations with African-descended men.[15] Yet we rarely question whether such encounters were consensual for the men involved. In some respects, this makes sense. In the early colonial period, British North American lawmakers penalized white women who crossed the color line for love or intimacy. In colonial Maryland, white women who had sex with enslaved African-descended men and gave birth to their mulatto children could be sentenced to a lifetime of servitude. Their offspring would also be enslaved for thirty years. When free white women gave birth to mixed-race children in colonial Virginia, court officials fined them, and if they could not afford to pay, the courts bound them out to the church for five years. They also sentenced their children to serve the church for thirty years.

While southern colonies like Virginia and Maryland enacted the earliest bans on interracial intimacy between white women and African-descended men, northern colonies, including Massachusetts, banned interracial marriage and relationships as part of its black codes in 1705, and Pennsylvania did the same in 1725. Pennsylvania lifted its ban as part of its gradual emancipation laws in 1780, but the prohibition in Massachusetts remained in effect until 1843. Additionally, as the nation expanded west throughout the nineteenth century, new states also implemented bans on interracial marriage that included a range of ethnic groups, such as the Chinese, Japanese, South Asians, and indigenous peoples. However, antimiscegenation laws in the west imposed the most stringent penalties for European- and African-descended couples.[16] These were stiff penalties to pay for loving, or at the very least having sex with, African-descended men.[17]

Bearing these laws in mind, many white women almost certainly weighed the advantages and disadvantages of interracial intimacy and decided that there was far too much at stake. But others continued to love and have sex with free and enslaved African-descended men long after southern laws criminalized these behaviors.[18] However, were these intimate encounters consensual for the African-descended men involved?

The very idea of a male victim of sexual violence is only beginning to gain traction in legal and social contexts. However, historians are uncovering instances in which individuals committed acts of sexual exploitation against enslaved men. In her study of gender and slavery in antebellum Georgia, Daina Ramey Berry argues that slaveholders' practice of forced breeding constituted one form of sexual violation against enslaved females and males.[19] She emphasizes the fact that enslaved men did not always desire or consent to have sexual or romantic relationships with the women their masters chose for them. The man who Emily Haidee compelled to have sex with Henrietta Butler, for example, may not have consented to this ordeal.[20] And while slave owners may not have forced these men to engage in nonconsensual sex with enslaved women under the threat or the actual infliction of brutal punishment, they understood that refusing their masters' demands could result in such discipline.

If we recognize the sexual victimization of enslaved men in the coercive and nonconsensual context of forced breeding when orchestrated by white men, and we acknowledge the sexual violation of enslaved men at the hands of other men, as historian Thomas Foster has done, we should be equally prepared to consider the possibility that white women subjected enslaved men to exploitative sex acts.[21]

On rare occasions, formerly enslaved people expressed their belief that white women had ulterior motives for complying with or accepting white men's sexual exploitation of enslaved females: their own sexual relationships with enslaved men. One formerly enslaved person told of how "in them times white men went with the colored gals and women bold . . . but the women went with the colored men too. That's why so many women slave owners wouldn't marry, 'cause they was goin' with one of their slaves."[22] Even when they did not proffer rationales for white women's sexual liaisons with enslaved men, they nevertheless spoke about them. J. W. Lindsay, a formerly enslaved man born in Washington, D.C., and raised in Tennessee, claimed that "there were cases where white women f[e]ll in love with their servants," and he offered an account of a married white woman who had sex with an enslaved male that her husband owned. She eventually gave birth to the enslaved man's child, and after rumors circulated around the community about the affair and the infant, the child was "sent off South."[23] While Lindsay talked of love on the part of white women, he said nothing about whether the enslaved objects of these women's affections reciprocated their feelings.

Matilda Henrietta Perry's experiences in slavery not only reveal how sexual violence shaped the lives of generations of white and black females, it elucidates the ways that slaveholding women could possess near absolute power over enslaved men's sexualized bodies as well. Matilda's mistress was also her great-aunt (her mistress's brother had sex with Matilda's grandmother). When Matilda came of age, a white man on the estate where she lived tormented her with sexual innuendos and threats and attempted to have sex with her. Matilda went to her great-aunt for protection, and her mistress's intervention ended this man's sexual advances. Matilda had no doubt that the outcome of this incident would have been very different had she not been related to her owner: "if I hadn't been kin, you understand, I would not come through like dat."[24]

Matilda was saved from coerced and nonconsensual sexual contact, but her father was not so lucky. During the Civil War, her father's master hired a local white man named Bud Robertson to be his substitute, and he sent Matilda's father to manage Robertson's estate and look after his wife while he was away. During that time, Robertson's wife and Matilda's father had sex and gave birth to a child. When Robertson returned home to find that his wife had given birth to a mixed-race baby, he gave her an ultimatum: give the child away or leave. Robertson's wife decided to stay with her husband and give the baby to Matilda's father. He subsequently gave the child to a local woman to raise as her own. As Matilda talked about the nature of the acts committed against her and those that happened to her father, she framed them all as coerced and nonconsensual: "it was slavery times and you had to do what the white man said or the white woman said. You understand."

Enslaved people's allegations about coerced and nonconsensual sex between slave owners and the individuals they kept in bondage were audacious for a number of reasons. These formerly enslaved people not only accused white slave-owning women of shirking nineteenth-century gender conventions and sexual mores, they also charged them with breaking southern laws. More profoundly, they spoke about the sexual relations between white slave-owning women and enslaved men in tandem with the exploitative acts of sexual violence that white men perpetrated against enslaved women. When these formerly enslaved people spoke of white women's potentially coercive sexual encounters with enslaved men alongside white men's sexual violation of enslaved women, they explicitly tied these instances of coercion together. Speaking of such things in an era and region marked by racial violence was a courageous act.

What does *nonconsensual* mean when black men undoubtedly possessed more physical strength than the white women in question? Would physical force and tactics of intimidation be necessary in order to make an enslaved man submit to nonconsensual sex acts? White men did not always use physical force to subdue their enslaved female victims, and white women did not have to utilize it either. When enslaved women refused white men's advances, these men often used the threat of violence and sale against these women. White men did this to create coercive and harassing circumstances that they hoped would compel enslaved women to relent to their sexual assaults, without ever using physical violence. White women had these tactics at their disposal as well and could mobilize them for the same purposes.

Furthermore, law and custom worked in white women's favor and against recognizing their possible victimization of enslaved men. African American men's racial identity and their enslaved status made it more likely that they would be accused, convicted, punished, and even executed for sexually violating white women or attempting to do so.[25] The common-law emphasis on male force and female resistance diminished enslaved men's chances of legal recognition as victims of sexual violence. And the cultural assumption that male dominance and force and female resistance characterized broader sexual relations, something that Sharon Block has called the "blurred divisions between consensual and coercive sexual relations," similarly decreased the likelihood that judicial officials or the general public would entertain the idea that enslaved men could be victims of sexual coercion. For example, the *Richmond Examiner* published a story about the 1862 arrest of a free white woman named Mary E. Sawyer. A police officer stormed into her home and discovered David, an enslaved man who belonged to Mary Smith, in Sawyer's bed. The paper did not suggest that Sawyer compelled David to have sex with her. The reportage found her brazen remark about David being "as good as any white man" to be more notable.[26]

Enslaved people repeatedly learned that their female owners' economic investments were equally bound up in their reproductive bodies, and the products of their sexual labor. These lessons sometimes came when white women compelled or forced them to have sex against their will for the purpose of breeding.[27] Some enslaved people merely surmised that their mistresses were engaging in breeding practices, but others possessed direct knowledge of their mistresses' intentions or heard their female owners articulate these ideas to others. Rhoda Hunt's owner, Eleanor Patton McGlaun, tied slave breeding to her female slave's freedom. She promised to free Rhoda's mother after she gave birth to twelve children. She never got the chance to keep her word. Rhoda was the twelfth child, and Eleanor died a month before she was born.[28] Another formerly enslaved woman recalled a conversation between her mistress and an individual who wanted to buy her when she was a little girl. Her mistress told the prospective buyer that she "wouldn't sell her for nothing," and "wouldn't take two thousand [dollars] for her," because she was her "little breeder." In response to her mistress's assertion, she cursed her and said, "damn you, I won't never be no breeder for you."[29]

Before she had even reached childbearing age, her female owner already declared her priceless simply because of the *future* promise of her womb.[30] Her mistress also clearly understood that enslaved females possessed an enhanced value because of their capacity to reproduce. She recognized that she possessed the ability to create conditions—sexually violent or otherwise—under which she could reap the rewards of owning an enslaved female. It is quite possible that this woman merely deployed breeding discourse as a way to acknowledge the enhanced value that coincided with this enslaved girl's childbearing potential. But it also suggests that she possessed a measure of comfort with the darker dimensions of breeding: the physical and psychological tolls breeding could have on the girl, the kind of sexual violence that typically characterized breeding practices, and the pecuniary advantages of selling any children that may have been born as a result of such acts.

Underlying this enslaved girl's refusal lay an implicit understanding of what being a breeder meant. Her staunch rejection of her mistress's plan suggests that she may have already known about the sexual violence inherent in forced breeding practices. It also hints at the possibility that she knew that enslaved people did not use the term *breeding* to refer to consensual sexual relations with a partner of their choice. Rather than acquiesce to her mistress's plans for her body, she was determined to make sexual choices for herself.

White slave-owning women invested their economic futures in the possibilities of enslaved female bodies, and when African-descended women and girls shattered their hopes, they paid a brutal price. As Eli West traveled through the South, he recalled his yearlong stay with slave owner Esquire Starky and his mother. They owned two hundred slaves, but one enslaved woman of childbearing age simply could not, or would not, conceive. After continuously failing to have children, her mistress had her stripped naked and then she whipped her severely. When this brutality proved ineffectual in remedying the problem, her mistress sold the enslaved woman to slave traders.[31] Eli West's testimony elucidates how important enslaved women's reproductive capacity was to some white women and the lengths to which they would go in order to reap the tangible rewards of owning female slaves.

Some enslaved women were not able to thwart their mistresses' plans for their wombs, however. Henrietta Butler's mistress, Emily Haidee, not only forced her to engage in nonconsensual sex with a man, she commanded Henrietta's mother to do the same. Emily Haidee knew the value that enslaved females in particular possessed, and she developed long-term financial strategies to maximize their worth. When those coerced sexual acts produced enslaved offspring, she was known for "sellin' the boys and keepin' the gals."[32] For Emily, sexual violence was part of a business strategy that made practical sense, and black female bodies lay at the heart of it. She understood that black women's sexualized bodies held a self-perpetuating, economic promise that black men's bodies did not possess. But she was not unwilling to use enslaved men's bodies too. She knew all too well that pairing enslaved male and female bodies together was the key to increasing her economic investments in the institution, and this is precisely what she did.

Deeply embedded in formerly enslaved people's testimony about slavery and sexual violence lies a more profound discussion about the ways in which white women sought to benefit financially from their capacity to reproduce. And the experiences of the white women and enslaved people discussed in this chapter compel us to reconsider how we define acts of sexual violence in a legal context that denied the very existence of female perpetrators and black victims. Formerly enslaved people's reflections about white women's involvement in sexually violent acts not only unveil dimensions of their enslavement that have heretofore remained obscured, they also reveal important new intersections among gender, violence, sex, and the marketplace of slavery.

White women throughout the slaveholding South resigned themselves to the acts of sexual violence that their white male kin and employees perpetrated against enslaved people. Some further traumatized enslaved women by committing acts of sexualized violence on them in an attempt to make these women submit to further violation. And others sanctioned and ordered enslaved people to have sex with each other against their will. Why did they do these things?

Historians such as Thavolia Glymph have shown that white southern women were far from the natural allies of enslaved women, or men for that matter. Yet the idea that white women sympathized with enslaved people because they considered themselves bound by the legal, economic, and political constraints of marriage continues to pervade studies of white women's relationships with enslaved people.[33] The experiences of the enslaved men, women, and children discussed in this chapter offer evidence to challenge this notion. The white women discussed were part of a society that was predicated on the perpetual subjugation of an entire group of people. White women owned and used them, bought and sold them, and sometimes brutalized them. They were part of a culture of violence, and for those women deeply invested in the institution of slavery, sexual violence was part of that culture—it was inseparable from bondage. But there was more to it than that. Raised in slaveholding households and communities, most of these women realized that enslaved females and males possessed different monetary values that were contingent on their biologically distinct bodies, and they banked on this knowledge. White women were members of the South's slaveholding community and their investments in white supremacy and African American enslavement frequently outweighed other sentimental alliances.

NOTES

1. Interview with Henrietta Butler, *Mother Wit: The Ex-Slave Narratives of the Louisiana Writers' Project* (New York: Peter Lang, 1990), 38.

2. See, for example, Thelma Jennings, "'Us Colored Women Had to Go through a Plenty': Sexual Exploitation of African-American Slave Women," *Journal of Women's History* 1, no. 3 (1990): 45–74; Adrienne D. Davis, "'Don't Let Nobody Bother Yo' Principle': The Sexual Economy of American Slavery," in *Sister Circle: Black Women and Work*, ed. Sharon Harley (New Brunswick, N.J.: Rutgers University Press, 2002), 103–27; Edward Baptist, "'Cuffy,' 'Fancy Maids,' and 'One-Eyed Men': Rape, Commodification, and the Domestic Slave Trade in the United States," *American Historical Review* 106, no. 5 (2001): 1619–50; Joshua Rothman, *Notorious in the Neighborhood: Sex and Families across the Color Line in Virginia, 1787–1861* (Chapel Hill: University of North Carolina Press, 2003); and Sharony Green, "'Mr Ballard, I Am Compelled to Write Again': Beyond Bedrooms and Brothels, a Fancy Girl Speaks," *Black Women, Gender & Families* 5, no. 1 (2011): 17–40. Thomas Foster's work on the sexual abuse of enslaved men is helping to move us beyond this paradigm. See Thomas A. Foster, "The Sexual Abuse of Black Men under American Slavery," *Journal of the History of Sexuality* 20, no. 3 (2011): 445–64.

3. Mary R. Block, "Rape Law in 19th-Century America: Some Thoughts and Reflections on the State of the Field," *History Compass* 7, no. 5 (2009): 1392; and Sharon Block, *Rape and Sexual Power in Early America* (Chapel Hill: University of North Carolina Press, 2006), 16. Kirsten Fischer defines sexualized violence as acts "that may not have involved intercourse or have aroused sexual feelings on the part of either victim or perpetrator." See Kirsten Fischer, *Suspect Relations: Sex, Race, and Resistance in Colonial North Carolina* (Ithaca, N.Y.: Cornell University Press, 2001), 161.

4. William Blackstone, *Commentaries on the Laws of England* (London: John Murray, 1862), 4:236.

5. On the juridical refusal to recognize black female victims of sexual violence, see Deborah Gray White, *Ar'n't I a Woman? Female Slaves in the Plantation South* (New York: W. W. Norton, 1985), 152; and Block, *Rape and Sexual Power*.

6. Fischer, *Suspect Relations*, 161.

7. Walter Johnson, *River of Dark Dreams: Slavery and Empire in the Cotton Kingdom* (Cambridge, Mass.: Belknap Press of Harvard University Press, 2013), 195.

8. Richard Godbeer, *Sexual Revolution in Early America* (Baltimore: Johns Hopkins University Press, 2002), 193; and Fischer, *Suspect Relations*, 160–61.

9. Harriet Ann Jacobs, *Incidents in the Life of a Slave Girl: Written by Herself*, ed. Lydia Maria Child (Boston: Published for the author, 1861), 45.

10. Interview with Chris Franklin, "Born in Slavery: Slave Narratives from the Federal Writers' Project, 1936–1938," U.S. Work Projects Administration (USWPA), Library of Congress, Manuscript Division, http://memory.loc.gov/ammem/snhtml/snhome.html (hereafter "BIS"); and interview with unidentified slave, "Compilation Richmond County Ex-Slave Interviews, Mistreatment of Slaves," Georgia Narratives, vol. 4, part 4, "BIS."

11. Interview with Annie Young, Oklahoma Narratives, vol. 13, "BIS."

12. Interview with Jacob Manson, North Carolina Narratives, vol. 11, part 2, "BIS."

13. "Mistreatment of Slaves," Georgia Narratives, vol. 4, part 4, "BIS." White women knew all too well what happened to the enslaved women they sent to be whipped in these establishments. See, for example, "Testimony of Angelina Grimke Weld" in Theodore Dwight Weld, *American Slavery as It Is: Testimony of a Thousand Witnesses* (New York: American Anti-Slavery Society, 1839), 52–54.

14. Interview with Fannie Moore, North Carolina Narratives, vol. 11, part 2, "BIS." Other women engaged in the same kinds of eroticized, sexually sadistic whippings. See "Slavery as It Is. Slavery Illustrated," *Frederick Douglass' Paper* (Rochester, N.Y.), May 11, 1855.

15. See Martha Hodes, *White Women, Black Men: Illicit Sex in the Nineteenth-Century South* (New Haven, Conn.: Yale University Press, 1999); and Loren Schweninger, *Families in Crisis in the Old South: Divorce, Slavery and the Law* (Chapel Hill: University of North Carolina Press, 2012), 22–27. See also Fischer, *Suspect Relations*, 164.

16. "For the Better Preventing of a Spurious and Mixt Issue, &c.," in *The Charters and General Laws of the Colony and Province of Massachusetts Bay* (Boston: T. B. Wait, 1814), 747–48; and "An Act for the Better Regulations of Negroes in This Province," in James T. Mitchell and Henry Flanders, *The Statutes at Large of Pennsylvania from 1682–1801*, vol. 4, *1724–1744*, chapter 222, [1725–26] section 8 (n.p.: Clarence M. Busch, State Printer of Pennsylvania, 1897), 62–63; Amber D. Moulton, *The Fight for Interracial Marriage Rights in Antebellum Massachusetts* (Cambridge, Mass.: Harvard University Press, 2015), 10–48; and Peggy Pascoe, "Race, Gender, and Intercultural Relations: The Case of Interracial Marriage," *Frontiers: A Journal of Women Studies* 12, no. 1 (1991): 6.

17. Maryland State Archives, Proceedings and Acts of the General Assembly January 1637/8–September 1664, "An Act Concerning Negroes & Other Slaves," 1:533–34, http://msa.maryland.gov/megafile/msa/speccol/sc2900/sc2908/000001/000001/html/am1—533.html; "Act XVI. An Act for Suppressing Outlying Slaves," in *The Statutes at Large, Being a Collection of All the Laws of Virginia, from the First Session of the*

Legislature in the Year 1619, ed. William Waller Hening (Philadelphia: Printed for the author, by Thomas Desilver, 1823), 3:86–88. See also Paul Finkelman, "Crimes of Love, Misdemeanors of Passion: The Regulation of Race and Sex in the Colonial South," in *The Devil's Lane: Sex and Race in the Early South*, ed. Catherine Clinton and Michele Gillespie (New York: Oxford University Press, 1997), 124–38; and Peter Bardaglio, "'Shamefull Matches': The Regulation of Interracial Sex and Marriage in the South before 1900," in *Sex, Love, Race: Crossing Boundaries in North American History*, ed. Martha Hodes (New York: New York University Press, 1999), 112–38.

18. Hodes, *White Women, Black Men*; and Schweninger, *Families in Crisis*, 22–27. See also Fischer, *Suspect Relations*, 164.

19. Daina Ramey Berry, *"Swing the Sickle for the Harvest Is Ripe": Gender and Slavery in Antebellum Georgia* (Urbana: University of Illinois Press, 2007), 77–88.

20. Butler interview, 38.

21. Foster, "Sexual Abuse of Black Men."

22. Interview with unidentified slave, "Compilation Richmond County Ex-Slave Interviews."

23. Interview with J. W. Lindsay, 1863, Canada, in John W. Blassingame, *Slave Testimony: Two Centuries of Letters, Speeches, Interviews, and Autobiographies* (Baton Rouge: Louisiana State University Press, 1977), 400.

24. Interview with Matilda Henrietta Perry, *Weevils in the Wheat: Interviews with Virginia Ex-Slaves* (Charlottesville: University Press of Virginia, 1976), 224–25.

25. Diane Miller Sommerville, *Rape and Race in the Nineteenth-Century South* (Chapel Hill: University of North Carolina Press, 2004); and "The Rape Myth in the Old South Reconsidered," *Journal of Southern History* 16, no. 3 (August 1995): 481–518.

26. Estelle B. Freedmen, *Redefining Rape: Sexual Violence in the Era of Suffrage and Segregation* (Cambridge, Mass.: Harvard University Press, 2013), 1–32; Blackstone, *Commentaries on the Laws of England*, 4:233–39, Block, *Rape and Sexual Power*, 18; *Richmond Examiner*, October 21, 1862, 16.

27. Historians have discussed slave breeding for decades and many have sought to address the questions of whether it really took place and how frequently it occurred. They have generally concurred that it did happen, but the matter of prevalence remains contentious. See, for example, Richard G. Lowe and Randolph B. Campbell, "The Slave-Breeding Hypothesis: A Demographic Comment on the 'Buying' and 'Selling' States," *Journal of Southern History* 42, no. 3 (1976): 401–12; Richard Fogel and Stanley Engerman, *Time on the Cross: The Economics of American Negro Slavery* (New York: W. W. Norton, 1974), 78–79; and John Boles, *Black Southerners: 1619–1869* (Lexington: University Press of Kentucky, 1984), 69. More recently, Gregory D. Smithers examined African American people and abolitionists' deployment of the idea of forced breeding as a metaphor through which they sought to articulate the horrors of slavery to various audiences. Gregory D. Smithers, *Slave Breeding: Sex, Violence, and Memory in African American History* (Gainesville: University Press of Florida, 2012). In this chapter I do not seek to revisit these questions. Rather, I examine actual incidents in order to suggest more expansive ways of conceptualizing the violent nature of those events and

to highlight white women's involvement in a practice we typically associate with male perpetrators.

28. Interview with Rhoda Hunt, *The American Slave: A Composite Autobiography, Mississippi Narratives*, part 2, supplement series 1, vol. 7 (Santa Barbara, Calif.: Greenwood Press, 1977), 1075.

29. Social Science Institute, Fisk University, *Unwritten History of Slavery: Autobiographical Accounts of Negro Ex-Slaves* (Washington, D.C.: Microcard Editions, 1968), 77.

30. Jennifer L. Morgan's examination of white slave owners' wills in colonial South Carolina and Barbados demonstrates the importance that enslaved women's childbearing potential held for these individuals as they sketched out their bequests to descendants. As recipients of these slave inheritances, white women understood that enslaved infants augmented their wealth just as white men did. See Jennifer L. Morgan, *Laboring Women: Reproduction and Gender in New World Slavery* (Philadelphia: University of Pennsylvania Press, 2004), 102.

31. Weld, *American Slavery as It Is*, 68–69.

32. Butler interview, 38.

33. Thavolia Glymph, *Out of the House of Bondage: The Transformation of the Plantation Household* (New York: Cambridge University Press, 2008).

CHAPTER 7

The Sexual Abuse of Black Men under American Slavery

THOMAS A. FOSTER

In 1787 an enslaved man in Maryland raped a free black woman. The story comes to us from the female victim in the incident, Elizabeth Amwood. One white man, William Holland, had her "Pull up her Close and Lie Down he then Called a Negrow Man Slave" "and ordered him to pull Down his Britches and gitt upon the said Amwood and to bee grate with her." A fourth individual in this horrific scene, a white man named John Pettigrew, operating with Holland, pointed a pistol at the unnamed enslaved man and Elizabeth Amwood. All the while, Holland taunted them both, asking if it "was in" and "if it was sweet." Afterward, William "went up into the Company and Called for Water to wash his hand, saying he had bin putting a Mare to a horse."[1]

Scholars have suggested that rape can serve as a metaphor for enslavement— thus applying to both men and women who were enslaved. As Aliyah I. Abdur-Rahman argues, "the vulnerability of all enslaved black persons to nearly every conceivable violation produced a collective 'raped' subjectivity."[2] The standard scholarly interpretation of how slavery affected black manhood is perhaps best captured by the comments of one former slave, Lewis Clarke, who declared that a slave "can't be a man" because he could not protect his female kin from being sexually assaulted by owners and overseers.[3] Clarke's concern, the rape and sexual assault of black women and girls, has been well documented by the historical record. Thelma Jennings and others have analyzed the literal sexual assault of enslaved women in a range of contexts.[4] Physical sexual abuse of women and girls under slavery ranged from acts of punishment to expressions of desire and from forms of forced reproduction to systems of concubinage. Slavery violated the masculinity of black men who were denied the ability to protect vulnerable female dependents. According to Deborah Gray White, "those who tried to protect their spouses were themselves abused."[5] The emasculating psychic toll, White further argued, could have led men to eschew monogamy or resist marriage altogether.[6]

The rape of Elizabeth Amwood reveals that black manhood under slavery was also violated in other ways that are less easily spoken of (then and now), namely, the sexual exploitation of enslaved men.[7] The historical sexual assault of men and boys is well known, if mostly unarticulated.[8] The scholarship on early America shows us numerous instances of rape and sexual assault of men and boys. Ramón Gutiérrez has argued that individuals of the Native American third sex, or berdaches, were frequently prisoners of war used for sex and emasculated. We also know through the handful of extant sodomy cases that males have been so abused. The seventeenth-century Connecticut gentleman Nicholas Sension, for example, sexually preyed on his male servants. Virtually all of the cases of sodomy that came to the courts in early America involved individuals violating status boundaries—instructors on students, masters on servants. None involved peers.[9]

In the context of slavery, literary scholars have shown that sexual abuse of men was part of the Spanish slave system in Cuba. Robert Richmond Ellis argues that the account of former slave Juan Francisco Manzano "has commonly been regarded as a searing indictment of a physical mistreatment of slaves" but "can also be read as silent testimony to a kind of abuse largely unacknowledged by historians of slavery and critics of slave narratives: the sexual violation of male slaves." As Ellis points out, the topic has largely gone unexplored for a wide variety of reasons, including the obvious barrier of the historical record in that "male victims of slave rape left behind no biological record in the form of offspring" as well as the prevalent homophobia in traditional Latin American societies, which would have prevented men from telling their stories given that "male sexual passivity . . . was particularly stigmatized insofar as it was seen as entailing a loss of masculinity."[10] This article uses a wide range of sources on slavery—early American newspapers, court records, slave owners' journals, abolitionist literature, and the testimony of former slaves collected in autobiographies and in interviews— to argue that enslaved black men were sexually assaulted by both white men and white women. It finds that sexual assault of enslaved men took a wide variety of forms, including outright physical penetrative assault, forced reproduction, sexual coercion and manipulation, and psychic abuse.

It is difficult to determine with certainty the prevalence of the sexual abuse of male slaves. Martha Hodes concludes that the sexual "coercion" of black men in antebellum America "lurked as a possibility regardless of how frequently it came to pass."[11] Antislavery movements documented relatively more instances of such abuse than did previous eras. Nineteenth-century sources discussing slavery in the South, for example, are more abundant given the abolitionist movement, which drew attention to sexual depravity to argue for the immorality of slavery as an institution. Given the variety of social and cultural barriers to documenting the sexual abuse of enslaved black men, however, it would be an error to assume that the pattern of surviving sources reflects the historical practice of abuse. Indeed, the unlikelihood that cases would have been documented at all suggests that it would be safe to say that, regardless of location and time period, no enslaved man would have been safe from the threat of sexual abuse.

In many ways the cases discussed here have been hidden in plain sight. This article revisits instances that other scholars have cited in their studies of sex and slavery. In particular, it is indebted to Martha Hodes's research on antebellum sex between white women and enslaved black men, Thelma Jennings's work on the sexual exploitation of enslaved women, and Deborah Gray White's study of plantation life for enslaved women.[12] Through their painstaking research in slave records, these and other scholars show that the sexual abuse of enslaved women was ubiquitous. Establishing this now widely accepted conclusion was itself a challenge, for historians had to argue against deep-rooted racist depictions of enslaved women as hypersexual. Turning to the sexual abuse and exploitation of enslaved men builds on the perspective of this recent literature to challenge the view of black men as hypersexual and white women as passive and asexual.

Although scholars have acknowledged the sexual assault of enslaved women, none to my knowledge have highlighted the sexual abuse of enslaved men. In part, we have taken our cues from the nineteenth-century abolitionist writers who drew on certain gender-, race-, and class-infused understandings of sexual assault to appeal to a particular audience. As Martha Hodes reminds us, though, it was not simply that sex between black men and white women was uninteresting to abolitionists. Individuals recognized that it was "dangerous to the cause" to insult the virtue of southern white womanhood.[13] The rape of slave men has also gone unacknowledged because of the current and historical tendency to define rape along gendered lines, making both victims and perpetrators reluctant to discuss male rape. The sexual assault of men dangerously points out cracks in the marble base of patriarchy that asserts men as penetrators in opposition to the penetrable, whether homosexuals, children, or adult women. This article, therefore, confronts our own raced, classed, and gendered perceptions of rape and argues that we have a moral imperative to recognize the coerced sexuality of enslaved men as rape. Narrowly defining sexual assault along gendered lines has obscured our ability to recognize the climate of terror and the physical and mental sexual abuse that enslaved black men also endured.

BLACK MALE BODIES

The sexual exploitation of enslaved black men took place within a cultural context that fixated on black male bodies with both desire and horror. Sexual assault

took a wide variety of forms, but the common factor in all was the legal ownership that enabled control of the enslaved body. Winthrop Jordan notes the
conflicting messages embraced by Anglo-American culture as it sought to control and circumscribe the bodies of enslaved men and women, on the one hand
voicing repulsion for Africans, framing them as beastly, ugly, and unappealing,
while on the other hand viewing them as hypersexual. Anglo-American culture
had a long-standing view of black men as "particularly virile, promiscuous, and
lusty."[14] Although this view is consistently framed as a negative one, given Anglo-
American cultural norms of moderation and self-control, it is clear that early
Americans also saw erotic possibilities and beauty in black bodies. We know,
for example, that some slave masters fetishized and objectified women of color,
understanding that sexual abuse was about power and not simply expressing sexual desire. The presence of antebellum "fetish" markets of light-skinned enslaved
women, in particular, has been well documented by scholars. Edward Baptist, for
example, argues that the antebellum domestic slave trade might be reconsidered
as a "complex of inseparable fetishisms" given the slave traders' "frequent discussions of the rape of light-skinned enslaved women, or 'fancy maids,'" and "their
own relentlessly sexualized vision of the trade."[15]

The evidence also leads us to speculate that an unusual interest in light-skinned
men may have paralleled the more formalized and documented fetish market
in "fancy maids" that Edward Baptist has analyzed. Such an interest is found in
testimony presented to the American Freedmen's Inquiry Commission (AFIC),
which was established by the secretary of war in 1863 to document the conditions of those freed by the Emancipation Proclamation. White abolitionist
Richard J. Hinton, for example, testified that "I have never yet found a bright
looking colored man" "who has not told me of instances where he has been compelled, either by his mistress, or by white women of the same class, to have connection with them." In another case, a man testified that a man who had been
"brought up in the family" was also coerced into sex by his mistress, his family connection suggesting that he was mulatto. We also have some evidence of
light-skinned black men as sexually prized. Testimony to the AFIC included reference to light-skinned men as "fine looking."[16] One man told the AFIC, "it was
an extremely common thing among all the handsome mulattoes at the South to
have connection with the white women."[17] In the antebellum divorce case of one
white couple, Dorothea and Lewis Bourne, Dorothea's chosen lover, an enslaved
man named Edmond, is described in the records by more than one neighbor as
"so bright in his colour, a stranger would take him for a white man."[18] Such testimony raises the possibility that in this patriarchal society the sexual abuse of
"nearly white" men could enable white women to enact radical fantasies of dom-

ination over white men with the knowledge that their victim's body was legally
black and enslaved, subject to the women's control.

Although we have no evidence for a sexual fetish market in black male flesh,
historical scholarship shows us that black male bodies might well be eroticized
by white observers. Jordan claims that Anglo-American culture long held a fascination with the penises of black men and projected both desire and jealousy
on an objectified and disembodied black phallus.[19] Colonial accounts abound
with recorded instances of masters and others commenting not only on the nudity of slaves but on their bodies with a certain fascination. As Philip Morgan
reminds us, "daily encounters had a sexual dimension" in part because slaves
"wore little or no clothing." One observer in 1781 named William Feltman remarked on the reaction this nudity might provoke among Virginia women, given
that "young boys of about Fourteen and Fifteen years Old" were "virtually naked." Feltman quipped, "I can Assure you It would Surprize a person to see these
d——d [damned] black boys how well they are hung."[20] Numerous abolitionist
images also fixate on the black male body as perfection, highlighting muscular
bodies and, in almost pornographic detail, exposed buttocks, enduring unjust
abuse and degradation. William Benemann and others maintain that the image
of whipping exposed male flesh carried a homoerotic charge—one that mirrored
the nearly obscene fixation on whipping nude enslaved women, as has been suggested by scholars such as Colette Colligan.[21] John Saillant's work on the eroti-
cization of the black male body in early abolitionist literature also contributes to
this view that whites found sexual appeal in black male bodies. He notes that this
literature idealized black male bodies in a manner that included an unusual focus
on height, musculature, and skin color. Accounts in late eighteenth-century and
early nineteenth-century U.S. publications like the *American Universal Magazine*
and the *Philadelphia Minerva* described black male characters as "the blackest,
the best made, the most amiable," "beautiful in shape as the Apollo of Belve-
dere," and "Tall and shapely."[22] Black men's bodies could be described in sympa-
thetic tones: "Jack knelt down—not a muscle of his countenance quivered—
he was entirely naked, and was a remarkably muscular and well made man. He
looked like a fine bronze statue."[23] Accounts also discussed the "strength of limb,
the roundness of muscle, mind, tender affection, sympathy" in efforts to com-
bat slavery; such details served to underscore the moral injustice of enslaving
these men.[24] It is also worth noting that, despite the homoerotic nature of these
accounts suggested by their content, women made up the backbone of the abolitionist movement and readily consumed such literature. Accordingly, these descriptions lead us to conclude that white women were exposed to cultural ideas
about black male beauty, desirability, and physical prowess.

Yet at the same time, black men's genitalia were subject to scrutiny and punishment. Castration and other genital mutilations served as punishment in the hands of overseers and owners as well as in popular depictions of public enforcement of "justice." Thus, the *Boston News-Letter* reported in 1718 the assault of a white woman but with a focus on black male genitalia that warned off "all Negroes meddling with any White Woman": "A Negro Man met abroad an English woman, which he accosted to lye with, stooping down, fearing none behind him, a Man observing his Design, took out his Knife, before the Negro was aware, cut off all his unruly parts Smack and Smooth, the Negro Jumpt up roaring and run for his Life, the Black is now an Eunuch and like to recover of his wounds & doubtless cured from any more such Wicked Attempts."[25] In 1762 a North Carolina enslaved black man convicted of raping a white woman had his "private parts cut off and thrown in his face" as part of his execution.[26] While these articles recall the depiction of black men as agents of sexual assault, still then a notion in formation but one that would long remain in the American tradition, they also underscore how punishments for perceived or actual sexual infractions, in the hands of whites, focused on black male bodies and in particular in maiming the genitalia of enslaved men.

Already in the era of slavery Anglo-American culture embraced a message about black men as particularly sexual, prone to sensual indulgence, and desiring white women. Such messages undoubtedly served to demonize and define the population of black men but would also have raised the radical possibility for some women of the desirability of such men as highly sexual and accomplished—a model of masculinity that highlighted power, strength, and mastery rather than one of moderation and self-control.

Objectification of black men affected bodies and minds. Depictions of sexual prowess and the myth of the black rapist constituted one form of sexual abuse. This myth contributed to the legal and political disenfranchisement of black men from the earliest days of the Republic.[27] Yet the psychic toll was also high. Being told that one is hypersexual and uncontrollable cannot be dismissed as mere racist caricaturing; for some men, such messages would have inflicted great emotional pain.

HOMOSEXUAL ASSAULT

Like heterosexual relations between white men and black women, sex between masters and male slaves undoubtedly occurred, sometimes in affectionate and close relationships but also as a particular kind of punishment. That we have a handful of documented instances is noteworthy, given the prohibitions against

sodomy in early America, the absolute power that owners wielded and that enabled them to keep such moments secret, and the shame that was attached to being sodomized by a master and that could ensure the victim's silence.

Abolitionist literature demonstrates the possibility of the sexual assault of
enslaved black men by slave-owning white men of what was called the planter
class. John Saillant's analysis of early abolitionist literature both shows the ho-
moerotics of the literature and provides examples of masters who were said to be
sexually abusing their slaves. In one such account, authored by Joseph LaVallée,
a slave named Itanoko was subjected to rape by a white slaver named Urban.
Urban was described as a "ravisher" who, Itanoko explained, was "struck by my
comeliness," and he did "violate, what is most sacred among men." As Saillant explains, although Itanoko was rescued, he found himself on a plantation in Saint-
Domingue, where he met Theodore, "whose 'criminal complaisance with the
overseer' allows him to give 'free scope to his irregular passions.'" As Saillant
explains, "the 'irregular passions' apparently include sexual activity with black
men, which LaVallée calls 'crime,' 'vice,' and 'rapine,' all 'enormities' resulting from
'unbridled disorders' and 'passion.'"[28]

Incidents in the Life of a Slave Girl, published in 1861 by abolitionist and escaped slave Harriet Jacobs (under the pseudonym Linda Brent), also included
mention of male slave owners sexually abusing male slaves. Jacobs alluded to this
abuse in the context of the rape of slave women and girls, lamenting that "no pen
can give adequate description to the all-pervading corruption produced by slavery." That corruption extended beyond female victims, for, as Jacobs wrote, "in
some cases they exercise the same authority over the men slaves."[29] Jacobs's autobiographical account also includes an incident between a slave named Luke and
his owner that Abdur-Rahman reads as "sadomasochistic" and one that "reveals
in general the entwinement of desire and coercion that typifies the master-slave
relationship." He writes: "Linda remembers Luke as a particularly degraded figure" sent to the master's son, a man described in coded terms as a depraved ho-
mosexually inclined individual. It was in this man's service that Luke "became
prey to the vices growing out of the 'patriarchal institution.'"[30] Abdur-Rahman
points, for example, to passages in Jacobs like the following:

> The fact that [the young master] was entirely dependent on Luke's care, and
> was obliged to be tended like an infant, instead of inspiring any gratitude or
> compassion towards his poor slave, seemed only to increase his irritability and
> cruelty. As he lay there on his bed, a mere wreck of manhood, he took into his
> head the strangest freaks of despotism; and if Luke hesitated to submit to his
> orders, the constable was immediately sent for. Some of these freaks were of a

nature too filthy to be repeated. When I fled the house of bondage, I left poor Luke still chained to the bed of this cruel and disgusting wretch.[31]

Even while most of the accounts illustrating sexual abuse of enslaved men came from the nineteenth century, eighteenth-century sources indicate the practice was not limited to that era. Slave owners' diaries, for example, also reveal instances of sexual assault perpetrated by masters, indicating that the literary examples reflected a certain social reality. The eighteenth-century diary of a Jamaican planter named Thomas Thistlewood tersely noted two incidents of homosexual assault. In one entry he recorded, "Report of Mr. Watt Committing Sodomy with his Negroe waiting Boy." The language is specific enough to indicate this was a case of sodomy—not the more common attempted sodomy found in the historical records. It also notes the power dynamic within a power dynamic by singling out a "boy" and not an adult man. Thistlewood's diary also noted "strange reports about the parson and John his man." While the term "strange reports" is not precise, Trevor Burnard interprets it as meaning homosexual activity.[32] Again it is worth noting that this act occurred between a slave owner and a close personal servant rather than with a field hand. As such, this type of abuse follows a broader pattern that suggests the closer the proximity to whites, the more likely that sexual abuse was to occur.

RECONSIDERING FORCED COUPLING

In the story from eighteenth-century Maryland that opened this article, it is clear that the unnamed enslaved man was also a victim of sexual assault. Yet such stories have rarely been told by historians, and this account itself was documented only by chance. One of the white perpetrators of the assault, William Holland, was convicted of assault and battery on the free black woman, Elizabeth Amwood. Holland petitioned the governor of Maryland for a pardon. Included in the pardon file was a memorandum from Amwood detailing the assault.[33] The case illustrates the sexual vulnerability of black women, to be sure. But we must also recognize the physical and psychological toll that such an event would have taken on the enslaved man, who was unnamed. Forced to rape this woman at the point of a gun, not only would he have had to deal with the legal and moral consequences of assaulting a free black woman—someone he may or may not have known—but his manhood was also usurped.

Other accounts of forced sex reveal that male slaves could also suffer punishment for a forced attack. An abolitionist newspaper, the *National Era*, reported in 1853 on the case of another unnamed man, described only as a "negro man, belonging to H. France." The man had been "burned at the stake" for having "attempted to commit rape" and for murder. What makes this case unusual, however, is that after the execution the "citizens of Pettis county" requested that the France family leave the community, "having some suspicion that the negro was instigated to the perpetration of the deed by his master." In addition to "aiding and abetting the murder," the master was criticized for his "bad examples set before slaves, by conversing with them in relation to the virtue and chastity of white women, and in defamation of their character; thereby influencing them to commit deeds of crime and rapine."[34] We must consider that France may well have forced his slaves to assault white women, since to take the story at face value is to accept the rhetoric of an ignorant, animalistic, and docile slave who, excited by France, was set loose on women.

At a minimum, this last story raises questions about how often slave masters used male slaves to inflict sexual punishment on women, whether free black, enslaved, or white, and about the toll that these forced rapes would have taken on those men, who could rarely resist the will of their masters. In this instance, it resulted in the punishment for the slave of death by being burned alive. It is important to note again that the man was unnamed. His designation as only a "negro" man dehumanizes him, rendering him in his assault on the woman a symbol perhaps of all black men, but we must rehumanize him as another type of victim in a multilayered sexual assault perpetrated by white men on both black men and white and black women.

Forced sex also took place within the context of so-called slave breeding. From what little documentation we have, we know the practice of forcing slaves to reproduce had colonial roots. Most scholars identify the early nineteenth century as the period of greatest expansion of this practice, coinciding with the growth of slavery in the United States and the maturation of the domestic slave trade. In his account of his experiences as a slave, William J. Anderson described what he knew about one master's attempts at forced breeding: "I have known him to make four men leave their wives for nothing, and would not let them come and see them any more on the peril of being shot down like dogs; he then made the women marry other men against their will. Oh, see what it is to be a slave? A man, like the brute, is driven, whipped, sold, comes and goes at his master's bidding."[35] Many slave owners allowed enslaved men and women to develop personal ties and to form relationships and families of their own choosing. Others, however, clearly took a more active role in selecting for the qualities they wanted in slaves, forcing some to have children or to live as husband and wife. The conclusions that historian Thelma Jennings draws about the power that slave owners held over enslaved women should be applied as well to enslaved men: "the white patri-arch had the *power* to force them to mate with whomever he chose, to reproduce or suffer the consequences, to limit the time spent with their children, and even to sell them and their children" (original emphasis). Masters could and did force couples to have sexual intercourse, and if "either one showed any reluctance, the master would make the couple consummate the relation in his presence."[36]

Testimony from a number of former slaves demonstrates how forced repro-duction had the dehumanizing effect of labeling certain enslaved men as "stock men" or "bulls." As Thelma Jennings explains with one example, "on Mary In-gram's plantation, the master made the decision on who could and could not get married." Or, in the words of Mary Ingram herself, "him select de po'tly and p'lific women, and de po'tly man, and use sich for de breeder an' de father ob de women's chillums."[37] In another example, one former slave recollected how "Joe was 'bout seven feet tall an' was de breedinges' nigger in Virginia." He continued: "Once ole Marsa hired him out to a white man what lived down in Suffolk. Dey come an' got him on a Friday. Dey brung him back Monday mo'nin.'"[38] Another former slave similarly noted how his master had prevented him from engaging in sexual relations with only one woman, forcing him to reproduce with about fifteen women and to father dozens of children.[39]

Forcing some enslaved men to reproduce with many different women denied to them a fatherly role even while it prevented their children from bonding with them. A Texas woman who had been enslaved attested to this result when she noted that "half of us young negroes didn't know who our fathers were." Sim-ilarly, one slave named Mary Young remarked, "we never hardly knew who our father was." Another slave, Millie Williams, also commented, "shuck's nobody knows who der father waz."[40] It is possible that African and African American men would have viewed this violation differently than Anglo-Americans, given Anglo-American norms of monogamy and traditional West African matrilineal kinship practices, although these differences would have become lessened within long-enslaved populations. Nonetheless, men from both cultures shared the val-ues of male independence and mastery in a broad sense.[41]

Forced coupling also placed a premium on young and healthy men and im-plied the lesser value of men who were beyond years thought suitable for repro-duction. As Thelma Jennings explains, the former slave Lulu Wilson noted that her father was forced off her plantation once the slave owner considered him to be "too old for breeding."[42] Other men who might be young enough to repro-duce but were deemed undesirable were prevented from fathering children. One Tennessee slave woman remarked that a "scrubby man" would not be permitted to father children. Another slave woman, Polly Cancer, noted that her suitor was forced by her master to discontinue seeing her and told "to git coz he didn't want no runts on his place."[43]

The scholarly focus, reflecting the sources, has generally viewed these forced couplings from the point of view of the assaulted woman, often wholly neglecting the male participant. Thus, for instance, despite the very rich testimony she mobilized to explain the sexual exploitation of enslaved women when discussing miscegenation, Thelma Jennings concludes that "only the bondwomen could be subjected to the white man's passion," overlooking the broader power that white men also held over enslaved black men's bodies and sexuality.[44] Still, the sources can provide that evidence. In one example, a slave woman named Rose Williams of Texas fought off a slave man, Rufus, despite their owner's decision to place them together. Rose described Rufus as a "bully" and explained, "I don't like Rufus." Accordingly, when he attempted to "crawl in" bed with her, she argued with him. He never responded with physical force but instead pleaded with her that she should "hush" and said to her, "dis am my bunk, too." Rose used physical violence to discourage Rufus from being intimate with her, giving him a "shove" and taking a "poker," with which she "lets him have it over de head." Rufus did not respond with force but did let her know that "dey's gwine larn you somethin'," indicating the punishment that would await her for disobeying their owner's intentions. The account as told by Rose rightly positions her as a victim, but we should not overlook that Rufus himself was placed in a position of powerlessness by his owner. Rufus did not retaliate physically even after being assaulted. In the end, however, Rose capitulated after being threatened by her mistress.[45]

In addition to being forced into sexual situations with women they did not choose, enslaved men could also face the emotional withdrawal and resentment of the women they were then supposed to seduce and marry. Rufus, for example, faced the physical resistance of Rose Williams. After the freeing of the slaves, she was able to leave Rufus, with whom she bore only two children, which some have taken to suggest a resistance to him throughout their "marriage." Jennings's observations on the psychic trauma of forced marriage for women should also be applied to men. Forced marriage, she argues, caused both "physical and mental anguish" and "may have even caused greater humiliation than concubinage . . . since marriage was long term."[46] A level of resentment and even hatred could more easily be aimed at the enslaved male husband than at the slave master or white overseer. One woman, Mary Gaffney, told her interviewer, "I just hated the man I married . . . but it was what Master said do."[47] In forced coupling, the levels of victimhood were multilayered.

Men, such as Joe in Virginia, who were forced to have children with many women might also have found themselves unwanted within the slave community. These unions might have led to children who would have been desired by the white planter class but certainly not always by enslaved women. Some slave women, for example, rejected husbands and lovers because of their promiscuity, as did one woman "on account of his having so Many Children."[48] Deborah Gray White notes in one example that after a slave named Molly lost her husband because he was sold for constantly running away, she was "given" a new husband—meaning forced into another arrangement to produce children. Despite having nine children together, however, Molly later rejected this man and exclaimed that he was not her "real" husband despite their years of cohabitation. "In Molly's heart her *real* husband was the man sold away by their master."[49] For such men, the rejection and resentment of their forced wives would have further compounded their dehumanized situation.

Records from the period immediately after slavery indicate the desire of former slaves both to find family members who had been sold away and to remove themselves from forced spouses. Men and women found themselves able to extricate themselves from sexual partners they had not selected and, in many cases, not wanted. The Florida General Assembly, for example, created legislation for those who sought to legalize their chosen families and spouses but came under fire for failing to address the problem of those who had previously been forced into marriage and who were "opposed to being regularly joined in the bonds of matrimony" with these unwanted spouses.[50]

The forced coupling of enslaved men and women denied the individuality of both. Continuing to overlook the victimization of men in such sexual assaults not only denies the full extent of that sexual abuse but also continues dangerously to draw on long-standing stereotypes of black male sexuality that positions black men as hypersexual. In some instances of forced coupling, undoubtedly, some men took pleasure, as did some women. In other instances, for both partners, it may have been a last resort to avoid punishment from masters or overseers. In all such cases, white men controlled the bodies of both black men and women.

WHITE WOMEN

The traditional denial of white women's sexual agency has contributed to our obscured view of those white women who sexually assaulted and exploited enslaved men. Indeed, the abuse of black men at the hands of white women stands on its head the traditional gendered views of racialized sexual assault. Yet as historians have demonstrated, despite the legal and cultural prohibitions against sex between black men and white women in early America, occurrences were far from rare. Many examples, from a wide range of sources, demonstrate no out-right violence or threat of physical harm to the black men (enslaved and free) but highlight that it was well understood that white women did at times take the ini-tiative in these interactions. As with relations between white men and enslaved women, sexual contact between white women and enslaved men ranged from af-fectionate to violent. Even presumably affectionate and long-term relationships must be reconsidered given the context of slavery. As scholars remind us, the ap-parently affectionate relationships of enslaved women and white men took place within the context of absolute power over life and limb and therefore must not be viewed as consensual. Few scholars, however, have viewed the relationships of enslaved men and free white women through the lens of sexual abuse in part be-cause of gendered assumptions about sexual power.

White women's desire for sexual intimacy with black men was noted by more than one early American observer, sometimes in the form of derisive attacks against the women involved. For example, in 1731 one white woman declared about another woman that she "would have Jumpt over nine hedges to have had a Negroe."[51] One Maryland planter commented in 1739 that a white woman who had heard about a slave rebellion from one of her slaves did nothing because "perhaps She had a mind for a black husband."[52] In 1769, after giving birth to a black child, one woman in Maryland was condemned in the newspaper for "pol-lut[ing]" her husband's bed.[53] Another woman in 1785 in Virginia was punished by her church for "committing fornication by cohabiting with a negro."[54] Thomas Thistlewood's eighteenth-century diary denounced a white woman in Jamaica who was "making free" with male slaves.[55] His comment, although brief, indi-cated her agency in the matter and reminds us that in such cases it is wrong for us to assume that the enslaved man would be necessarily perceived as the sexual aggressor in such encounters.

Philip Morgan's research on the eighteenth-century Chesapeake and Low-country regions of the American colonies revealed numerous instances of white women engaged in sexual relationships with enslaved men. In early eighteenth-century Maryland, for example, one woman who lived with an enslaved man had seven children, although Morgan emphasizes the man's agency in this instance by noting that *she* "bore *him*" seven children (emphasis added).[56] The divorce case of Dorothea and Lewis Bourne, a focus of Hodes's study and mentioned above, reveals another instance that tells us that such cases were far from rare. In this 1825 divorce, testimony from neighbors and friends revealed that Dorothea had enjoyed a long-term relationship with a neighbor's slave, Edmond, with whom she had probably had several children. Neighbors revealed themselves to be well aware of her conduct and, perhaps more surprisingly, did not frame it as wholly unusual. Martha Hodes argues that this incident provides yet more evidence that black men were not necessarily assumed to be the initiators in such relationships and that the figures of the aggressive black man and the sexually passive white woman had not yet emerged as cultural stereotypes. Indeed, Judith Richardson, who owned Edmond, testified that Dorothea was often seen "lurking about her negroes houses."[57]

Abolitionist literature also occasionally drew attention to white women's agency in depictions of interracial intimacy. Harriet Jacobs noted in her account that sex between white women and black men was not all that unusual, as did another former slave named J. W. Lindsay, who said, "There are cases where white women fall in love with their servants."[58] Martha Hodes explains that one African American told the AFIC that when he had worked as a steward on the Mississippi River, it was common for black men who worked on the river to exchange information about "the desires of certain white women to 'sleep with them.'"[59] Another told the AFIC that during his time in Tennessee he observed that "planters here in Tennessee have sometimes to watch their daughters to keep them from intercourse with the negroes. This, though of course exceptional, is yet common enough to be a source of uneasiness to parents."[60]

That it was understood that white women at times took the initiative in interracial sex is not, of course, in itself evidence of the sexual abuse of enslaved men, although it is worth repeating that the enslaved status of black men in such interactions made them necessarily vulnerable. Other evidence more clearly points to instances of coercion and sexual exploitation and should lead us to conclude that white men were not the sole perpetrators of sexual coercion or the sexual abuse of enslaved black men and women. Hinton told the AFIC that one slave recounted to him a story of being "ordered" "to sleep with" his mistress within a year of her husband's death, something that he said had happened "regularly."[61] Testimony from Hinton before the AFIC also told of hearing that "colored men on that river knew that the women of the Ward family of Louisville, Kentucky, were in the habit of having the [black] stewards, or other fine looking fellows, sleep with them when they were on the boats."[62] There is hint of the men's coercion in these comments, and certainly much more than a hint of the women's agency.

Hinton's testimony also revealed something about the variety of tactics that women employed toward the men in such circumstances, many of them strikingly similar to the strategies employed by white owners against black women. "I have generally found that, unless the woman has treated them kindly, and won their confidence, they have to be threatened, or have their passions aroused by actual contact."[63] Here we see that direct threats or indirect manipulation, with a more subtle threat of violence, accompanied some of these relationships. Even in the physical contact and arousal that Hinton mentioned, once made, the man would have little recourse to resist.

Other sources supported the testimony before the AFIC and show the possibility of the exploitation of enslaved men by white women, even in seemingly benign relationships. Court testimony from an 1841 Kentucky case likewise involved an enslaved man and a white woman who lived together as husband and wife and whose case had come to court over the woman's ability to sell her own land. The court declared that their relationship was not marriage but was instead one of "concubinage," given the power imbalance between them. Moreover, the case included testimony that revealed the power dynamic within the relationship, since it was reported that the white woman *sometimes threatened to sell* her concubine, James (original emphasis).[64]

As Hodes argues, white women of the planter class were certainly able to wield power over black men, although all white women could coerce enslaved black men given the legal and social setting in which they lived. Planter-class women might more easily and more believably have persuaded the community to view them as innocent victims of their sexual contact with black men. One black man who recruited black Union soldiers told the AFIC that another black man had told him how white women could assume the mantle of white female purity to facilitate the sexual assault of black men. Even women who may have been physically smaller and weaker than their victims thus wielded a powerful threat. The recruiter testified about "a young girl" who "got him out in the woods and told him she would declare he attempted to force her, if he didn't have connection with her." Others testified that this sort of coercion was not unusual, and one Patrick Minor, for example, told Hinton that he knew of "several cases of the same kind."[65]

As an alternative to or in conjunction with threats of retribution, some white women may have wielded the purse as a means of coercing enslaved men to have sex with them. That is to say, some men may have been paid for their sexual services to white women. One black steward reported that a white woman from Louisville, Kentucky, "offered him five dollars to arrive at her house in Louisville at a particular time."[66] The words suggest that she was negotiating a way to discretely engage in sex with him. Others may have done the same. Enslaved men, like enslaved women, may well have negotiated opportunities that sex under slavery presented them to their advantage. One black man testified to the AFIC precisely how such encounters might have begun: "I will tell you how it is here. I will go up with the towels, and when I go into the room the woman will keep following me with her eyes, until I take notice of it, and one thing leads to another. Others will take hold of me and pull me on to the sofa, and others will stick out their foot and ask one to tie their boot, and I will take hold of their foot and say 'what a pretty foot!'"[67]

Regardless of the circumstances that prompted these varied arrangements, many of them clearly took place in the context of servitude and highlighted the power of the slave-owning mistress over the enslaved man. Harriet Jacobs, in her mention of a white woman who preyed on a male slave, wrote that she had picked a man who was "the most brutalized, over whom her authority could be exercised with less fear of exposure."[68] Anecdotes such as these suggest that some white women initiated sexual encounters and made clear what they wanted, knowing that their cultural role, the sexual innocence expected of them, helped to hide their actions. Jacobs's account noted that she was personally familiar with this household, and she suggested that the woman preyed on more than one man, saying that the woman "did not make advances . . . to her father's more intelligent servants" but singled out for sexual assault instead a man "over whom her authority could be exercised with less fear of exposure" because he was so traumatized. Such a man, it is suggested, had been terrorized into submission on the plantation, and she took advantage of his state of mind to force herself on him—with the threat of additional punishment if he did not accept her assault and if he did not keep it clandestine.

Wives and daughters of planters who formed these sexual relationships were simply taking advantage of their position within the slave system. Having sex with their white counterparts in the insular world of the white planter class, if exposed, would certainly have risked opprobrium, and even gossip about their public actions might have marred their reputations. Daughters of planters could use enslaved men in domestic settings, however, and retain their virtue and maintain the appearance of passionlessness and virginity while seeking sexual experimentation. In other words, one of the ways that some southern women may have protected their public virtue was by clandestine relations with black men. Hinton also told the AFIC that a white doctor reported to him that in Virginia and Missouri, "white women, especially the daughters of the smaller planters, who were brought into more direct relations with the negro, had compelled some one of the men to have something to do with them."[69]

Sons of planters also engaged in such conduct, as Hinton also noted, even suggesting that young women imitated the behavior of their brothers. Daughters of wealthy individuals on the American frontier, he explained, where interaction with male suitors was also relatively limited as it was for planters' daughters given social constraints, noted that they "knew that their brothers were sleeping with the chambermaids, or other servants, and I don't see how it could be otherwise than that they too should give loose to their passions."[70] Another man reported that the conditions of slavery brought about not only the "promiscuous intercourse among blacks, and between black women and white men," but also created a context that encouraged white women to be "involved" in the "general depravity."[71] Harriet Jacobs wrote that daughters "know that the women slaves are subject to their father's authority over men slaves" and use their example to coerce certain male slaves into being their sexual partners. Although Hinton and Jacobs perhaps could not conceive of women taking the initiative on their own and so understood them as following the example set by their fathers and brothers, we should note that the women seem to have engaged in the same behavior as the men, if not perhaps as many women as men.

As historians have often pointed out, the widespread presence of persons of mixed racial ancestry across the U.S. South in the era of slavery has stood as firm evidence, in the face of denials, that sex between white men and black women took place on plantations. Madison Jefferson, for example, who was himself a slave in Virginia, pointed out already in 1841 that "the proof" of the rape of enslaved black women by white men was that "a very considerable portion of the slaves are of the mixed race."[72] One major difference between white male exploitation of enslaved women and white female exploitation of enslaved men is that white women, including daughters of planters, risked giving birth. We do know that some white women became pregnant, as did Dorothea Bourne. To be sure, white women risked less than their black female counterparts, with their far greater control over their sexual partners and greater access to contraceptive information and technologies. Still, the risks were there. Although by law the status of a child followed that of its mother, in many cases when a white woman had a child who was fathered by an enslaved man, the child was taken away and placed with the local slave community or sold into slavery elsewhere. Lewis Jenkins, for example, was raised as a slave although his mother was a white woman. As he told his family's story, when his mother became pregnant, she was "taken away from her playmates and kept in the attic hid. They took me soon as I was born from her."[73]

The sexual assault of enslaved black men was a component of slavery and took place in a wide variety of contexts and in a wide range of forms. Given the current and historical obstacles to documenting and recognizing the abuse, the examples described here should be seen as the tip of the iceberg and the abuse as far from rare. In addition to the direct physical abuse of men that happened under slavery, this sexual exploitation constituted a type of psychological abuse that was ubiquitous. Without recognizing male sexual abuse, we run the risk of

reinscribing the very stereotypes used by white slave owners and others who reduced black men to bestial sexual predators and white women to passionless and
passive vessels. The cases discussed here show that the use of physical force and
direct threats of violence as well as implicit power imbalances worked against
enslaved men as well as enslaved women. The documentary record confronts our
own gendered perceptions of rape and creates a moral imperative for historians
to recognize the sexual assault of enslaved black men. The cases here should also
help us to rethink male sexual abuse in general not only in the antebellum American South but also elsewhere, and future research could further refine these findings along geographic and chronological lines of examination. This article, therefore, is offered as a contribution to our understanding of the experience of black
masculinity in early America.

NOTES

I would like to thank all those who helped with the development of this article, including Ramón A. Gutiérrez, Mathew Kuefler, and the participants in the history of the
intersection of race and sexuality conference hosted by the Center for the Study of Race
and Ethnicity at the University of California, San Diego. I would also like to thank Estelle Freedman and Margaret Storey for feedback on earlier versions of this article.

1. Petitions for William Holland, March 1787, Governor and Council, Pardon Papers, box 4, folder 47, Maryland State Archives (hereafter MDSA). For the first discussion of this case, see Sharon Block, *Rape and Sexual Power in Early America* (Chapel
Hill: University of North Carolina Press, 2006), 85.

2. Aliyah I. Abdur-Rahman argues, "More than simply a condition of black women's
experience under slavery, rape serves as a useful paradigm for assessing and describing the
position and experience of black people in total under slavery's brutal regime." Aliyah I.
Abdur-Rahman, "'The Strangest Freaks of Despotism': Queer Sexuality in Antebellum
African American Slave Narratives," *African American Review* 40, no. 2 (2006): 230–31.

3. Lewis Clarke, "Leaves from a Slave's Journal of Life," *National Anti-Slavery Standard*, October 20 and 27, 1842, reprinted in *Slave Testimony: Two Centuries of Letters,
Speeches, Interviews, and Autobiographies*, ed. John W. Blassingame (Baton Rouge: Louisiana State University Press, 1977), 156–58.

4. Thelma Jennings, "'Us Colored Women Had to Go through a Plenty': Sexual
Exploitation of African-American Slave Women," *Journal of Women's History* 1, no. 3
(1990): 45–74.

5. Deborah Gray White, *Ar'n't I a Woman? Female Slaves in the Plantation South*
(1985; New York: Norton, 1999), 146. See also, for example, Daina Ramey Berry, *"Swing
the Sickle for the Harvest Is Ripe": Gender and Slavery in Antebellum Georgia* (Chicago:
University of Illinois Press, 2007), 81.

6. White, *Ar'n't I a Woman?*, 147.

7. The rape of adult men in conflict and war today, for example, goes underreported

and is much less discussed than rape of women as a weapon of war. In 2005, for example, in eastern Congo and northern Uganda, rape of boys and men was a notable feature of the conflicts there. This has been documented by the United Nations, Human Rights Watch, and Amnesty International. See, for example, its *2005 Annual Report for Congo (Dem. Rep. of)*, available online at http://www.amnestyusa.org/annualreport .php?id=ar&yr=2005&c=COD (accessed August 1, 2010). Also muted in discussions of the rape and sexual assault of men is prison rape. See, for example, Human Rights Watch, "No Escape: Male Rape in U.S. Prisons," 2001, available online at http://www .hrw.org/legacy/reports/2001/prison/report.html (accessed August 1, 2010). On the history of sex and sexual abuse behind bars, see, for example, Regina Kunzel, *Criminal Intimacy: Prison and the Uneven History of Modern American Sexuality* (Chicago: University of Chicago Press, 2008). More often than not, rape of men in prison is the subject of derisive humor in popular culture, masking a deep discomfort and homophobia. But dismissive humor also hides the deeper threat that male rape exposes—the penetrability and vulnerability of men.

8. Michael Scarce, *Male on Male Rape: The Hidden Toll of Stigma and Shame* (New York: Plenum, 1997).

9. See Thomas A. Foster, ed., *Long before Stonewall: Histories of Same-Sex Sexuality in Early America* (New York: New York University Press, 2007), introduction and essays by Ramón Gutiérrez and Richard Godbeer.

10. Robert Richmond Ellis, "Reading through the Veil of Juan Francisco Manzano: From Homoerotic Violence to the Dream of a Homoracial Bond," *PMLA* 113, no. 3 (1998): 422–35.

11. Martha Hodes, *White Women, Black Men: Illicit Sex in the Nineteenth-Century South* (New Haven, Conn.: Yale University Press, 1997), 139.

12. Ibid.; Jennings, "'Us Colored Women'"; White, *Ar'n't I a Woman?*

13. Hodes, *White Women, Black Men*, 128.

14. Winthrop D. Jordan, *White over Black: American Attitudes toward the Negro, 1550–1812* (Chapel Hill: University of North Carolina Press, 1968), 151.

15. Edward E. Baptist, "'Cuffy,' 'Fancy Maids,' and 'One-Eyed Men': Rape, Commodification, and the Domestic Slave Trade in the United States," *American Historical Review* 106, no. 5 (2001): 1620.

16. Richard Hinton testimony, quoted in Hodes, *White Women, Black Men*, 130–31.

17. James Redpath testimony, quoted in Hodes, *White Women, Black Men*, 127.

18. Lewis Bourne divorce petition, Louisa County, Virginia, January 20, 1825, quoted in *American Sexual Histories*, ed. Elizabeth Reis (Malden, Mass.: Blackwell, 2001), 166–67.

19. Jordan, *White over Black*, 34–35.

20. Military journal of Lt. William Feltman, June 22, 1781, HSP, quoted in Philip D. Morgan, *Slave Counterpoint: Black Culture in the Eighteenth-Century Chesapeake and Lowcountry* (Chapel Hill: University of North Carolina Press, 1998), 398–99.

21. William Benemann, *Male-Male Intimacy in Early America: Beyond Romantic Friendships* (New York: Harrington Park, 2006), 68–69; Colette Colligan, "Anti-Abolition Writes Obscenity: The English Vice, Transatlantic Slavery, and England's

Obscene Print Culture," in *International Exposure: Perspectives on Modern Pornography, 1800–2000*, ed. Lisa Z. Sigel (New Brunswick, N.J.: Rutgers University Press, 2005), 67–99.

22. John Saillant, "The Black Body Erotic and the Republican Body Politic," in Foster, *Long before Stonewall*, 314.

23. *Colored American*, October 5, 1839.

24. *North Star*, November 17, 1848.

25. *Boston News-Letter*, March 3, 1718.

26. Morgan, *Slave Counterpoint*, 405.

27. See, for example, Leslie Harris, "From Abolitionist Amalgamators to 'Rulers of the Five Points': The Discourse of Interracial Sex and Reform in Antebellum New York City," in *Sex, Love, Race: Crossing Boundaries in North American History*, ed. Martha Hodes (New York: New York University Press, 1999), 191–212.

28. Saillant, "Black Body Erotic," 303–30, 310.

29. Linda Brent [Harriet Jacobs], *Incidents in the Life of a Slave Girl, Written by Herself* (1861), quoted in Abdur-Rahman, "Strangest Freaks of Despotism," 236n13.

30. Abdur-Rahman, "Strangest Freaks of Despotism," 231. See also Benemann, *Male-Male Intimacy*, 149–50.

31. Jacobs, *Incidents in the Life*, 233.

32. Trevor Burnard, *Mastery, Tyranny, and Desire: Thomas Thistlewood and His Slaves in the Anglo-Jamaican World* (Chapel Hill: University of North Carolina Press, 2004), 216.

33. Petitions for William Holland, March 1787, Governor and Council, Pardon Papers, box 4, folder 47, MDSA. See also Block, *Rape and Sexual Power*, 85.

34. *National Era*, August 4, 1853.

35. William J. Anderson, *Life and Narrative of William J. Anderson, Twenty-Four Years a Slave* (Chicago: Daily Tribune Book and Job Printing Office, 1857), 24.

36. Jennings, "'Us Colored Women,'" 46, 50. See also, for example, Berry, *"Swing the Sickle,"* 76–103.

37. Quoted in Jennings, "'Us Colored Women,'" 50.

38. Quoted in Brenda E. Stevenson, "Slave Marriage and Family Relations," in *Major Problems in the History of American Sexuality: Documents and Essays*, ed. Kathy Peiss (Boston: Houghton Mifflin, 2001), 169.

39. Jennings, "'Us Colored Women,'" 51.

40. Quoted in ibid., 50.

41. See, for example, Daniel P. Black, *Dismantling Black Manhood: An Historical and Literary Analysis of the Legacy of Slavery* (New York: Garland, 1997); and Herbert G. Gutman, *The Black Family in Slavery and Freedom, 1750–1925* (New York: Vintage, 1977).

42. Jennings, "'Us Colored Women,'" 51.

43. Quoted in ibid.

44. Jennings, "'Us Colored Women,'" 61.

45. Rose Williams interview, in *When I Was a Slave: Memoirs from the Slave Narrative Collection*, ed. Norman R. Yetman (Mineola, N.Y.: Dover, 2002), 146–49.

46. Jennings, "'Us Colored Women,'" 49.

47. Quoted in ibid., 47.

48. Quoted in White, *Ar'n't I a Woman?*, 156–57.

49. White, *Ar'n't I a Woman?*, 149.

50. Untitled letter from 1st Lt. F. E. Grossman to the Actg. Asst. Adjt. General, October 1, 1866, quoted in *Families and Freedom: A Documentary History of African-American Kinship in the Civil War Era*, ed. Ira Berlin and Leslie S. Rowland (New York: New Press, 1997), 171.

51. *Anne Batson v. John Fitchet and Wife Mary* (1731), quoted in Morgan, *Slave Counterpoint*, 401–2.

52. Stephen Bordley to Matt Harris, Annapolis, Maryland, January 30, 1739, quoted in Jordan, *White over Black*, 154.

53. *Maryland Gazette*, October 12, 1769, quoted in Morgan, *Slave Counterpoint*, 402.

54. Hartwood Baptist Church, June 25, 1785, quoted in Morgan, *Slave Counterpoint*, 402.

55. Burnard, *Mastery, Tyranny and Desire*, 216.

56. Morgan, *Slave Counterpoint*, 400.

57. Bourne divorce petition, 165–67. See also Hodes, *White Women, Black Men*, 68–95.

58. Hodes, *White Women, Black Men*, 133; Lindsay interview in ibid., 400–401.

59. Hodes, *White Women, Black Men*, 128–29.

60. Testimony of Maj. George L. Stearns, Nashville, Tennessee, November 23, 1863, quoted in ibid., 127.

61. Hinton testimony in Hodes, *White Women, Black Men*, 131.

62. Ibid., 130.

63. Ibid., 131.

64. *Armstrong v. Hodges*, from Franklin County, Kentucky (1841), quoted in Hodes, *White Women, Black Men*, 133–34.

65. Hinton testimony quoted in Hodes, *White Women, Black Men*, 135.

66. Hodes, *White Women, Black Men*, 130.

67. Redpath testimony in ibid., 130.

68. Jacobs, *Incidents in the Life*, quoted in Hodes, *White Women, Black Men*, 133.

69. Hinton testimony in Hodes, *White Women, Black Men*, 131.

70. Hodes, *White Women, Black Men*, 132.

71. Samuel Gridley Howe, *The Refugees from Slavery in Canada West: Report to the Freedmen's Inquiry Commission* (1864), quoted in ibid., 132.

72. Madison Jefferson interview (1841), quoted in Blassingame, *Slave Testimony*, 221.

73. Lewis Jenkins interview, quoted in Yetman, *When I Was a Slave*, 77.

CHAPTER 8

Manhood, Sex, and Power in
Antebellum Slave Communities

DAVID DODDINGTON

Over the last few decades, historians have become increasingly attuned to the centrality of sex to U.S. slavery and the ways in which reproductive, bodily, and intimate practices were deeply enmeshed in the power dynamics of bondage. Pioneering work by Deborah Gray White, Darlene Clark Hine, Thelma Jennings and other scholars emphasizes the gendered dimensions to slave life and the diverse ways in which enslaved women and men sought to shape human lives in an inhumane institution. While not restricted to sexual matters, these historians highlight the particular difficulties enslaved women faced in the intimate sphere, proving that "the institution of slavery created for slaveholders the possibility of unrestrained sexual access and control" and that many white men of the period, master or not, embraced this possibility.[1] The ubiquity of such abuse has been starkly and stubbornly revealed, with Catherine Clinton arguing that this should put to rest forever early southern protestations that "slavery was one big happy family."[2]

Much of this scholarship emphasizes the degree to which coerced sex reflected and consolidated white supremacy.[3] In her influential study of the sexual exploitation of enslaved women, for example, Jennings notes that WPA respondents commonly "blamed the white people for forcing a behavior that many of them characterized as similar to that of animals."[4] Much excellent work has since furthered this analysis, but this chapter aims to develop the literature by looking at sexual dynamics within slave communities, thinking, in particular, about how some enslaved men exerted or expected dominance over enslaved women in sexual encounters.[5] White men were the principal instigators of coerced sex—of this there is no doubt. However, gendered discrepancies relating to power and agency could be reflected in sexual interactions within the slave quarters: sex could be a terrain of struggle in slave communities. Although important historical work demonstrates that many enslaved relationships could be "characterized as broadly egalitarian and supportive," Deborah Gray White, Brenda Stevenson,

Christopher Morris, and other scholars have also shown less positive dynamics in slave communities. Stevenson, for example, notes that enslaved men could "gain control of and manipulate black women's sexuality."[6] However, such instances have also been described as the acts of men denied manhood elsewhere, taken as evidence of men left broken by bondage, or, more recently, placed within a framework that suggests sexual exploitation was understood by enslaved people as another shared burden of enslavement.[7]

However, former slaves recalled some enslaved men, as well as white men, forcing enslaved women to do "what they wanted them to do"; the WPA respondents' use of "want" when discussing these encounters indicates at least some perception of male agency and a belief that not all enslaved men were equally victimized by sexual encounters in slavery.[8] All slaves were brutalized by the racial oppression of U.S. bondage, but tension over expressions of male dominance in the quarters can illustrate that the enslaved population of the antebellum South conceived of their struggles beyond a racial dichotomy. In spite of the ostensible unity of racist oppression, layers of patriarchal thinking could also manifest in interactions between enslaved men and women. When Charles Ball described an intimate relationship in which an enslaved man "often beat and otherwise maltreated his wife," the man in question expected unquestioned dominance, bemoaning that he had "but one woman to do any thing for him." Such instances highlight limitations to the idea that enslaved men collectively faced emasculation. Indeed, shared expectations of patriarchal privilege could transcend racial divisions. Ball's overseer did nothing to stop this man's abuse of his wife, seemingly normalizing claims of intimate strife by claiming that he "never interfered in the family quarrels of the black people."[9] Scholars have challenged the enduring myth that enslaved men uniformly rejected compassion and care for others, showing that many felt that their identity as men came through protecting enslaved women from the horrors of slavery. However, we need not replace this myth with an idyllic version of enslaved manhood. Enslaved men took individual routes when constructing a sense of self, and these were not always routes worthy of applause.

Of course, much contemporary abolitionist material aimed to elevate enslaved men in public discourse, challenging persistent beliefs in their inferiority or bestial nature in order to attack the injustices of bondage. One such way in which enslaved men were applauded was through highlighting their heroic efforts to protect enslaved women from the sexual exploitation committed or controlled by hypocritical white men.[10] Indeed, according to Henry Bibb, southerners defended "their 'peculiar institution'" so strongly because "licentious white men could not carry out their wicked purposes among the defenceless colored population as they now do, without being exposed and punished by law, if slavery was abolished."[11] When black men were described as abusive by antislavery contemporaries, they could be depicted as having been dehumanized by slavery. Sambo, a brutal slave driver in Harriet Beecher Stowe's novel *Uncle Tom's Cabin*, was "given" an unwilling enslaved woman and expected her submission to him, declaring, "wal, Lucy, yo my woman now." However, Stowe emphasized how the drivers on the plantation had been trained by Simon Legree "in savageness and brutality as systematically as he had his bull-dogs," until they were willing to do his bidding. This power dynamic was reinforced by Legree's comments to Sambo, after he initially failed to get the enslaved woman to accept this arrangement: "'I'd a flogged her into 't,' said Legree, spitting, 'only there's such a press o' work, it don't seem wuth a while to upset her jist now.'"[12] Other antislavery authors acknowledged that enslaved men were expected to fulfill their masters' sexual demands in forced marriages, but maintained that honorable men still strove to protect enslaved women. For example, in a postbellum interview with "Uncle Stephen," a former slave from Louisiana, he recalled how he was split from his wife and forced to take a new partner by his master. But rather than accept this he secretly maintained his previous relationship and helped his new wife and others to see their lost loved ones.[13] Another enslaved man chose to suffer heroically rather than accept his master's demands to marry an enslaved woman from his plantation, continually making illicit trips to his first wife. The sense of admiration for this man's refusal to accede to his master's sexual demands is clear in the narrative, as is the suggestion that this related to his sense of honor as being conjoined with fidelity and faithfulness: "Sometimes they would catch Richard and drive four stakes in the ground, and they would tie his feet and hands to each one and beat him half to death. I tell you, sometimes he could not work. Marster did not care, for he had told Richard to take some of our women for a wife, but Richard would not do it. Richard loved Betty, and he would die for her."[14] With depictions of enslaved men fighting against the sexual demands of their masters or looking for intimate relationships based on respect and care, much antislavery material therefore painted a picture in which enslaved men sought to protect women from the sexual exploitation endemic to U.S. slavery.

Yet while enslaved men were certainly capable of such heroic actions, they were trapped in an institution that legitimized sexual abuse, as well as within a society that expected men to dominate sexual encounters, even accepting a degree of force at times.[15] Although historians have explored this in relation to white men of the period, studies on enslaved men rarely suggest similar attitudes could influence identities and intimate encounters in slave communities.[16] Much scholarly work on enslaved men, has, in fact, focused on refuting the common, if contradictory, depictions of black men as either emasculated victims or bestial rapists by stressing the more positive attributes associated with enslaved masculinity.[17] Yet to argue that some enslaved men considered the pursuit of unwilling women or assertions of sexual dominance as an element of manhood is not to make the claim that they were hypersexual "bucks" unable to control their sex drives. Instead, it is to suggest that multiple ideals and behaviors could be associated with masculinity in the antebellum United States and that enslaved men could take different paths in the construction of a masculine self. Some enslavers, and enslaved men alike, viewed sexual dominance as an acceptable expression of manhood. Gendered discrepancies relating to sex, power, and agency could, however, lead to tension in the slave quarters.

Although Rebecca Fraser has noted how "few personal texts are available that truly reveal the intimate lives of the enslaved," this chapter makes use of select testimonies from former slaves interviewed during the 1930s as part of the Works Progress Administration (wpa), in order to address sex within slave communities.[18] The aim is not to claim these interviewees spoke for everyone, but instead to use their stories to showcase the diversity of experience in slavery and note that sexual exploitation was not necessarily understood as a shared burden of bondage. While the wpa collections have been described as "an indispensable source" for historians of slavery, they have also been the subject of fierce critiques.[19] Although many were enslaved only as children, Paul Escott, and, more recently, Gregory Smithers, highlight that a significant number of respondents experienced or were willing to discuss sexual matters, while also noting that "likely reticence caused some underreporting."[20] This reticence may have come from the conditions of the interviews, with the racial tension of the era no doubt influencing some, but it may also have come from a morality or a "culture of dissemblance" imposed by the respondents themselves.[21] Despite these limits, the formerly enslaved were not completely cowed into silence. Historians have made significant use of their testimony in order to discuss both intimacy and exploitation within slave communities.

With regard to enslaved men's role in intimate unions, Fraser has argued that some wpa respondents painted a picture of black male morality "far removed from white images of the sexually menacing and aggressive black male[;] . . . the men in these narratives were defined as both unassuming and modest in the context of a relationship that was intimately connected to sexual desire."[22] Emily West has suggested that wpa accounts from South Carolina showcase the loving nature of intimate relationships. According to West, the testimony "provides virtually no cases of slave husbands abusing wives" and that such abuse was, moreover, "so completely against the positive tone of the slave testimony that it seems inconceivable that it could have been a significant part of the inner thoughts of ex-slaves."[23] West later addressed sexual abuse and violence in enslaved families while noting that enslaved men "did not seek to imitate the behavior of white men by systematically abusing enslaved females."[24] Yet, while enslaved men may not have systematically abused enslaved women, the language employed by some WPA respondents suggests that concerns with masculine dominance extended into the quarters and could affect how some enslaved men, as well as white men, perceived intimate power dynamics.

As Gregory Smithers shows, WPA respondents offered particular insights into sexual coercion in slavery when discussing forced marriages and "breeding."[25] Although debates exist over the mechanisms employed and the extent of white control, enslavers were deeply interested and depressingly invested in their slaves' reproductive lives, particularly following the closing of the Atlantic slave trade.[26] Slaves strove for agency in intimacy, but their sexual lives were rarely free from white interference and marriage was frequently predicated on fecundity. Historians generally suggest that these pressures "made men and women 'victims of reproductive abuse.'"[27] Daina Ramey Berry has shown how "forced breeding in the slave quarters manifested itself as an indirect form of rape where *powerless* enslaved males and females became the victims of reproductive abuse to which they did not *willingly* give their consent" (original emphasis), and there are certainly clear examples of this dual burden.[28] One former slave stated that "Massa, he bring more women to see me. He wouldn't let me have jus' one woman," while other respondents maintained that male "stockmen" were rented out to those slave owners who had "some young women he wanted to raise children from."[29]

These unions could entail a shared loss of autonomy for men and women, but the language some former slaves used to describe these encounters suggests that expectations of male dominance could permeate such encounters. Willie Mc-Cullough described how his mother reached the age of sixteen and was forced to marry an enslaved man; although both individuals were dehumanized through the process, the enslaver seemed to expect male sexual control and that the male slave would be appreciative of this: "[Master] told this negro he could take her to a certain cabin and go to bed. This was done without getting her consent or even asking her about it."[30] This assumption of normative male dominance and desire—that she was his to "take"—as well as the reference to her lack of consent but not his, challenges the idea that enslaved men were consciously emasculated by their enslavers when it came to establishing sexual relationships in the quarters. The use of the word "could," as opposed to "should," potentially speaks to a perception of sex as reward. This man may not have shared his enslaver's view on the matter, but in similar arrangements enslaved men apparently took the lead, believing that slaveholders would acquiesce to their requests. Katie Blackwell Johnson, a former slave from Virginia, informed her interviewer that "if a man saw a girl he liked he would ask his master's permission to ask the master of the girl for her. If his master consented and her master consented then they came together." Tellingly, Johnson went on to note that "the woman had no choice in the matter."[31]

While ultimate control clearly rested with the white slaveholder, enslaved men appeared to hold a greater degree of intimate agency than enslaved women did. Other historians have noted this gendered power dynamic. Jennings, for example, argues that men frequently played the central role in determining intimate relationships: "most often some young male selected his partner and then asked the master if she could become his wife." More recently, Kathleen M. Brown has stated that enslaved men frequently took the lead in asking for wives, suggesting that this could "tell us about enslaved men's desires for intimacy and connections with women."[32] However, these requests were not always viewed in a positive light by the enslaved women involved. The fact that Katie Blackwell Johnson went on to note that "some good masters would punish slaves who mistreated their womenfolk and some didn't," implies that enslaved men did not inevitably treat well the women they requested.[33] Some former slaves also felt that, rather than being victimized by their master in intimate matters, enslaved men could make requests of them. Moses Jeffries, for example, highlighted competitive male sexual agency and a lack of concern for female consent in his description of how marriage worked in slavery: "If I went on a plantation and saw a girl I wanted to marry, I would ask my master to buy her for me. It wouldn't matter if she were somebody else's wife; she would become mine."[34] The recollections by Jerry Eubanks of his youthful sexual endeavors underscore how shared expectations between black and white men of the acquisitive nature of male sexuality could inform sexual access to enslaved women. Eubanks, formerly an enslaved carriage driver from Mississippi, told his interviewer: "I didn't marry, you know—dere was a boss over dere and a boss over here. If one had a woman I wanted, my boss would send a note and tell him—den I'd visit dat plantation on sich and sich a nights."[35] The emphasis on "want" suggests a degree of agency, as opposed to unrelenting pressure.

Some enslaved men who were involved in relationships that could fulfill historical definitions of breeding articulated these activities as examples of their standing above others: rather than evidence of emasculation or dependency, these roles were public recognition of virile manhood. Rias Body, enslaved in Georgia, suggested that "stud bucks"—including eight of his brothers—"were allowed to roam anywhere they pleased at night, without passes and with no questions asked," claiming that these men would compete with one another in order to "beget the largest number of children in a year." While Body admitted this was unpopular among other men, he painted their displeasure as jealousy: "of course, they were the envy of all the average sized and under-sized men who did not enjoy any such considerations."[36] Although it is clearly possible that some of these tales were boasts or exaggerations, this also implies a belief that the men involved were not powerless victims. Rather than accept such a role as evidence of their dehumanization and degradation, these slaves, or those around them, occasionally used these practices to craft homosocial hierarchies based on sexual prowess. Zeno John, who was enslaved as a small child in Louisiana, stated that "when de marsters see a good big nigger sometime dey buy him for a breeder." John's father purportedly held and fulfilled such responsibilities, as, "befo' he die he say he had sebenty chillen, gran'chillen, and great-gran-chillen."[37] Although it seemed as though his parents had little attachment to one another, with his mother choosing another man in freedom, the sexual prowess of John's father appeared worth emphasizing. Rather than evidence of his father's powerlessness, John saw this role as direct recognition of his manhood: according to John, "my daddy was much of a man, yessir."[38]

Other respondents emphasized a comparative and competitive element to male sexual dominance in their communities, with the men chosen for "breeding" roles depicted as more deserving than others. William Matthews noted that "if a unhealthy nigger take up wit' a healthy, stout woman, de white folks sep'rate 'em," but that "if a man was big, stout, man, good breed, dey give him four, five women. Dat's de God's truth."[39] Andrew Boone stated that his father was ranked in such a way and "had several women besides mother," as well as exclusive rights to them: "no udder man wus allowed to have anything to do wid 'em."[40] While bound within the broader exploitation of slavery, the emphasis on the prowess of these slaves compared with other men in the community suggests that these men were not automatically considered controlled or powerless by their peers. Furthermore, the depiction of intimacy as a "reward"—of women being given or owned—is infused with patriarchal rhetoric. Ex-slave John Cole, whose testimony has been used by Smithers to highlight the "master's disregard for courtship and nurturing family networks among the enslaved," also suggested that a degree of disregard could come from within the slave quarters.[41] The idea that men's desires—white and black—could take precedence over female consent was highlighted in Cole's recollections that "if the woman wasn't willing, a good, hard-working hand could always get the master to make the girl marry him—whether of [*sic*] no, willy-nilly."[42] These testimonials, while addressing intimate arrangements that could correspond to historical definitions of breeding, offer little sense of male sexual victimhood or a feeling of shared oppression. Instead, some contemporaries felt that select enslaved men could "earn" sexual access to enslaved women, occasionally irrespective of whether their female counterparts agreed.

Although the previous respondents did not always address consent in these encounters, enslaved women who had faced sexual pressure occasionally stressed that their resistance was directed at black men as well as at white men. Others felt that there was cooperation between enslaved men and owners in establishing intimate relationships and, tellingly, appeared to resent this. The references to the agency of the men involved offer insights into how enslaved women could perceive coerced sex as more than simply a shared oppression of bondage, making this an aspect of slavery where they felt victimized by gender as well as by race. Mary Gaffney, taken to Texas as part of her master's plan to "get rich," offered one such example.[43] On arrival, and despite knowing this was against her wishes, Gaffney's master "put another negro man with my mother, then he put one with me." Despite acknowledging her master was in control overall, she described how she "hated the man I married." Furthermore, she also suggested there was a degree of contest with regards to a sexual encounter, informing her interviewer: "I would not let that negro touch me." Gaffney was cruelly whipped into submission by her master, but she placed at least some of the blame for this on the enslaved man: "he told Maser and Maser gave me a real good whipping, so that night I let that negro have his way." While absolutely condemning her master, the initial hatred of her enslaved partner, and, perhaps more importantly, the suggestion that this sexual encounter was "*his* way," suggests her belief that his desires actively helped in the enforcement of sexual activity against her wishes.[44] Other female respondents detailed how they fought both master and slave in order to prevent unwanted intimacy, and the disdain with which they described the enslaved men suggests they did not believe they were equally powerless in the process. Silvia King was sold to a planter in Texas and, despite having told her master that she had a "man and three chillen back in de old country," was nonetheless forced to take a new husband. She attempted to refuse, and the inference in King's testimony was that her given partner tried to force her into sex. Indeed, she "fit him good and plenty" before the overseer ultimately forced her to submit.[45]

Enslaved men faced enormous pressures in bondage, including the threat of physical punishment and sale if they failed to do their enslaver's bidding. This undoubtedly affected their actions in the intimate sphere. However, enslaved women who expressed anger at the role some enslaved men took in enforcing intimacy within slavery appeared to believe that these behaviors spoke to broader expectations of dominance over others, and that this had negatively affected the women's lives. Their testimonies offer insight into the ways in which gender and race intersected and influenced relationships in slavery, and, perhaps, in freedom. Women's anger is evident in the testimony of Rose Williams, a formerly enslaved woman who had been sold as a teenager with the expectation that she "will make de good breeder." Williams's story is well known to scholars of slave intimacy, but there are elements of the story that illuminate contests over intimate agency within the slave quarters. Having turned sixteen, Williams was placed in a cabin with Rufus, an enslaved man on the plantation, and explained her confusion when he attempted to join her in bed. Rather than accept this, Williams kicked him out. Historian Deborah Gray White has noted that Rufus was "infuriated" by Williams's response. Although historian Thomas Foster insists that Rufus did not attempt to use physical force, his argument understates the level of conflict Williams's refusal occasioned.[46] Having kicked Rufus off the bunk, Williams explicitly went on to describe his anger at her, as well as the extreme lengths to which she defended herself: "Dat nigger jump up and he mad. He look like de wild boar. He starts for de bunk and I jumps quick for de poker." The language employed by Williams indicated a real perception of threat: "*when he comes at me* I lets him have it over de head" (emphasis added). Williams was eventually forced into a sexual relationship with Rufus after her master threatened her with whipping as well as the sale of her family. When Williams eventually yielded, it was because she "'cides to do as de massa wish." Yet she also clearly believed this encounter was shaped by more than just the desires of her enslaver. When Williams initially described her refusal to have sex, she claimed this was "what Rufus wants."

Rufus, of course, has no say in this story; he may have endured threats and terrible suffering that we will never know. However, despite having been told by her mistress that this relationship was "de massa's wishes," and after more than seventy years of reflection, Williams hardly felt his behavior was symptomatic of the shared hardships of slavery. Before recounting her experiences of forced sex, she described Rufus as a bully who expected his dominance to extend across the plantation: "He am big and 'cause he so he think everybody do what him say." Her insistence that she was unwilling to have "truck with any man" after emancipation implies that she felt her oppression was gendered as well as racial and that this had lasting consequences for her.[47] Williams's story, as well as other stories described in this essay, do not conform easily to the model of enslaved men enforcing intimacy in order to prove a subversive manhood denied elsewhere by emasculatory white men. Nor do they easily reflect the notion that such abuse was unquestionably recognized as evidence of a shared powerlessness that punished

men and women equally. The agency that some slaves attributed to enslaved men
in matters of sexual coercion, while by no means unproblematic, demonstrates
the complexity to intimate relations in slavery, as well as how gendered power
dynamics could disrupt or challenge the solidarity of slave communities.

Scholars are increasingly highlighting the complex legacies of sexual encounters
in U.S. slave societies, and, in this vein, it is worth considering the complications
attached to enslaved intimacy. Sexual coercion within the slave quarters cannot
be explained solely as a consequence of emasculation or oppression; enslaved
men were not hypersexual "bucks" unable to control their sex drive, but neither
were they all equally victimized through an institutionalized emasculatory regime. Some enslaved men were understood, and understood themselves, as being the beneficiaries of a form of masculine privilege in the intimate realm, using sexual dominance to construct a homosocial hierarchy in which they placed
themselves above other men, sometimes at the expense of enslaved women. Historians have done significant work in restoring enslaved men to the historical
picture as loving and caring husbands and fathers, but there was not an idyllic or
singular version of enslaved manhood. Conflict in the quarters, boastful descriptions of "breeding," and implicit or explicit suggestions of a lack of concern for
consent demonstrate that enslaved men could have different perceptions as to
what manhood entailed and that this could divide slave communities. Coerced
sexual activity could be articulated as an expression of masculinity by some enslaved men. This fact should not demonize all enslaved men, but it does highlight the complex and multiple understandings of manhood among the enslaved.
Sexually domineering enslaved men may have been viewed with hatred and scorn
by others in their community, but they did not invariably see themselves as low
in a masculine hierarchy. While undeniably victimized and constrained in their
actions by slavery, some enslaved men felt that manhood meant they could be,
and even should be, dominant in sex, even if this came at the expense of others
in their community.

NOTES

1. Dorothy Roberts, "The Paradox of Silence and Display: Sexual Violation of Enslaved Women and Contemporary Contradictions in Black Female Sexuality," in *Beyond Slavery: Overcoming Its Religious and Sexual Legacies*, ed. Bernadette J. Brooten
(New York: Palgrave Macmillan, 2010), 41–61, 43. Pioneering work on gender and
slavery includes Angela Davis, *Women, Race and Class* (1981; rpt., London: Women's
Press, 1982); Jacqueline Jones, *Labor of Love, Labor of Sorrow: Black Women, Work, and*

the Family, from Slavery to the Present (New York: Basic Books, 1985); Deborah Gray White, *Ar'n't I a Woman? Female Slaves in the Plantation South* (New York: W. W. Norton, 1985); Darlene Clark Hine, "Rape and the Inner Lives of Black Women in the Middle West: Preliminary Thoughts on the Culture of Dissemblance," *Signs* 4, no. 4 (1989): 912–21; Thelma Jennings, "'Us Colored Women Had to Go through a Plenty': Sexual Exploitation of African American Slave Women,'" *Journal of Women's History* 1, no. 3 (1990): 45–74; Catherine Clinton, "'Southern Dishonour': Flesh, Blood, Race and Bondage," in *In Joy and Sorrow: Women, Family, and Marriage in the Victorian South, 1830–1990,* ed. Carol Bleser (New York: Oxford University Press, 1991), 52–68; Brenda E. Stevenson, *Life in Black and White: Family and Community in the Slave South* (New York: Oxford University Press, 1996).

2. Catherine Clinton, "Breaking the Silence: Sexual Hypocrisies from Thomas Jefferson to Strom Thurmond," in Brooten, *Beyond Slavery,* 213–28, 223.

3. Although ideas on consent and coercion are not ahistorical, I define sexual coercion in a similar fashion to Sharon Block, who has applied the label to "acts not necessarily identified as rape in early America that nevertheless contained some degree of extorted or forced sexual relations." For the purposes of this essay I will primarily discuss sexual encounters in which some form of unwillingness to engage in sex was acknowledged or expressed. See Sharon Block, *Rape and Sexual Power in Early America* (Chapel Hill: University of North Carolina Press, 2006), chapters 1–2.

4. Jennings, "'Us Colored Women,'" 53.

5. Although outside the remit of this essay, scholars are increasingly exploring same-sex encounters in slavery, both consensual and otherwise. See Thomas A. Foster, "The Sexual Abuse of Black Men under Slavery," *Journal of the History of Sexuality* 20, no. 3 (2011): 445–64; John Saillant, "The Black Body Erotic and the Republican Body Politic, 1790–1820," in *Long before Stonewall: Histories of Same-Sex Sexuality in Early America,* ed. Thomas A. Foster (New York: New York University Press, 2007), 303–23.

6. Stevenson, *Life in Black and White,* 206–58, 240; Christopher Morris, "Within the Slave Cabin: Violence in Mississippi Slave Families," in *Over the Threshold: Intimate Violence in Early America,* ed. Christine Daniels and Michael V. Kennedy (New York; London: Routledge, 1999), 268–87.

7. Bertram Wyatt-Brown, "Mask of Obedience: Male Slave Psychology in the Old South," *American Historical Review* 93, no. 5 (1988): 1228–52, 1246; Foster, "Sexual Abuse of Black Men," especially 454–58. Some commentators have used the idea of emasculation in slavery to explain rape in the twentieth century. See Robert Staples, *Black Masculinity: The Black Male's Role in American Society* (San Francisco: Black Scholar's Press, 1985), 64.

8. George P. Rawick, gen. ed., *American Slave: A Composite Autobiography* (Westport, Conn.: Greenwood Press, 1972), vol. 9, pt. 3, 218.

9. Charles Ball, *Fifty Years in Chains; or, The Life of an American Slave* (Indianapolis: H. Dayton, 1859), 197.

10. For more on the abolitionist construction of enslaved men as pure, see Maria Diedrich, "'My Love Is Black as Yours Is Fair': Premarital Love and Sexuality in the Antebellum Slave Narrative," *Phylon* 47 (1986): 238–47.

11. Henry Bibb, *Narrative of the Life and Adventures of Henry Bibb, an American Slave, Written by Himself* (New York: H. Bibb, 1849), 199, accessed at http://docsouth .unc.edu/neh/bibb/bibb.html.

12. Harriet Beecher Stowe, *Uncle Tom's Cabin* (1852; New York: Oxford University Press, 1998), 354–63.

13. Octavia V. Rogers Albert, *The House of Bondage, or, Charlotte Brooks and Other Slaves, Original and Life Like, as They Appeared in Their Old Plantation and City Slave Life; Together with Pen-Pictures of the Peculiar Institution, with Sights and Insights into Their New Relations as Freedmen, Freemen, and Citizens* (New York: Hunt & Eaton, 1890), 106–8, accessed at http://docsouth.unc.edu/neh/albert/menu.html.

14. Ibid., 25.

15. Block, *Rape and Sexual Power*, 20; Kirsten E. Wood, "Gender and Slavery," in *The Oxford Handbook of Slavery in the Americas*, ed. Robert L. Paquette and Mark M. Smith (New York: Oxford University Press, 2010), 513–34, 524.

16. See, for example, Kathleen M. Brown, *Good Wives, Nasty Wenches, and Anxious Patriarchs: Gender, Race, and Power in Colonial Virginia* (Chapel Hill: University of North Carolina Press, 1996), 333; Bertram Wyatt-Brown, *Southern Honor: Ethics and Behavior in the Old South* (New York: Oxford University Press, 1982), 226, 283; Clare Lyons, *Sex among the Rabble: An Intimate History of Gender and Power in the Age of Revolution, Philadelphia, 1730–1830* (Chapel Hill: University of North Carolina Press, 2006); Craig Thompson Friend, "Sex, Self, and the Performance of Patriarchal Manhood in the Old South," in *The Old South's Modern Worlds: Slavery, Region, and Nation in the Age of Progress*, ed. L. Diane Barnes, Brian Schoen, and Frank Towers (New York: Oxford University Press, 2011), 246–65.

17. Daniel P. Black, *Dismantling Black Manhood: An Historical and Literary Analysis of the Legacy of Slavery* (New York: Routledge, 1997), 127. We could note, for example, the generally positive tone and emphasis on work, family life, and resistance as evidence for black manhood in essays in Darlene Clark Hine and Earnestine Jenkins, eds., *A Question of Manhood: A Reader in U.S. Black Men's History and Masculinity*, vol. 1, *"Manhood Rights": The Construction of Black Male History and Manhood, 1750–1870* (Bloomington: Indiana University Press, 1999).

18. Rebecca Fraser, *Courtship and Love among the Enslaved in North Carolina* (Jackson: Mississippi University Press, 2007), 11.

19. Paul D. Escott, "The Art and Science of Reading WPA Slave Narratives," in *The Slave's Narrative*, ed. Charles T. Davis and Henry Louis Gates Jr. (New York: Oxford University Press, 1985), 40–48, 40. For methodological discussions on the uses and limitations of WPA sources, see Paul D. Escott, *Slavery Remembered: A Record of Twentieth-Century Slave Narratives* (Chapel Hill: University of North Carolina Press, 1979); Donna Spindel, "Assessing Memory: Twentieth-Century Slave Narratives Reconsidered," *Journal of Interdisciplinary History* 27, no. 2 (1996): 247–61; Stephanie Shaw, "Using the WPA Ex-Slave Narratives to Study the Impact of the Great Depression," *Journal of Southern History* 69, no. 3 (2003): 623–58; Edward E. Baptist, "'Stol' and Fetched Here': Enslaved Migration, Ex-slave Narratives, and Vernacular History,"

in *New Studies in the History of American Slavery*, ed. Edward E. Baptist and Stephanie M. H. Camp (Athens: University of Georgia Press, 2006), 243–74.

20. Escott, *Slavery Remembered*, 45; Gregory D. Smithers, *Slave Breeding: Sex, Violence, and Memory in African American History* (Gainesville: University Press of Florida, 2012), 101.

21. For more information on sexual morality, "principle," and the culture of dissemblance, see Brenda E. Stevenson, "Gender Conventions, Ideals and Identity among Antebellum Virginia Slave Women," in *More than Chattel: Black Women and Slavery in the Americas*, ed. David Barry Gaspar and Darlene Clark Hine (Bloomington: Indiana University Press, 1994), 169–93, 171; Anthony Parent Jr. and Susan Brown Wallace, "Childhood and Sexual Identity under Slavery," *Journal of the History of Sexuality* 3, no. 3 (1993): 363–401; Hine, "Rape and the Inner Lives of Black Women," 915.

22. Fraser, *Courtship and Love*, 80.

23. Emily West, "The Debate on the Strength of Slave Families: South Carolina and the Importance of Cross-Plantation Marriages," *Journal of American Studies* 33, no. 3 (1999): 221–41, 238.

24. Emily West, "Tensions, Tempers, and Temptations: Marital Discord among Slaves in Antebellum South Carolina," *American Nineteenth Century History* 5, no. 2 (2004): 1–18, 7.

25. Smithers, *Slave Breeding*, esp. chapter 5.

26. See, for example, Wilma Dunaway, *The African American Family in Slavery and Emancipation* (Cambridge: Cambridge University Press, 2003), 274–77; Jennifer L. Morgan, *Laboring Women: Reproduction and Gender in New World Slavery* (Philadelphia: University of Pennsylvania Press, 2004), 3; Richard L. Sutch, "The Breeding of Slaves for Sale and the Westward Expansion of Slavery, 1850–1860," in *Race and Slavery in the Western Hemisphere: Quantitative Studies*, ed. Stanley L. Engerman and Eugene D. Genovese (Princeton, N.J.: Princeton University Press, 1975), 173–211; Richard H. Steckel, "Demography and Slavery," in Paquette and Smith, *Oxford Handbook of Slavery*, 643–63. Two prominent scholars of the internal slave trade, Michael Tadman and Steven Deyle, are skeptical of widespread "stud farms" but acknowledge the coercive power slaveholders wielded. Michael Tadman, *Speculators and Slaves: Masters, Traders, and Slaves in the Old South* (Madison: University of Wisconsin Press, 1989), 122–29; Steven Deyle, *Carry Me Back: The Domestic Slave Trade in American Life* (New York: Oxford University Press, 2005), 47. For an assessment of breeding as an integral part of enslaved women's experiences, see Pamela D. Bridgewater, "Ain't I a Slave: Slavery, Reproductive Abuse, and Reparations," *UCLA Women's Law Journal* (2005): 90–161. For wide-ranging discussions on the rhetoric, experiences, memories, and contested historiography on the topic, see Smithers, *Slave Breeding*.

27. Wood, "Gender and Slavery," 523.

28. Daina Ramey Berry, *"Swing the Sickle for the Harvest Is Ripe": Gender and Slavery in Antebellum Georgia* (Urbana: University of Illinois Press, 2007), 79.

29. Rawick, *American Slave*, vol. 4, pt. 1, 299; Rawick, *American Slave*, vol. 10, pt. 6, 223.

30. Rawick, *American Slave*, vol. 15, pt. 2, 78.

31. Charles Perdue Jr., Thomas E. Barden, Robert K. Phillips, eds., *Weevils in the Wheat: Interviews with Virginia Ex-Slaves* (Bloomington: Indiana University Press, 1980), 161.

32. Jennings, "'Us Colored Women,'" 47; Kathleen M. Brown, "'Strength of the Lion . . . Arms Like Polished Iron': Embodying Black Masculinity in an Age of Slavery and Propertied Manhood," in *New Men: Manliness in Early America* (New York: New York University Press, 2011), ed. Thomas A. Foster, 172–95, 180.

33. Perdue et al., *Weevils in the Wheat,* 161.

34. Rawick, *American Slave,* vol. 9, pt. 4, 39.

35. George P. Rawick, gen. ed., *American Slave: A Composite Autobiography, Supplement, Series 1* (Westport, Conn.: Greenwood Press, 1977), vol. 7, pt. 2, 689.

36. Rawick, *American Slave, Supplement, Series 1,* vol. 3, pt. 1, 69.

37. Rawick, gen. ed., *American Slave: A Composite Autobiography, Supplement, Series 2* (Westport, Conn.: Greenwood Press, 1979), vol. 6, pt. 5, 1950.

38. Ibid.

39. Rawick, *American Slave, Supplement, Series 2,* vol. 7, pt. 6, 2616.

40. Rawick, *American Slave,* vol. 14, pt. 1, 136.

41. Smithers, *Slave Breeding,* 115.

42. Rawick, *American Slave,* vol. 12, pt. 1, 228.

43. Rawick, *American Slave, Supplement, Series 2,* vol. 5, pt. 4, 1453.

44. Gaffney eventually grew to accept the relationship, stating that after slavery she "just kept on living with that negro." However, the reference to initial hatred in the interview was clear, suggesting the importance of critically addressing the continuation of families postemancipation. White also notes this need for caution in *Ar'n't I a Woman?,* 150.

45. Rawick, *American Slave,* vol. 4, pt. 2, 291.

46. White, *Ar'n't I a Woman?,* 102–3; Foster, "Sexual Abuse of Black Men," 457.

47. All Rose Williams quotations are from Rawick, *American Slave,* vol. 5, pt. 4, 175–78.

CHAPTER 9

What's Love Got to Do with It?

Concubinage and Enslaved Women and
Girls in the Antebellum South

BRENDA E. STEVENSON

> I was a little girl, not fourteen years old. One day Mr. Cook told me
> I must come to his room that night, and take care of him.
>
> —LOUISA PICQUET

Louisa Picquet's and her mother's stories of concubinage chart experiences that they shared with thousands of other enslaved women in the antebellum South, and hundreds of thousands in the Atlantic world. Born in the late 1820s on a plantation outside of Columbia, South Carolina, Louisa was sold as an infant, along with her mother, Elizabeth Ramsey. Elizabeth was about twenty years old when Louisa was born. A seamstress and domestic for her mistress by day, Elizabeth was the "quadroon" concubine of her owner, James Hunter Randolph, by night. Although James Randolph had sworn Elizabeth to secrecy regarding the paternity of her "white" baby, Mrs. Randolph could see for herself that Louisa had a remarkable resemblance to her own infant, born only two weeks earlier. Mrs. Randolph insisted that Elizabeth and her child be sold.[1]

David R. Cook, a cotton planter in Jasper County, Georgia, bought the twenty-year-old mother and her baby. It was not long before Elizabeth again became the concubine of her owner, and had three children by him. Louisa was raised as a child domestic in the Cook home, caring for his children by his wife, Pheba, and no doubt those of her mother. When Cook, a drinking, gambling man, literally "lost the farm" to creditors, he went into hiding. He sent his wife, Pheba, and their children to live with a cousin, and took his concubine, Elizabeth, her children, including Louisa, and a few of his other bond people to Mobile, Alabama, where he rented them out to earn income for him. By the time Louisa was fourteen, her owner, the father of Louisa's step-siblings, was determined now to "have" her. Louisa resisted, receiving two brutal whippings at Cook's hand as a result. She had just decided to submit to her owner's demand when the Georgia sheriff, bent on bringing Cook to justice, caught up with him.

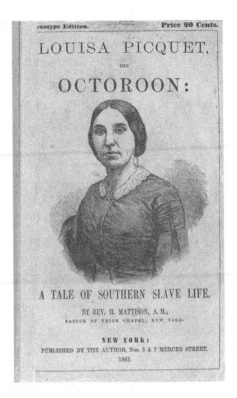

Book cover, *Louisa Picquet, the Octoroon.*
Documenting the American South,
UNC—Chapel Hill Library

Cook's "property," including Elizabeth, her son John, and daughter Louisa, were
sold for his debts.[2]

The family was separated. Mother and son went to Texas. Their new owner,
Texas's first lieutenant governor and a founder of Baylor University, Colonel Albert Horton, tried to purchase Louisa, bidding $1,400 for her. But the beautiful
youth had captured the sexual imagination of another purchaser. John Williams,
a divorced man in his late forties from New Orleans, had planned to buy the "virtuous" Louisa and make her his concubine.[3] The bidding war ended with Williams successful. He paid $1,500 for the young teen. Glad that she had escaped
Cook, Louisa soon had cause to lament that she had "jump[ed] out of the fryin'-
pan into the fire." Williams had bought her for sex. On the trip to New Orleans,
by boat on the Mississippi, "Mr. Williams told me what he bought me for. He
said he was getting old, and when he saw me he thought he'd buy me, and end his
days with me. He said if I behave myself he'd treat me well: but, if not, he'd whip
me almost to death." Louisa had four children by the "grey haired" man who was
at least thirty years her senior.[4]

Sexual contact between slave masters and their bonded female "property" was a common experience in the Atlantic world. These relations ran the gamut from rape and sodomy to romance, from chance encounters to obsession, concubinage and even "marriage." They could be hetero- or homosexual in nature. They included, but were not limited to, pedophilia, incest, sadomasochism, and voyeurism. One need only peruse the travel literature, diaries, church records, letters, and even colonial newspapers produced throughout the French, British, Dutch, Portuguese, and Spanish American colonies to find ample evidence. Whether one reads the diary of William Byrd of early eighteenth-century Virginia or Thomas Thistlewood of eighteenth-century Jamaica, Olaudah Equiano's writings descriptive of his life in Montserrat, or John Steadman's account of his life in late eighteenth-century Suriname provide details and descriptions. In the travel accounts of other curious European onlookers in the Americas; ecclesiastical records of the Catholic Church in Florida, Brazil, Cuba, New Orleans, and New Spain; printed abolitionist attacks on the immoral consequences of slavery, and, for that matter, Thomas Jefferson's *Notes* on the same topic; as well as the hundreds of recollections and autobiographical accounts of enslaved people in the Atlantic world, one is confounded by the prevalence of sexual contact between European or European American men and African or African American women bound by the institution of slavery.[5] It was a common occurrence by any measure, widespread and obvious.

In North America, sexual relations across the color line may have been more prevalent, or at least more public, in the cities of the lower South such as New Orleans, Mobile, Biloxi, and Charleston. There, systems of plaçage, and other forms of concubinage—sustained sexual contact between an enslaved woman and her master—were part of the publicly acknowledged, circum-Caribbean legacy of interracial sex.[6] Still, this particular type of slave labor also existed in smaller cities, in the countryside and on the frontier territories of the U.S. South. Indeed, the practice of concubinage in these smaller southern locales has been woefully underestimated largely because rural isolation permitted an invisibility on isolated farms and plantations where these women toiled.[7]

"It wus a hard job to find a marster dat didn't have women 'mong his slaves," one former antebellum bondsman recalled. "Dat wus a ginerel thing 'mong de slave owners."[8] Federal census enumerators did not typically identify mixed-race bond people in their descriptions of the free black or enslaved populations during the antebellum era. They did so for the first time in 1850, offering substantial evidence of interracial sexual contacts—11 percent of enslaved persons were designated as "mulatto," along with 37 percent of "free blacks."[9] Indeed, there is no more sufficient marker of the commonality of a slave experience than its recording in popular song. Throughout the South, as in Kentucky, South Carolina, and

Louisiana, for example, enslaved men sang, to the accompaniment of banjo and guitar, the appropriately titled song "Massa Had a Yaller Gal." This version, from South Carolina, suggests the competition between enslaved and slaveholding men for the affections of these women.

> Ol' Mars'er had a pretty yaller gal, he bought her fum de Souf;
> Her hair it curled so berry tight she couldn't shet her mouf.
> Chorus: Way down in Mississippi
> Where de gals dey are so pretty,
> W'at a happy time, way down in ol' Car'line!
> Dis darkey fell in love
> Wid a han'some yaller Dinah.
> Higho—higho—higho![10]

Levi Pollard, a former slave from Virginia, remembered singing a song of similar theme:

> Black gal sweet,
> Some like goodies dat de white folks eat;
> Don't you take 'n tell her name,
> En den if sompin' happen, you won't ketch de blame.
>
> Yaller gal fine
> She may be yo'ne, but she oughter be mine,
> Lemme git by
> En see what she mean by de cut er dat eye . . .[11]

Likewise, concubinage was not just a phenomenon practiced in the Americas during the slave era. Rather, it was an institution as old, widespread and diverse as systems of human bondage. Just as some form of slavery has manifest itself in virtually every major civilization in recorded history, including those of ancient Rome, Greece, Israel, China, Persia, India, various European and pre-Columbian American societies, as well as throughout Africa, so too did some form of sexual relations exist between owners and those owned in these societies. Indeed, historians believe that sexual slavery was practiced in those West and Central African societies from which many of the female captives who arrived in the Americas were drawn. Paul Lovejoy, for example, notes of concubinage in northern Nigeria that almost all enslaved women who worked in the domestic sphere "spent at least part of their sexually mature years as concubines."[12] Martin Klein likewise asserts that in French West Africa enslaved "women were sexually available to be commanded rather than courted."[13] Joseph Miller concurred, concluding that in West Central Africa, "girls and young women who struck male purchasers as sexually attractive were universally prized."[14] As for eastern Africa, Frederick Cooper reported that there too, "any female slave was legally at the sexual disposal of her master."[15]

The practice and experience of concubinage is important to understand, therefore, because of its place within the range of experiences that helped to define the southern female slave's emotional and psychological development, domestic life, and work routine. It also deepens the connection between her experiences to those of other enslaved people across time, place, and culture. Opening the door to this aspect of a female slave's sexual experiences exposes her ideas about her body as a location of pleasure, production, and procreation as well as a site of exploitation, alienation, loss, and shame. A study of concubinage also can suggest much about the internal dynamics of the slave family and community. Were concubines, for example, considered members of the enslaved community? or were they ostracized and regarded as fundamentally different from other bonded women? Equally important is what concubinage can tell us about sexual attitudes and relations in southern black communities; marital relations among the enslaved and their owners; the place of mixed-race children in slave and white families; and the location of mixed-race people in a society in which its residents commonly derived their legal status from being either white or black, not both. Interracial sexual relations, later referred to as "miscegenation," raised explosive issues of force, female purity, and sexual sanctity in both black and white families, all the while creating a class of women (and men) whom both bonded and slaveholding men and women found physically desirable. Color consciousness and stratification among African Americans resulted from a combination of factors surrounding interracial sexual contact, voluntary and coerced, which produced a large mixed-race population among enslaved and free African Americans. The popularity of racist ideologies about color differences and racial hierarchies and their practical application in antebellum southern society was widespread. The remainder of this essay explores two topics: the nature of enslaved women's sexual work, with an emphasis on concubinage; and the responses of various factions of the antebellum southern community to the presence of sustained sexual relationships between white men and enslaved African American women.

BRED AND SOLD FOR SEX

"When my sister was 16 years old," Lewis Clarke of Madison County, Kentucky, explained, "her master sent for her." It was a meeting that changed the young woman's life, and that of her family, forever. According to Clarke, his sister was "pretty" and near white. "She was whiter than I am, for she took after her father," he explained of his sibling. "When he sent for her again," Clarke continued, "she cried, and didn't want to go." Finally she confided her troubles to their mother, who had lived through the same experience. Their female parent could offer little advice or comfort. Try to "be decent, and hold up [your] head above such things, if [you can]," she told the girl. Their master, William Campbell, enraged by both Clarke's sister's public exposure of his desire for her, and her rejection of him, "sold her right off to Louisiana." "We were told afterwards," Lewis added, that "she died there of hard usage."[16] Elizabeth Keckley, the famed seamstress of Mary Todd Lincoln, Mrs. Jefferson Davis, and other politicians' wives in the 1850s and 1860s, described her adolescent experiences as a bonded female in North Carolina. "I was regarded as fair-looking for one of my race, and for four years a white man— . . . had base designs on me. . . . I do not care to dwell upon this subject, for it is one that is fraught with pain," Keckley declared. "Suffice it to say, that he persecuted me for four years, and I—I became a mother."[17]

Mary Reynolds had been enslaved in Concordia Parish, Louisiana, and recalled of the arrival of the mulatto woman Margaret around 1850. "Once massa goes to Baton Rouge and brung back a yaller girl dressed in fine style. . . . She was a seamster nigger." Reynolds explained that everyone on the plantation of fifty or so slaves soon noticed how their master, Dr. A. H. Kilpatrick, treated his new bondwoman. They also understood why. "He builds her a house way from the quarters," Mary noted, "and she done fine sewin' for the whites. Us niggers knowed the doctor took a black woman quick as he did a white and took any on his place he wanted, and he took them often. But mostly the chillun born on the place looked like niggers. Aunt Cheyney allus say four of hers were massas, but he didn't give them no mind. But this yaller gal breeds so fast and gits a mess of white young'uns." Indeed, the 1860 census from Concordia indicates that Dr. Kilpatrick did own one twenty-seven-year-old "mulatto woman" and three "mulatto" children, a six-month-old boy, a six-year-old girl, and a nine-year-old boy. "She larnt them fine manners and combs out they hair," Mary Reynolds recalled. "Onct two of them goes down the hill to the doll house where the Kilpatrick chillun am playin'. They wants to go in the dollhouse and one the Kilpatrick boys say, 'That's for white chillun.' They say, 'We ain't no niggers, cause we got the same daddy you has.'"[18]

A profoundly important difference between the experiences of enslaved females and males as laborers in the antebellum South is that most bondsmen did not face the constant sexual harassment or battery that many enslaved girls and women such as Elizabeth Ramsey, Louisa Picquet, Elizabeth Keckley, Margaret Kilpatrick, and Lewis Clarke's mother and sister (whose stories are recounted above), confronted during their most vulnerable years. Nor could slave men

ELIZABETH KECKLEY.

Elizabeth Keckley. *Documenting the American South,* UNC–Chapel Hill Library.

expect that their physical attractiveness and sex appeal were likely to gain them the same access to "emancipation" or material well-being as some of these women.

The prices of enslaved females reveal the "value" slaveholders placed on their feminine "assets." Bonded men generally cost more than females, skilled laborers more than field hands, and the young more than the elderly.[19] The only real exception to these rules of the market was the "fancy girl" trade and "good breeding" women, two categories of sexual commodification of enslaved females that were not mutually exclusive, particularly since many of the women targeted for this trade were mixed race. Indeed, historian Lawrence Kotlikoff concludes in his study of slave prices in New Orleans from 1804 to 1862 that "light skin color added over 5.3 percent to the female's price; while only 2.29% to the price of enslaved males."[20] If these women proved to be fertile and were impregnated by a white male, the child they bore would be even lighter, and thereby, more valuable monetarily as "slave property" for their owners, particularly if the offspring were female. "Marie was pretty, dat's why he took her to Richmond to sell her. You see, you could git a powerful lot of money in dose days for a pretty gal," Carol Anna Randall explained of her sister's sale to the Carolinas. Joe Bruin, of the Alexandria, Virginia, slave trading firm of Bruin and Hill, placed Emily Russell, a beautiful young girl whom he planned to sell as a prostitute in New Orleans, on the market in 1850 for $1,800. Mr. J. Davenport was offered $2,500 for Harriet, his enslaved woman who looked like a white girl and was likely considered a "quadroon."[21] In his autobiography, James Pennington, who had been enslaved in Queen Anne's County, Maryland, explained: "It is under the mildest form of slavery, as it exists in Maryland, Virginia and Kentucky, that the finest specimens of coloured females are reared. . . . for the express purpose of supplying the market [to] a class of economical Louisiana and Mississippi gentlemen, who do not wish to incur the expense of rearing legitimate families, they are, nevertheless, on account of their attractions, exposed to the most shameful degradation."[22] Pennington went on to illustrate his claims by presenting the case of Mary Jane and Emily Catherine Edmondson, enslaved girls aged fourteen and sixteen, priced together at $2,250. There was such an exorbitant fee, Pennington argued, because they intended to sell Mary Jane and Emily as prostitutes in the Deep South.[23] Louisa Picquet fetched a price of $1,500. Elizabeth Ramsey's master asked $1,000 for her, even when she was in her forties, but settled for $900, noting of the pale-skinned domestic, "it's true she is getting old but she carries her age well, and looks as young as she did twenty years ago."[24]

THE CONCUBINE AND HER DUTIES

Most enslaved females and girls were, at some time during their working lives, destined to at least experience some sexual harassment, if not an outright sexual assault, from a male authority figure. Oftentimes being white was the only badge of authority necessary, but this pressure also emanated from male drivers, white overseers, and others with a modicum of "power." But what typically distinguished those enslaved women who were targeted for occasional or random sexual contact from those whom slaveholding males viewed as potential concubines? When one looks closely at the documents that describe slave concubinage and concubines, females with certain physical, cultural and sometimes intellectual characteristics emerge as desirable. Many were mixed race—African, Native American, European—but the vast majority also were young, beautiful, culturally adept, skilled, sometimes literate, and, most important, physically accessible.

Most concubines were forced or lured into sexual relationships soon after reaching puberty. As such, slaveholding men could assure the "sexual purity" of their conquests and impose a type of psychological control. George Carter of the elite Carter clan in Virginia, for example, was notorious for buying "likely" virgins of "about age 14 or 15."[25] Sally Hemings became Jefferson's concubine at that age, bearing her first child when she was sixteen years old.[26] Harriet Jacobs's "troubles" started at about the same age. "I now entered on my fifteenth year—a sad epoch in the life of a slave girl," Harriet began her tale of sexual harassment. "My master began to whisper foul words in my ear. Young as I was, I could not remain ignorant of their import."[27] In Georgia, David Dickinson raped his mother's enslaved girl Julia when she was twelve and then made her his long-term concubine.[28]

The physical similarity of these mixed-race girls to those considered the most beautiful Euro-American women of the era was strikingly obvious in the written descriptions, paintings, and drawings. Skin tone and hair texture were especially highlighted, but facial features resembling those of northern Europeans (thin lips and noses, for example) also were important. The general measure was that the lighter the skin and the straighter the hair, the more attractive the woman or girl. "Marse Sid ain't got but one weakness an' dat am pretty yaller gals," Chaney Spell of North Carolina admitted. "He just can't desist them."[29] Uncle Cephas, "who used to live in Tennessee before the war," told a late nineteenth-century interviewer "a very pathethic [*sic*] story of a colored girl, . . . whose master had bought her in Carolina and brought her to Tennessee." He went on: "Her name was Lizzie Beaufort. She was a most beautiful girl. She had large black eyes, long black hair, a beautiful oval-shaped face, and was of a fine oily brunette complexion. She might have easily passed for a Cuban."[30]

Another enslaved woman, "Nellie Johnson, . . . was sold to a mighty bad man," her unofficial biographer noted. "Nellie was almost white, and had pretty, long, straight hair."[31] Louisa Picquet was described as "medium height. . . of fair complexion and rosy cheeks, with dark eyes, a flowing head of hair with no perceptible inclination to curl. . . No one. . . would suspect that she had a drop of African blood in her veins." Louisa's mother, also a concubine, was described as "pretty white" with "long hair" that was "wavy." Another enslaved seamstress named Lucy who belonged to a member of Louisa's mistress's family, and was a concubine, was described as "right white—light hair and blue eyes."[32] Lewis Hayden's mother also was "chosen" to be the concubine of a local white man in Kentucky. She was biracial but had no African ancestry, rather Native American and Caucasian, and she was described as "very handsome," with "long, straight black hair."[33] And while no known drawings or paintings exist of perhaps the most famous concubine in southern history, Sally Hemings, bondman Isaac Jefferson described the woman who lived at Monticello with him as "very handsome," "mighty near white," with "long straight hair down her back." Isaac also described Sally's mother, who had been the concubine of John Wayles and at least one other white man at Monticello, as a "bright mulatto woman."[34]

The desire for a woman whose appearance resembled that of white women was also echoed in the preferences for a potential concubine's cultural accoutrements. Most slaveholding men chose slave consorts who were house servants or skilled laborers (seamstresses were particularly popular). Domestics, after all, had to be more culturally similar to whites than field slaves. Indeed, slaveholding men so typically chose domestic servants to be their concubines that the term "house-keeper" became a popular euphemism that encompassed these women's physical, sexual, and emotional labor as their masters' consorts.[35] These women, because they typically lived around their owners' children and older kin, had to possess a degree of sophistication and cultural knowledge. Domestics and other skilled women certainly had more access to literacy than those whose work did not require that they have an intimate familiarity with southern white females' culture and conventions. Enslaved domestics, moreover, had been reared to maintain a comfortable home—one that slaveholding men could appreciate. Slave masters preferred that their concubines, therefore, not only look like white women, but also dress, speak, clean, sew, cook, and worship like them as well. Louisa Picquet, for example, was described as "easy and graceful in her manners" and appeared as "an accomplished white lady."[36]

An advertisement appearing in the July 4, 1835, *American Beacon* for the escaped woman Harriet Jacobs reiterates the traits most slaveholding men desired in their concubines. In that advertisement Dr. James Norcom describes Harriet as "a light mulatto, 21 years of age, about 5 feet 4 inches high, of a thick and corpulent habit, having on her head a thick covering of black hair that curls naturally, but which can be easily combed straight." Norcom went on to depict other aspects of Harriet's appearance that indicate her attractiveness to him. Of her dress, the doctor noted: "Being a good seamstress, she has been accustomed to dress well, had a variety of very fine clothes, made in the prevailing fashion, and will probably appear, . . . tricked out in gay and fashionable finery." Norcom added, with regard to Jacob's demeanor and presence, "she speaks easily and fluently, and had an agreeable carriage and address."[37] In other words, Harriet, the enslaved woman he wanted so desperately to be his concubine, was young, beautiful, charming, and refined. Is it any wonder then that Norcom was desperate to get her back? Equally desperate was another slaveholder, Mr. J. Davenport of Mississippi, who advertised in 1839 for the return of his domestic Harriet Powell, who escaped during their trip to Syracuse, New York. Davenport was willing to pay $200 for the return of the twenty-four-year-old "Bright Quadroon" whom he described as "of a full and well proportioned form, straight light brown hair, dark eyes, approaching to black, of fresh complexion, and so fair that she would generally be taken for white. . . . Her demeanor is very quiet, and her deportment modest."[38]

The daily routine of these "housekeepers" was the same as with other domestics, with the additional burden of sex on demand. On the farms and smaller plantations, some of these women worked in the house and the field. "What did I do?," one former Alabama concubine responded to a question about her work routine. "I spun an' cooked, an' waited, an' plowed; dere weren't nothin' I didn't do."[39] Most began learning their skilled trades as children, sometimes as the companion of planter youths, or in the kitchen, sewing room, and barnyard with older domestics. Like other domestics, as well, they had extremely limited privacy and often were at the beck and call of their owners, and other members of the owners' families, day and night.

The labor and domiciles for domestics, of course, also allowed slaveholding men greater physical access. It was not unusual for enslaved girls, raised in the main house or in the adjacent yard as the children of older domestics (some of whom also had been concubines), to become the sexual targets of the planter boys and men who also resided there. Rose Maddox, an enslaved woman raised in Mississippi and Louisiana, emphasized that "a white man laid a nigger gal whenever he wanted her. Seems like some of them had a plumb craving for the other color. Leastways they wanted to start themselves out on the nigger women."[40] Rose's suggestion that slaveholding men first began demanding sexual favors from enslaved African American women as adolescents was quite true. Under the control of teenaged boys seeking sexual pleasure and experience when no respectable white woman could afford to participate in such an activity, slave girls and women were forced to comply, and those who worked in the house were most vulnerable.

The double sexual standard in slaveholding families, which rewarded patriarchs and their male heirs with the right to demand sexual favors of their bondwomen as part of their duties, was a tradition passed down from one generation of slave-owning men to the next. Judge John Maddox, for example, grew up with his enslaved half sister working in his home. Once married and settled on his own plantation in Marion County, Georgia, he bought a "pretty mulatto ... seamstress" for himself.[41] Ethel Mae, a "yaller gal, told me 'bout Marsa bringing his son Levey ... down to the cabin," one former bondman confessed. "They both took her—the father showing the son what it was all about—and she couldn't do nothing 'bout it."[42]

Sexual relations with enslaved girls and women did not just involve white males of several generations in the slave family. It also included bonded women of the same family across time. For example, Ary was raised as a domestic in the home of her white father's brother. By her midteens, she had become the concubine of her young master, who also was her paternal first cousin.[43] Sally Hemings became the concubine of Jefferson while living in his household in Paris during the early republic period. Her mother, Elizabeth, had been the domestic servant of John Wayles during the colonial era and had served as maid to his two wives before she became his consort and bore him six children. Elizabeth's African mother had been the consort of an English sea captain named Hemings.[44] Both Louisa Picquet and her mother were concubines. When Louisa reached puberty, the father of four of her mother's children also tried to seduce her.[45] Incest, of course, was the most extreme and perverse example of how physical intimacy lent itself to serial concubinage and sexual predatorship. The quadroon woman Celia Bryan, for example, was repeatedly raped by her biological father Jacob Bryan in Duval County, Florida, in the late 1840s.[46]

SLAVEHOLDING MEN AND
CONCUBINAGE RELATIONS

Despite the commonality of enslaved women's sexual harassment, not all slave-holding men actually sought a concubine among their bondwomen. Some pursued no sexual relations with their bond people. Of those who did, however, the costs of concubinage—monetary, social, and moral—were high. To pursue such a relationship was least troublesome if a man was single, wealthy, and socially inconspicuous. Concubinage became more problematic for the master as well as the enslaved female if he was married, of modest holdings, or was in the public eye. Still, many who had public roles as legislators and clergymen, for example, sometimes maintained enslaved concubines and the offspring of the arrangement. While rejecting Norcom's incessant demands that she be his consort, Harriet Jacobs did become the concubine of Samuel Treadwell Sawyer. Sawyer was a young, wealthy, single lawyer building for himself a political career when he and Jacobs began their intimate relationship. He subsequently became a North Carolina state legislator while involved with Harriet and continued to have contact with her while serving as a member of the U.S. House of Representatives in the late 1830s.[47] Likewise, then President Thomas Jefferson continued his relationship with Sally Hemings even after it had been publicly exposed by James Callendar in 1802.[48] Henry Grimke, politically and socially prominent in Charleston, South Carolina, maintained Nancy Weston as his slave mistress for nineteen years. She had three children by him. Jefferson and Grimke, however, wisely maintained their slave women in rural isolation, and Sawyer eventually did leave Edenton for Washington, D.C., and later Norfolk, Virginia. All three men were either widowed or single when they began these relationships.

While many of the slaveholding men who established lengthy sexual relationships with enslaved women were wealthy and powerful, most were not. The experience of prolonged sexual relations between owner and owned was so typical as to encompass middling planters as well as overseers. The power of the southern

Nancy Weston, concubine of Henry Grimke of South Carolina. Weston had three children by Grimke: Archibald, Francis, and John. Henry Grimke's heir and white son, Montague, refused to free them on his father's death. Moorland-Spingarn Research Center, Manuscript Division, Howard University, Washington, D.C.

white patriarchy over the bodies of enslaved females sometimes even extended beyond the rich and powerful to white males, regardless of class status. "Marsters an' overseers use to make slaves dat wuz wid deir husbands git up, [and] do as they say," one former bondman noted. "Send husbands out on de farm, milkin' cows or cuttin' wood. Den he gits in bed wid slave himself. Some women would fight an' tussel. Others would be [h]umble—feared of dat beatin.'"[49] Jacob Manson, who was formerly enslaved in Warren County, North Carolina, recalled that many of the slaveholding men in his area held enslaved women as concubines. Remembering his own master, Colonel Bun Eden's, sexual exploits in the quarters, Manson was clear: "Marster had no chilluns by white women. He had his sweethearts among his slave women. I ain't no man for tellin' false stories. I tells de truth, an' dat is de truth."[50] None of the slaveholding men with sexual designs on Louisa Picquet, or her mother, were particularly famous or wealthy. Louisa's father was a middling planter; David Cook, the father of her mother's other children, went bankrupt. Louisa became the concubine of John Williams, a man who was neither a planter nor wealthy enough to purchase the beautiful woman himself—he had to borrow the money from his brother.[51]

John Sella Martin, born in 1832, the child of a concubine, recalled bitterly his mother's story and that his family's sale and dispersal were fueled by his father's limited financial means. "Like too many girls," he began, "my mother had been a victim of the selfish designs of her mistress in securing an eligible match in marriage for the heir of her property." Mr. Martin, John's father, was not wealthy, but the family had arranged for him to marry someone of substantial property. His betrothed, however, was several years younger and it would be at least a decade before she was ready to marry. In order to persuade her nephew to wait to marry the heiress, Martin's aunt, "Mrs. Henderson," arranged a concubinage relationship for her nephew with Winnifred, John's mother. Accordingly, "Mrs. Henderson, by methods known only to the system of slavery, encouraged, and finally secured a relationship between Mr. Martin and my mother, of which my sister Caroline and myself were the fruits."[52] Mrs. Henderson arranged for Winnifred, who was white or a "griff," to have a separate cabin, "nominal" housekeeping duties for her master and mistress, and food from the "big house." In exchange, Winnifred was Mr. Martin's concubine for the next ten years. Then, it was time for him to marry his betrothed. According to John, Martin had grown attached to his enslaved family members over the years and refused to marry. Mrs. Henderson would hear nothing of this. He needed a wealthy, respectable wife, not an enslaved concubine. Henderson sent her nephew on a family errand to Virginia, and while he was away, she sold Winnifred and her two children to slave traders in Georgia.[53]

OF MISTRESSES AND CONCUBINES

Most slaveholding women's responses to sexual relations that the men in their families had with enslaved women ran the gamut from violent outrage to quiet, perhaps tortured, compliance. Slaveholding mistresses had to do so, keep in mind, while working side by side with these women in their households. A few stepped forward to help those victimized, but the women who did so were not usually the wives of offending males. Louisa Picquet, for example, recalled that one of the women she was hired out to tried to save her from her owner's grasp. Mrs. Bachelor seemed aware of Cook's intentions toward the girl and helped her, on more than one occasion, to avoid being left alone with him. She was, Louisa recalled, "the best friend I had."[54] Still, efforts like Mrs. Bachelor's were rare. Others responded quite differently from Louisa's protector, and some actually were enablers. Mrs. Henderson, John Martin recalled for example, both created and later destroyed the concubinage arrangement of her nephew with John's mother, Winnifred.[55] "One of de slave girls on a plantation near us went to her missus and tole her 'bout her marster forcing her to let him have somethin' to do wid her," one former North Carolina slave related, "and her missus tole her, 'Well, go on. You belong to him.'"[56]

While most slaveholding women did not openly deter or enable concubinage, these relationships disturbed them deeply. Mary Chesnut, for example, was completely disgusted with her grandfather-in-law's sexual liaison with one of his enslaved women, complaining in her famed diary on one of many occasions, "Rachel and her brood make this place a horrid nightmare to me."[57] Wives, no doubt, were the most disturbed and opposed to these relations. "In them times white men went with colored gals and women bold," another bondman recounted. "Any time they saw one and wanted her, she had to go with him, and his wife didn't say nothin' 'bout it."[58]

The white wives' public responses were, as expected, muted. Gendered decorum demanded that slaveholding women exercise a strong sense of propriety, especially in the face of an enslaved person's humiliating accusation of such damnable acts. Silence, many believed, was their only acceptable public response unless they were willing to risk loss of face within their households and standing in their communities. Some wives were afraid to confront their husbands, a fear that did not escape the knowing eyes of their bondmen and women. "Before my old marster died," one former enslaved man recalled, "he had a pretty gal he was goin' with and he wouldn't let her work nowhere but in the house, and his wife nor nobody else didn't say nothin' 'bout it; they knowed better. She had three chillun for him."[59] But after all, it was the wife's duty to obey her husband. On this point, Mary Chesnut was particularly incensed, expressing her utter disdain for men who hypocritically subjected their wives to this kind of shame and humiliation, while still insisting that slaveholding women's moral compass be above reproach.

> But what do you say to this—to a magnate who runs a hideous black harem, with its consequences, under the same roof with his lovely white wife and his beautiful and accomplished daughters? He holds his head high and poses as the model of all human virtues to these poor women whom God and the laws have given him. From the height of his awful majesty he scolds and thunders at them as if he never did wrong in his life. Fancy such a man finding his daughter reading Don Juan. 'You with that immoral book!' he would say, and then he would order her out of his sight. You see Mrs. Stowe did not hit the sorest spot. She makes Legree a bachelor.[60]

Interracial marriage was outlawed as a criminal offense everywhere in the South since the colonial era, but rarely was the law enforced, particularly during the antebellum era, unless it involved white women and nonwhite men. Indeed, the Virginia state legislature granted its first two divorce settlements, in 1802 and

1803, respectively, to white male petitioners who claimed their wives had been sexually involved with black men and bore their children.[61] Few divorces were granted when the tables were turned. This, however, was not always the case. In 1814 and 1848, for example, white women in Virginia successfully petitioned for divorces based on eyewitness accounts that their husbands had committed acts of adultery with enslaved black women.[62] Still, a husband's adultery with an enslaved woman was far from a certain call for divorce in many southern states, particularly if the aggrieved wife could not prove paternity of a child as a result. Given the popular notion that enslaved women were so promiscuous that no one could be certain of their children's paternity (consider for example the number of historians who argued against Jefferson's paternity of Hemings's children until DNA evidence proved otherwise), it was virtually impossible to document a husband's affair with an enslaved women through the presence of mixed-race children.[63]

Indeed, some slaveholding men, but probably not in large numbers, made little or no effort to hide their extramarital relations with their enslaved girls and women. As the family patriarch, they believed their behavior was beyond open reproach, especially by their female "dependents." When George Carter's sister Sophia found out about his reputation as a pursuer of his enslaved girls and women, for example, she wrote to him, accusing the longtime bachelor of moral debauchery. The Virginia planter's reply was swift and to the point. "My habits," he wrote to her in June 1816, "like most men are vicious & corrupt . . . a Sin, [but for which I am] only answerable to God."[64] One former North Carolina bondman recalled that slaveholder Jimmie Shaw "owned a purty slave gal, nearly white, a' he kept her. His wife caught 'im in a cabin bed wid her. His wife said somethin' to him 'bout it, an' he cussed his wife."[65] When wives actually caught their husbands "in the act," however, they were much less likely to mask their pain and outrage. "She went back to de greathouse an' got a gun," the slave continued. "When de marster come in de greathouse, she tole 'im he must let de slave girls alone, dat he belonged to her. He cussed her agin an' said she would have to tend to her own damn business an' he would tend to his."[66] After more heated words, the bondman said, "She grabbed de gun an' let him have it. She shot 'im dead in de hall." Mrs. Shaw purportedly escaped prosecution by taking her two sons and leaving the area.[67]

Hurt and angry wives, however, were much more likely to act violently against the enslaved girls and women or their children, or both, than their errant husbands. One former bondwoman recalled that when she finally found out that she was her owner's child, she began to understand why her mistress had been so cruel to her. "When I was eight years old, Old Mistress died," she explained, "and Grandmammy told me why Old Mistress picked on me so. She told me about me being half Master Ned's blood. Then I knowed why Master Ned would say, 'Let her alone, she got big, big blood in her,' and then laugh."[68] Oftentimes slavehold-ing women demanded that these women and their children be sold away immedi-ately, as did Elizabeth Ramsey's and Louisa Picquet's mistresses.[69] If their spouses refused to do so, some acted quickly to deprive them of their concubine's plea-sures. A Georgia former bondman, Jack Maddox, recalled, his master brought home "a pretty mulatto gal. She was real bright and she had long black hair and was dressed neat and good."[70] The mistress was immediately suspicious. "What you bring that thing here for," she snapped. Judge Maddox's reply that the enslaved woman would do all of his wife's "fine needle work" was less than convincing. "Fine needlework, your hind leg," she retorted.[71] As soon as the judge left the plan-tation, his wife cut off the woman's hair "to her skull."[72] Others attacked offspring of these unions. As a formerly enslaved man who lived in Georgia reported, "one white lady that lived near us at McBean slipped in a colored gal's room and cut her baby's head clean off 'cause it belonged to her husband. [The baby's father] beat her 'bout it and started to kill her, but she begged so I reckon he got to feelin' sorry for her. But he kept goin' with the colored gal and they had more chillun."[73] Lulu Wilson's mistress was "special mean to me," she recalled. Lulu was the offspring of her master, Wash Hodges. "She beat me and used to tie my hands and make me lay flat on the floor and put snuff in my eyes."[74] Wilson eventually became blind.

THE CONCUBINES' RETORT

"Maybe you think, because they're slaves, they ain't got no feelings and no shame?," declared Lewis Clarke of Kentucky, whose mother was a concubine and whose sister was sold because she refused to become one. "A woman's being a slave, don't stop her having genteel ideas; that is, according to their way, and as far as they can."[75] Certainly, many of those former bond people who commented on concubinage relationships characterized them as abusive and forced. As one formerly enslaved man succinctly put it, "white men got plenty chilluns by the nigger women. They didn't ask them. They just took them."[76] Sexual desire and obsession, backed by racial and male privilege and pride, often led to physical brutalization for those who dared to resist. "Granny," who had been enslaved in Alabama, recalled that she never developed anything close to a romantic, or even emotionally supportive, relationship with her owner who was the father of her five children. Always afraid that she would be tortured if she refused him, Granny revealed, "I didn't want him, but I couldn't do nothin'. I uster say, 'What do yer want of a woman all cut ter pieces like I is?' But 'twant no use. I was a dog in dose days, a dog. Nothin' to eat, an' all day long work an' plow, an' allus [jeal-ous] ole missus."[77]

Blond, blue-eyed Henry Gerald recalled of his owner and father, "He beat my mama. He beat her until the blood ran down her back. . . . He beat her because she refused to have relations with him." Henry knew because he remembered, "he make me wash her back off with salt water." Born in 1853 in Gallivant's Ferry in Horry County, South Carolina, Henry Gerald reluctantly told the story of his mother's forced concubinage. She had four children for her owner before general emancipation.[78] David Cook also beat Louisa Picquet brutally because she refused to have sex with him.[79] Harriet Jacobs was brutalized for the same reason, and the list goes on.[80] Even Thomas Jefferson, a man who was involved with an enslaved woman for decades, had to admit that "the whole commerce between master and slave is a perpetual exercise of the most boisterous passions, the most unremitting despotism on the one part, and degrading submissions on the other."[81]

Brutal whippings, however, were not all these girls and women faced if they dared to resist. Some women who refused the sexual overtures of slaveholding men also experienced shaming, sale, loss of their children, or even death. One former bondman, for example, reported the story of a beautiful young woman who was sold for $2,100 to a man who "compelled her to enter into [carnal] relations with him, and when he discovered that she was in a delicate condition, had her tied up and whipped, with a view of producing the death of the child."[82] Sukie Abbott's master sold her when she refused him.[83] Dehumanization and defeminization were ready responses. Nellie, "who was almost white and had long straight hair," was made to wear men's pants, and work in the fields with deer horns and bells attached to her head, all because she refused the slaveholder's sexual demands.[84]

Most enslaved women quickly learned that to resist these sexual demands meant some sort of harsh punishment. Still, the reactions of enslaved women who were pursued by slaveholding men for sexual favor varied substantially. Some committed suicide, while others murdered their assailants; many tried to escape or begged to be sold; and it is likely that they all suffered emotional scars throughout their lives. Some women became resigned to their status, while others came to appreciate the material benefits and promises of freedom that were sometimes proffered and received in exchange. However, the bulk of the evidence points to forms of resistance. Harriet Jacobs secreted herself in a small attic for years to avoid her master's sexual demands.[85] Sukie Abbott slapped her master and pushed his naked buttocks into a pot of boiling soap.[86] The famous (or infamous) Celias—Celia Bryan of Florida and Celia Newsome of Missouri—never reconciled themselves to being sex slaves and resisted mightily. Both killed their masters and were tried and hanged for it.

Robert Newsome, of Calloway County, raped his slave girl Celia on the way back to his plantation immediately after he bought her. It was 1850, and Celia was fourteen years old; Newsome was sixty. Celia had just been torn from her family and friends in what was likely her first sale. Celia was to be the only black female on his farm for the duration of her stay, and Newsome built a separate house for her on his property, a short distance from his home. Over the next five years, he visited her regularly for sexual relations, which resulted in two children. When the opportunity arose to marry a bondman whom she loved, Celia acted forcefully to rid herself of Newsome. According to court testimony, Celia, who was then pregnant a third time (by Newsome or perhaps by her black lover), used her pregnancy to try to get Newsome to leave her alone, but he refused. Celia even asked his adult daughters to intervene on her behalf, and they also refused. The next time Newsome tried to rape Celia, she killed him, crushing his skull with a heavy stick. She then burned his body to hide evidence of the crime.[87]

No one knows when Celia Bryan, who lived and worked on a small plantation outside of Jacksonville, Florida, was first forced into concubinage. What is known is that her mother, Susan, had been the concubine of their master, Jacob Bryan, and Susan bore him at least six children. Celia was the oldest. Once Celia became an adolescent, Bryan began making sexual demands and when she refused, he promised Celia's mother, his "retired" concubine, that he would free the entire family if Celia agreed to have sex with him regularly. Susan insisted that Celia comply. The girl purportedly bore her biological father four children. Then on December 7, 1847, Celia and her owner-father got into a fight while working a field together. Celia picked up a hoe and bludgeoned Jacob Bryan to death.[88]

Obviously, concubinage could be a tremendous burden physically and emotionally for enslaved women. For some, it was a matter of "Christian morality." Many adolescent black girls, like Minnie Folkes, had been taught to be sexually chaste, to "let nobody bother yo' principle; 'cause dat wuz all yo' had," —since at the time a woman's sexual purity was as prized an asset among the enslaved as among the free. Older kin and even white mistresses instructed them to marry first, then commit to sexual relations. Louisa Picquet, for example, recalled that her mistress had taught her about proper Christian female behavior. She had explained to Louisa that sexual promiscuity—"to stay with any one without bein' married"—was a sin. When Louisa's master forced her into a concubinage relationship, she was tortured by her belief that she was committing a great sin. "I thought of what Mrs. Cook told me," she noted, "and I thought, now I shall be committin' adultery, and there's no chance for me, and I'll have to die and be lost."[89] There also was the heartfelt belief and desire of many to choose the man, or men, with whom they would share their bodies. "It seems less degrading to give one's self, than to submit to compulsion," Harriet Jacobs explained of her decision to become the concubine of Samuel Treadwell Sawyer, instead of her master James Norcom.[90]

Despite the abundance of evidence supporting the notion that large numbers of women resisted in any and every way that they could, not all of these relationships were physically coerced, just as not all "marriages" between bonded men and women were voluntary. Slave owners had many ways to gain control of, and manipulate, an enslaved woman's sexual loyalties. These men approached them when they were young girls, naive, vulnerable, and certainly frightened. Others took advantage of enslaved girls who were without the advice and support of family and friends because they were in strange new surroundings. Some females were convinced by the material incentives offered, and particularly by the promise of emancipation for them, their children, and perhaps other family members.

The abundant evidence of sexual compliance comes from Louisiana, where the system of concubinage was institutionalized and was already at least a century old by the 1800s. According to Joan Martin, one of the leading historians of New Orleans plaçage, there were an estimated fifteen hundred placées in New Orleans alone in 1788.[91] While these kinds of relationships were very likely financially beneficial to the women and their children, other forms of concubinage also could provide some limited benefit to the women. In 1842 Lewis Clarke pointed out that while enslaved women would cry, become depressed, and even suicidal as a result of particularly dehumanizing experiences of sexual abuse, such as gang rape, they responded more positively to slaveholding men interested in courtship and romance. At the same time, however, "they [knew] they must submit to their masters; besides, their masters, maybe, dress 'em up, and make 'em little presents, and give 'em more privileges, while the whim last." Even Harriet Jacobs, the icon of resistance, was attracted to a man who romanced her and promised to help free their children.[92]

Some concubinage relationships obviously developed over time, and could even mimic a marriage in some significant ways such as emotional attachment; financial support; better food, clothing, and furnishings; and sometimes freedom for the woman and her children. James Norcom told Harriet Jacobs, "I would cherish you. I would make a lady of you."[93] Louisa Picquet's "master" promised to emancipate her and their children and to bequeath to her his belongings.[94] Andrew Moss of Georgia recalled that his grandmother had been his master's concubine, and the couple had five children. "She was his house woman; dat's what he call her," Moss noted. "And when he died he willed her and all dem chillens a house, some land, and a little money."[95] At his death, Isaac Matthews freed his "negro wench Jen" and allowed her an annual allowance of thirty dollars.[96] John Chesnut of Camden, South Carolina, the grandfather-in-law of diarist Mary Chesnut, freed two of his enslaved children and left instructions that they be educated. According to Chesnut's will, Edward Burke was to be taught "some useful occupation" and emancipated at age twenty-one. His sister, Juliana, was "to be brought up as a mantua maker" or given some "useful occupation" as well, and to be free at age sixteen. Chesnut also bequeathed the eventual freedom of his "faithful woman and servant Sue," along with a $30 annuity.[97] Thomas Jefferson convinced Sally Hemings to return to a life of slavery in Virginia after he promised her that he would free their children. Although Madison Hemings's testimony indicates that Jefferson never openly embraced his enslaved children, some slaveholding fathers did.[98] When Margaret Fitzpatrick's enslaved children confronted their white half brothers and sisters at their Louisiana plantation dollhouse, they were quick to set the record straight regarding the father whom the two sets of children shared: "He comes to see us near every day and fotches us clothes and things from town. He is our daddy and we call him daddy when he comes to our house to see our mama."[99]

The unavailability of marriageable black or mixed-race men, particularly on small holdings where women outnumbered men, could also have served as a contributing factor in enslaved women's compliance in relationships with slaveholding men. Some slave owners made certain that other white or black men stayed away from their concubines. Louisa Picquet, for example, recalled the story of a woman held in concubinage in Mobile, Alabama; even though her owner did not reside with her, he still demanded her exclusive sexual attention. When a bondman began a false rumor that she was being visited by a specific enslaved man, the owner had both whipped brutally and sent the woman to be sold in the slave market in New Orleans.[100] Some bondwomen, Picquet added, never had an opportunity to have a bondman for a husband because their masters "[had] them all the time."[101] When speaking of her concubinage relationship, the enslaved woman Ary noted that her "young master" had assumed that she would remain sexually exclusive to him. He had insisted in particular that she have nothing to do with "colored men" because they "weren't good enough" for her.[102] Some masters worried more about white male competitors than the enslaved men they owned and more easily controlled. Colonel Eden, for example, was so taken with his enslaved women that he refused to hire white overseers, and used black drivers instead. Jacob Manson, a former slave, recalled that "Col. Eden liked some of de nigger women too good to have any uder white man playin' arou' wid 'em."[103]

One also cannot discount the impact that a combination of contemporary racial beliefs and attitudes and a desire to be a part of the "white" world could have had on a bonded woman's feelings about entering into a concubinage relationship. Under such circumstances, it is possible some enslaved women may have more readily agreed to become concubines, or may have even desired white male sexual partners. Harriet Jacobs's experiences are again instructive. Although she initially fell in love with a free man of color whom her owner would not allow her to marry, she became sexually involved with Samuel Sawyer. When describing her attraction to him, she explained: "So much attention from a superior person was, of course flattering; for human nature is the same in all. I also felt grateful for his sympathy, and encouraged by his kind words. It seemed to me a great thing to have such a friend. By degrees, a more tender feeling crept into my heart. He was an educated and eloquent gentleman."[104]

AGED CONCUBINES AND THE COMMUNITY

The responses of other African Americans to women who served as their masters' concubines were mixed and complicated. Clearly, slave testimony supports the assertion that most of these women had been forced into these relationships and that the shame, degradation, and abuse they experienced usually was not worth whatever payment they reaped, except perhaps emancipation. Because other enslaved people knew or were related to these girls and women, they understood their trials and often expressed great sympathy toward them. "A slave woman ain't allowed to respect herself," Lewis Clarke concluded bitterly after recalling the experiences of his mother, sister, and other enslaved women he knew who were ordered such sexual duties.[105]

Some, however, were less than comfortable embracing an enslaved woman who appeared to prefer the sexual attention of white, rather than African American, men. Even those who clearly were forced to have sexual relations with slaveholding men sometimes received a mixed reception, particularly if having such a relationship brought them obvious material reward, or inordinate power over other enslaved people. Slaveholding men sometimes made matters worse for these women when they disciplined those among their bond people who dared to expose, criticize, or oppose their concubinage relationships or their concubines. For example, one former bondman told the story of a wealthy slave owner in Kentucky who punished the enslaved women on his property who ridiculed his concubine for sleeping with him. The owner punished these women by forcing all of them to have sex with him. When they complained, he changed their status from that of domestic to field worker. Those who then complained of the hard labor were "tied up naked, and flogged, for disobeying orders."[106]

The children of these relationships, in particular, were caught between the world of their enslaved mothers and their slave-owning fathers, sometimes find-

ing no place to really belong. Life became even more difficult when they had
to contend with the various factions of their two worlds that complicated even
more their treatment and identity. Lizzie Williams, who had been enslaved on a
cotton plantation located fifteen miles outside of Selma, Alabama, for example,
remembered the triangulated identity of Emily, a mixed-race bondwoman who
simultaneously lived among her mistress, her father, and the other slaves on the
property. "Emily, she look like a white gal," Lizzie noted. "She was treated just
like she white. Her daddy was a white man." Emily, who was related to her mistress, found it difficult living between the relative privilege her mistress allowed
her, the complete invisibility to her father (Lizzie reported that "Her pappy pay
no more attention to her dan to de rest of the niggers"), and the ridicule of the
bond people. "But Emily had de saddest look on her yaller face," Williams concluded, "'cause de other niggers whisper about her pappy."[107]

Mothers and other kin who were sensitive to the kinds of teasing, insults, and
rough treatment that their children might receive at the hands of both blacks
and whites, often would lie to their children about their paternity or teach them
to avoid the issue when questioned about it. There was little solace, however,
for many since the color of their skin and other features told much of the story.
Dora Franks of Mississippi spoke openly of her painful experiences as the child
of her master. Her mother, Harriet Brewer, had come from Virginia where she
had been the concubine of her young master, George Brewer. Harriet never hid
Dora's paternity from the child. Although treated well by the Brewer family, her
father largely ignored her, and she felt rejected by fellow bond people. "Lord, it's
been to my sorry many a time," she noted, "'cause de chillen used to chase me
round and holler at me, 'Old yallow nigger.' Dey didn't treat me good, neither."
One day the cook violently slapped Dora, causing her nose to bleed because the
child had asked her for a piece of white bread, "like the white folks eat." When
her father returned to the house, the cook was severely whipped and then sold.
Still, Dora had to call her father "Marse George," and he eventually married a local white woman, his longtime sweetheart, "Miss Martha Ann." Dora prayed for
freedom during the Civil War and left "Marse George's" plantation after the war
without telling anyone.[108]

Even those women who eventually were able to establish marriages or long-
term relations with bondmen still found their mixed-race children at risk of being rejected by the new men in their lives. These stepchildren, after all, were a
constant reminder to bondmen of the power white men held over their wives and
their inability, as men, to protect them. Their frustration and anger sometimes
surfaced as resentment and rejection of these youngsters. Lulu Wilson recalled,
"[my] step-paw never did like me, but he was a fool for his own younguns." Lulu

also was treated badly by her owner's wife but was never sold. Her master-father, however, did sell many of her step-siblings.[109]

Some concubinage relationships, such as that of Sally Hemings and Thomas Jefferson, endured until either person died. Wills, letters, and court documents reveal that some slaveholding men provided for the continued financial support of their concubines and the children born to those relationships. Some also freed them. These same documents, however, also betray a legacy of denial of support and freedom for most. Even those who promised to do so sometimes went back on their word and failed to follow up on all the necessary legal procedures and payments, or had heirs who refused to honor such bequests. Moreover, many concubines did not benefit from special support or privileges even when the men were still alive. The illegality of these relationships, and the low status of enslaved women, despite their color, meant that slaveholding men could abandon them and their children whenever they desired. Many elected to do so when they married, as did Dora Frank's father.[110] These women suffered the loss of home, and sometimes children, when they were sold, as did Elizabeth Ramsey and Winnifred Martin.[111] Others, like Lulu Wilson's mother, lost their children when the slaveholding man they served lost interest.[112] Most, however, lived out their lives as other domestic servants with the distinction that, as they aged, their sexual duties declined.

Louisa Picquet was lucky. Her master died when she was in her early twenties. His brother, who was her true owner, honored the wishes of his deceased sibling and allowed Louisa and her two surviving children to move north with funds from the sale of their household effects. Louisa Williams, as she was then known, moved to Cincinnati. There, she met and married Henry Picquet, a mixed-race man from Georgia whose mother also had been a concubine. Louisa was determined to find her own mother, who had been sold with her brother to Texas, and she eventually did locate them. Louisa raised $900—largely through the sale of her autobiography and lectures about her life—to purchase and free her mother and brother.[113] Few survived concubinage so well—with their children and themselves in freedom and able to have a life with family, friends, and a modicum of dignity.

NOTES

This chapter is derived from a paper given at the Huntington Conference, "Legacies of Family, Labor and Reform: Women in the Atlantic World, 1600–1900," March 18–19, 2011, San Marino, California.

   1. Louisa Picquet and Hiram Mattison, *Louisa Picquet, the Octoroon: Or Inside Views*

of Southern Domestic Life, electronic edition, Manuscripts, Archives and Rare Books Division, Schomburg Center for Research in Black Culture, New York Public Library, Astor, Lenox and Tilden Foundations; Reginald H. Pitts, "Louisa Picquet, c. 1829– 1896," *Legacy* 24, no. 2 (2007): 294–95.

2. Picquet and Mattison, *Louisa Picquet, the Octoroon*, 15.

3. Some of the females were examined to determine whether or not they were virgins. Louisa notes that she was stripped only to her shoulders because she was labeled "virtuous" by a potential buyer when she was inspected prior to being placed on the auction block. Picquet and Mattison, *Louisa Picquet, the Octoroon*, 16.

4. Picquet and Mattison, *Louisa Picquet, the Octoroon*, 15, 18; Pitts, "Louisa Picquet," 294–95.

5. Primary sources and personal documents from the era of enslavement are rife with references to black sexual bondage in the Americas, including the United States. See, for example, Lewis and Marian Wright, eds., *The Secret Diary of William Byrd of Westover, 1709–1712* (Richmond, Va.: Dietz Press, 1941); Picquet and Mattison, *Louisa Picquet, the Octoroon*; Trevor Burnard, *Master, Tyranny, and Desire: Thomas Thistlewood and His Slaves in the Anglo-Jamaican World* (Chapel Hill: University of North Carolina Press, 2003); Richard and Sally Price, eds., *Stedman's Surinam: Life in Eighteenth-Century Slave Society; An Abridged Edition of the Narrative of a Five Years' Expedition against the Revolted Negroes of Surinam* (Baltimore, Md.: Johns Hopkins University Press, 1992); Shelly Eversley, ed., *The Interesting Narrative of the Life of Olaudah Equiano: or, Gustavus Vassa, the African* (1789; rpt., New York: Modern Library, 2004); Thomas Jefferson, *Notes on the State of Virginia* (1781; rpt., Charleston, S.C.: NABU Press, 2010), 162.

6. Much has been written on the extralegal custom of plaçage, which reached its peak in the eighteenth- and nineteenth-century Atlantic world, particularly in those areas colonized by the French and Spanish, that "placed" beautiful young women of color in long-term sexual relationships with well-to-do white men. Males provided financial and material support for their "placées" and any children born of the union. The women provided sexual and emotional care as well as raised their children. See, for example, Joan M. Martin, "Plaçage and the Louisiana Gens de Couleur," in *Creole: The History and Legacy of Louisiana's Free People of Color*, ed. Sybil Kein (Baton Rouge: Louisiana State University Press, 2000), 57–70; Sybil Kein, "One-Drop Rules: Self-Identity and the Women in the Trial of Toucoutou," *Louisiana Culture from the Colonial Period to Katrina*, ed. John Lowe (Baton Rouge: Louisiana State University Press, 2008), 138–46.

7. Sexual relations in the early national and antebellum eras between slaver and enslaved are examined in a number of secondary texts, including Deborah Grey White, *Ar'n't I a Woman? Women and Plantation Slavery* (New York: Norton Press, 1985), 27–61; Darlene Clark Hine, "Rape and the Inner Lives of Black Women in the Middle West," *Signs* 14 (1989): 912–20; Helene Lecaudey, "Behind the Mask: Ex-Slave Women and Interracial Sexual Relations," in *Discovering the Women in Slavery*, ed. Patricia Morton (Athens: University of Georgia Press, 1996), 260–77; Catherine Clinton and Michelle Gillespie, eds., *The Devil's Lane: Sex and Race in the Early South* (New York:

Oxford University Press, 1997); Martha Hodes, *White Women, Black Men: Illicit Sex in the Nineteenth Century South* (New Haven, Conn.: Yale University Press, 1999); Joshua Rothman, *Notorious in the Neighborhood: Sex and Families across the Color Line in Virginia, 1787–1861* (Chapel Hill: University of North Carolina Press, 2007).

8. James Mellon, ed., *Bullwhip Days: The Slaves Remember, an Oral History* (New York: Weidenfeld and Nicolson, 1988), 219–20.

9. Among free blacks, a majority were mixed race in Alabama, Arkansas, Georgia, Louisiana, North Carolina, Ohio, Tennessee, Texas, Virginia, Mississippi, and the territory of Oregon. Mixed-race people were close to 50 percent of the free black populations in Illinois, Michigan, and South Carolina. Among the slave population, the largest numbers of mulattoes were found in Alabama, Georgia, Kentucky, Louisiana, Mississippi, Missouri, North Carolina, Tennessee, and Virginia. Virginia had, by far, the largest number of mulatto slaves, numbering 44,299, or 10.3 percent, of its slave population. The nearby District of Columbia had one of the largest percentages of mixed-race people in its urban slave population—27.8 percent. Arkansas, Kentucky, and Texas all had slave populations that were more than 15 percent mulatto. J. D. B. DeBow, *Seventh Census of the United States, 1850: Embracing a Statistical View of Each of the States and Territories, Arranged by Counties, Towns, Etc.* (Washington, D.C.: Robert Armstrong, Public Printer, 1853), table 72, Black and Mulatto Population of the United States, 83.

10. Henry D. Spalding, *Encyclopedia of Black Folklore and Humor* (1972; rev. ed., Middle Village, N.Y.: Jonathan David Publishers, 1978), 239–41.

11. Charles L. Perdue Jr., Thomas E. Barden, and Robert K. Phillips, eds., *Weevils in the Wheat: Interviews with Virginia Ex-Slaves* (Charlottesville: University Press of Virginia, 1976), 232.

12. Paul Lovejoy has written on the use of young slave women as concubines in the Sokoto Caliphate. Paul E. Lovejoy, "Concubinage and the Status of Women Slaves in Early Colonial Northern Nigeria," *Journal of African History* 29, no. 2 (1988): 245–46.

13. Martin Klein, for one, exposed the widespread use of African women as slaves, noting their experiences in the western Sudan (Senegal, Guinea, Mali). Martin Klein, *Slavery and Colonial Rule in French West Africa*, (New York: Cambridge University Press, 1998), 2–3.

14. Joseph C. Miller, "Women as Slaves and Owners of Slaves: Experiences from Africa, the Indian Ocean World, and the Early Atlantic," in *Women and Slavery*, ed. Gwyn Campbell, Suzanne Miers, and Joseph C. Miller, vol. 1, *Africa, the Indian Ocean World, and the Medieval North Atlantic* (Athens: Ohio University Press, 2007), 11.

15. Cooper also notes, however, that "apparently" these slave women in eastern Africa had to consent to the relationship. Frederick Cooper, *Plantation Slavery on the East Coast of Africa* (Portsmouth, N.H.: Heinemann, 1997), 195.

16. Lewis Clarke, *Leaves from a Slave's Journal of Life*, ed. Lydia Maria Child, reprinted from *Anti-Slavery Standard*, October 20 and 27, 1842, 78–79, 83, accessed January 4, 2011 at Documenting the American South, http://docsouth.unc.edu/neh/clarke/support1.html. Also see Lewis Clarke, *Narrative of the Sufferings of Lewis Clarke during a Captivity of More than 25 Years* (Boston, Mass.: E. H. Ela, 1845).

17. Elizabeth Keckley, *Behind the Scenes or, Thirty Years a Slave, and Four Years in the White House*, ed. James Olney (1868; rpt., New York: Oxford University Press, 1988), 38–39.

18. George P. Rawick, ed., *The American Slave: A Composite Autobiography* (Westport: Conn.: Greenwood, 1972), vol. 5, *Texas Narratives*, parts 3 and 4, 236–46.

19. Inventory of Adam Shover's Estate, October 13, 1817, Shover Family Papers, Virginia State Library, Richmond; promissory note, Samuel DeButts, October 29, 1838, DeButts Family Papers, 1784–1962, Virginia Historical Society, Richmond; Benjamin Drew, ed., *North-Side View of Slavery, the Refugee: or the Narratives of Fugitive Slaves in Canada Related by Themselves with an Account of the History and Condition of the Colored Population of Upper Canada* (Boston: John P. Jewett, 1856), 74; Charles Poland Jr., *From Frontier to Suburbia* (Maceline, Mo.: Heritage Books, 2006), 139.

20. Lawrence J. Kotlikoff, "The Structure of Slave Prices in New Orleans, 1804 to 1862," *Economic Inquiry* 17, no. 4 (1979): 496–518.

21. Dorothy Sterling includes in her discussion of Emily Russell a quote from a letter sent by Bruin and Hill in 1850 in which they request $1,800 for Emily, described as "'the finest-looking woman in the country." Russell died on the way to New Orleans. Dorothy Sterling, ed., *We Are Your Sisters: Black Women in the Nineteenth Century* (New York: W. W. Norton, 1984), 48; advertisement of Davenport's escaped slave woman Harriet Powell, accessed January 13, 2011, at "The Civil War and Central New York," http://cnycivilwar.com/Erie%20Canal/eriecanal.html.

22. The first owner of the Edmondson girls sold them in 1848 because they had tried to escape. They were to be sold as prostitutes. Their father did raise the money to purchase them with the help of the Methodist Episcopal Church, North. James W. C. Pennington, *The Fugitive Blacksmith; or, Events in the History of James W.C. Pennington*, 3rd. ed. (1850; rpt., Westport, Conn.: Negro Universities Press, 1971), v; Perdue, Barden, and Phillips, eds., *Weevils in the Wheat*, 236.

23. Pennington, *Fugitive Blacksmith*, v, v–x.

24. Picquet and Mattison, *Louisa Picquet, the Octoroon*, 34–35. Elizabeth Ramsay was probably about forty-five years old at the time, well past the age of a prime worker, particularly a concubine. Horton indicated she was, however, still "as fine a washer, cook, and ironer as there is in the United States."

25. William Forbes to George Carter, May 20, 1805, Carter Family Papers, Virginia State Library.

26. Annette Gordon-Reed, *The Hemingses of Monticello: An American Family* (New York: W. W. Norton, 2008), 670.

27. Harriet Jacobs, *Incidents in the Life of a Slave Girl*, ed. Valerie Smith (1861; rpt., New York: Oxford University Press, 1988), 44.

28. "Amanda America Dickson," Oct. 24, 2009, accessed January 10, 2011, at Civil War Women, http://www.civilwarwomenblog.com.

29. Rawick, ed., *American Slave, North Carolina Narratives*, vol. 15, part 2, 140.

30. Octavia Rogers Albert, *The House of Bondage, or Charlotte Brooks and Other Slaves* (1890; rpt., New York: Oxford University Press, 1988), 120–21.

31. Ibid., 20.

32. Picquet and Mattison, *Louisa Picquet, the Octoroon*, 5, 8, 20.

33. John W. Blassingame, ed., *Slave Testimony: Two Centuries of Letters, Speeches, Interviews and Autobiographies* (Baton Rouge: Louisiana State University Press, 1977), 695–96.

34. Isaac Jefferson, "Life of Isaac Jefferson of Petersburg, Virginia, Blacksmith, containing a full and faithful account of Monticello and the family there, with notices of the many distinguished characters that visited there, with his Revolutionary experience and travels, adventures, observations and opinions, the whole taken down from his own words," 3, Thomas Jefferson Papers, Small Library, University of Virginia.

35. Cynthia Kennedy-Haflett, "'Moral Marriage': A Mixed-Race Relationship in Nineteenth-Century Charleston, South Carolina," *South Carolina Historical Magazine* 97, no. 3 (1996): 220–21.

36. Picquet and Mattison, *Louisa Picquet, the Octoroon*, 5.

37. Harriet Jacobs Fugitive Slave Advertisement Image Copy from *American Beacon*, July 4, 1835, North Carolina Division of Archives and History.

38. "$200 Reward," advertisement of Davenport's escaped slave woman, Harriet Powell, "Harriet Powell's Escape from Slavery," http://www.nyhistory.com/central /harriet.htm.

39. Blassingame, ed., *Slave Testimony*, 540.

40. Mellon, ed., *Bullwhip Days*, 122.

41. Ibid., 121.

42. Perdue, Barden, and Phillips, eds., *Weevils in the Wheat*, 301.

43. Henry Swint, ed., *Dear Ones at Home: Letters from Contraband Camps* (Nashville, Tenn.: Vanderbilt University Press, 1996), 55–56.

44. Gordon-Reed, *Hemingses of Monticello*, 11–13, 668–71.

45. Picquet and Mattison, *Louisa Picquet, the Octoroon*, 5.

46. "Celia's Sad Fate," *JacksonvilleStory.com: Local & Family History in Jacksonville, Florida*, http://www.jaxhistory.com, accessed January 10, 2011.

47. Jean Fagan Yellin, *Harriet Jacobs: A Life* (New York: Basic Books, 2004), 27; "Sawyer, Samuel Tredwell, (1800–1865)," in *Biographical Directory of the United States Congress, 1771–Present*, accessed January 13, 2011, at Infoplease, http://www .infoplease.com/biography/us/congress/sawyer-samuel-tredwell.html.

48. "James Thomson Callender, Scandalmonger," Digital History: Using New Technologies to Enhance Teaching and Research, http://www.digitalhistory.uh.edu, accessed September 10, 2010.

49. Perdue, Barden, and Phillips, eds., *Weevil in the Wheat*, 117, 207.

50. Mellon, ed., *Bullwhip Days*, 220.

51. Picquet and Mattison, *Louisa Picquet, the Octoroon*, 18–23.

52. Blassingame, ed., *Slave Testimony*, 703–6.

53. Ibid.

54. Picquet and Mattison, *Louisa Picquet, the Octoroon*, 14.

55. Blassingame, ed., *Slave Testimony*, 703–6.

56. Mellon, ed., *Bullwhip Days*, 220.

57. Mary Boykin Chesnut, *Mary Chesnut's Civil War*, ed. C. Vann Woodward (New Haven: Yale University Press, 1993), 72.

58. Rawick, ed., *American Slave, Georgia Narratives*, vol. 13, part 1, 292.

59. Ibid., 295.

60. Mary Boykin Chesnut, *A Diary from Dixie, as Written by Mary Boykin Chesnut, Wife of James Chesnut, Jr., United States Senator From South Carolina, 1859–1861, and Afterward an Aide to Jefferson Davis and a Brigadier-General in the Confederate Army*, ed. Isabella D. Martin and Myrta Lockett Avary (New York: D. Appleton and Company, 1905), electronic version, accessed August 15, 2011, at Documenting the American South, http://docsouth.unc.edu/southlit/chesnut/maryches.html.

61. Glenda Riley, "Legislative Divorce in Virginia, 1803–1850," *Journal of the Early Republic* 11, no. 1 (1991): 57–58.

62. Ibid.

63. Dinitia Smith and Nicholas Wade, "DNA Test Finds Evidence of Jefferson Child by Slave," *New York Times*, November 1, 1998, http://www.nytimes.com/1998/11/01/us/dna-test-finds-evidence-of-jefferson-child-by-slave.html, accessed November 10, 2010.

64. George Carter to Sophia Carter, June 20, 1816, Carter Family Papers, Virginia Historical Society.

65. Mellon, ed., *Bullwhip Days*, 220.

66. Ibid.

67. Ibid.

68. Norman Yetman, ed., *Voices from Slavery: 100 Authentic Slave Narratives* (Mineola, N.Y.: Dover, 2000), 327.

69. Picquet and Mattison, *Louisa Picquet, the Octoroon*, 6.

70. Mellon, ed., *Bullwhip Days*, 121.

71. Ibid.

72. Ibid.

73. Rawick, ed., *American Slave, Georgia Narratives*, vol. 13, part 2, 295; Helen T. Catterall and James J. Hayden, eds., *Judicial Cases Concerning American Slavery and the Negro* (Buffalo, N.Y.: William S. Hein, 1998), 3:243.

74. Yetman, ed., *Voices from Slavery*, 323.

75. Blassingame, ed., *Slave Testimony*, 157.

76. Mellon, ed., *Bullwhip Days*, 121.

77. Blassingame, ed., *Slave Testimony*, 540.

78. Author's oral history interview of Emma Gerald Stevenson, conducted in Portsmouth, Virginia, November 20, 1985. Mrs. Stevenson was the paternal granddaughter of Henry Gerald. The story was passed orally via Mrs. Florence Gerald, daughter-in-law to Henry Gerald, Mullins, South Carolina.

79. Picquet and Mattison, *Louis Picquet, the Octoroon*, 12, 15.

80. Norcom threatened to both beat and kill Jacobs on numerous occasions. See, for example, Jacobs, *Incidents in the Life of a Slave Girl*, 50.

81. Jefferson, *Notes on the State of Virginia*, 162.

82. Blassingame, ed., *Slave Testimony*, 506–7.

83. Works Progress Administration (WPA), "A Slave Named Sukie Resists a Master's Advances," accessed July 22, 2011, at HERB by ASHP, item 1638 http://herb.ashp.cuny .edu/items/show/1638.

84. Albert, *House of Bondage*, 20.

85. Jacobs, *Incidents in the Life of a Slave Girl*, 145–236.

86. WPA, "Slave Named Sukie."

87. Melton A. McLaurin, *Celia, a Slave* (Athens: University of Georgia Press, 1991), 20–30.

88. "Celia's Sad Fate."

89. Picquet and Mattison, *Louis Picquet, the Octoroon*, 20, 22.

90. Jacobs, *Incidents in the Life of a Slave Girl*, 84–85.

91. Martin, "Plaçage and the Louisiana Gens de Couleur," 58.

92. "Harriet Powell's Escape from Slavery," New York History Net, www.nyhistory .com/central/harriet.htm; Jacobs, *Incidents in the Life of a Slave Girl*, 84–86.

93. Ibid., 56.

94. Picquet and Mattison, *Louisa Picquet, the Octoroon*, 24.

95. Yetman, ed., *Voices of Slavery*, 232.

96. Isaac Matthews Will, MSS Will: Estate Record Book A, 106, S108093, South Carolina Will Transcripts, microcopy no. 9, South Carolina State Archives and Libraries, Columbia.

97. John Camden Will, MSS Will: Estate Record Book A1, 147, S108093, South Carolina Will Transcripts, microcopy no. 9, South Carolina State Archives and Libraries.

98. Blassingame, ed., *Slave Testimony*, 486.

99. Rawick, ed., *American Slave, Texas Narratives*, vol. 16, part 3, 236–46.

100. Picquet and Mattison, *Louisa Picquet, the Octoroon*, 9.

101. Ibid., 21.

102. Swint, ed., *Dear Ones at Home*, 56.

103. Mellon, ed., *Bullwhip Days*, 219–20.

104. Jacobs, *Incidents in the Life of a Slave Girl*, 84.

105. Blassingame, ed., *Slave Testimony*, 156.

106. Ibid.

107. Yetman, ed., *Voices from Slavery*, 317.

108. Ibid., 127.

109. Ibid., 323.

110. Ibid., 127.

111. Picquet and Mattison, *Louisa Picquet, the Octoroon*, 15; Blassingame, ed., *Slave Testimony*, 703–6.

112. Picquet and Mattison, *Louisa Picquet, the Octoroon*, 15.

113. Pitts, "Louisa Picquet," 296–98.

CHAPTER 10

When the Present Is Past

Writing the History of Sexuality and Slavery

JIM DOWNS

One problem that flummoxes both historians of sexuality and of slavery is the paucity of sources. Scholars of sexuality struggle to find archival references that detail the sexual and romantic lives of people from the past, often working against political, religious, social, and economic forces that prevented details about sexuality from entering into the historical record in the first place. Scholars of slavery, despite the avalanche of books, articles, and dissertations that have been written in the last half century, struggle to excavate details about the history of enslavement, or at the very least, make sense of the surviving evidence.

Compounding matters, only within the last few decades have archivists and research librarians begun to create searchable subject headings that included slavery; sexuality remains virtually absent from these catalogs. Even with the advent of online databases and the creation of sophisticated word searches that enable scholars to skim through millions of records in a few nanoseconds, the search for primary-source material remains difficult for both groups of historians, particularly for scholars of sexuality, as the language that contemporary scholars employ to describe these conditions and experiences often does not have a clear and direct antecedent in the past.[1] Even though both groups have devised theoretical and methodological ways to address the silences and to investigate with more sophistication the extant evidence, the lack of sources remains a challenge for historians of slavery as well as historians of sexuality.[2] As historian Marisa Fuentes astutely notes in her work on slavery in the eighteenth-century Caribbean, "the very call 'to find more sources' about people who left few if any of their own reproduces the same erasures and silences they experienced."[3]

For scholars—many whose work appears in this volume—whose work straddles both of these fields, the struggle to find a manuscript collection, a diary or journal, or an unabridged correspondence that chronicles an enslaved person's romance, desires, or definition of their sexuality remains deeply challenging. The limitation of available records has led to fewer scholars pursuing these subjects, which has led to fewer books and articles published on sexuality and slavery. Since the majority of the surviving records on slavery detail labor conditions, the historiography has followed this lead and reproduced the major themes that mattered to slaveholders—the number of enslaved people employed on a particular plantation, the power dynamics that undergirded masters and enslaved people's relationship, the economic value of the enslaved population, the status of the crops, and so on. In general, when many historians write on these topics, all of which are critically important to understanding the slaveocracy, these historians unwittingly propagate the planters' logic. Historians of slavery and capitalism— which has emerged as a leading theme in the field of late—potentially risk reproducing the logic of slaveholders by emphasizing economics, even when their aim is to restore humanity to enslaved people and to demonstrate their contribution to the broader economy. More to the point, since slavery created a major business, it left behind a major archive of financial transactions, bank records, notes of sales, monetary ledgers, promissory notes, wills, and estate records, which facilitate the scholarship on slavery and capitalism in ways that many scholars have underappreciated. Doing this research, even if it is part of larger recuperative historiography, reanimates the South in the way that slaveholders created it, even if the historian's motivation stems from a higher moral calling.[4]

Writing the history of sexuality inherently pushes against the archival grain and attempts to provide a counter-narrative, to expose a hidden history.[5] Sexuality studies, encompassing a wide range of subjects from reproduction to physical and romantic intimacy, seeks to unearth details about people's lives, refusing to see enslaved people as slaveholders did, as simply capital to be exploited for profit. It implicitly aims to redirect the gaze from the sites of economic production— the fields, the master's home, the farms—to the interiority of enslaved people's lives: their intimacies, desires, sexual and reproductive bodies, feelings, and loves. It seeks to observe their bodies moving in ways that pleased them and were not used directly or innately for profit.[6]

Writing a history of sexuality often invariably leads to new methods and broader definitions of evidence. When historians of capitalism research their topics, the archive is more complicit with their questions than it is for historians of sexuality. Rape, for example, was endemic during slavery but was often not articulated in the historical record. Due to the dearth of sources, the historiography on sexuality and slavery, in turn, continues to be marginalized within the larger historiography on slavery because it cannot marshal the same number of sources that economic, social, or even political historians can posit. As a result, the historiography on sexuality and slavery is less empirical, appears thinner, and, by many counts, less significant.

While these struggles continue to mount within the academy, making the history of sexuality during slavery difficult to chronicle, outside of the academy the subject of slavery and sexuality thrives. Novelists, poets, artists, and filmmakers have circumvented the problems of the archive and produced some of the most compelling, daring, and insightful work on the history of slavery and sexuality in the last few decades. Fiction writers and artists have centered sexuality in their depictions of slavery by bypassing the historical profession's strict and often provincial notion of evidence. From Elizabeth Alexander's ventriloquized narrative of Sarah Baartman, known as Saartjie, to the haunting images of rape and sexual abuse in Toni Morrison's *Beloved* to Kara Walker's highly sexualized rendering of *Uncle Tom's Cabin* to the banality of sex in Edward Jones's *The Known World*, those in the arts cover a panoply of topics related to sexuality. Unlike historians who offer more strict interpretations of primary sources, these writers and artists also use primary sources but are less interested in quibbling over historiographical debates and more invested in using these rare documents as a springboard to launch into more creative explorations. The artists' imaginations embroider the work, while the historical evidence forms its core, revealing how the past can be engaged through a combination of archival recovery and imaginative reconstruction.

Given that historians of sexuality do not have the archive of sources available to them that historians of capitalism and other subfields do, this chapter turns to the proliferation of depictions of slavery in the arts to offer new ways of reading existing sources. Certainly, those in the arts abide by a completely different system of writing and creation; their work, nonetheless, ought not to be dismissed purely based on disciplinary or professional differences. Artists' works can be used by historians in order to think through quagmires that have otherwise halted the study of sexuality or even prevented it from advancing. Further, this important, often public work, which typically provides many students and fellow scholars with their first impression of slavery, will help historians bridge the gap between the mainstream public's interpretation of the past and their own work. Even more importantly, the artists and writers I discuss here have all been influenced and informed by academic scholarly analyses as well as by archival material, making their work that much more relevant to historians.

Poet Elizabeth Alexander excavates the untold story of Sarah Baartman, the early nineteenth-century African woman who was placed on display in circuses throughout Europe based on imperialists' fascination with her buttocks, in her poem "The Venus Hottentot." Deemed as monstrous and subhuman, Baartman appears in both anthropological literature and the historiography on scientific racism, yet few empirical facts are known about her life; what has survived only reifies her alleged aberrance. No matter how diligently historians dig into the archives, there are limits to historical excavation. By drawing on what evidence does exist—namely details about the display and the notes from scientists who studied her while she was alive and then dissected her after her death—Alexander crafts a poem that imaginatively reconstructs Baartman's experience. She ventriloquizes Baartman's voice where the record remains silent. As Alexander once explained, "poetry can speak with a power and can color in the spaces that the archives cannot."[7] Alexander, in turn, refutes the passivity and unintelligence that many scientists and European audiences projected onto Baartman by claiming,

> He complains
> at my scent and does not think
> I comprehend, but I speak
>
> English. I speak Dutch. I speak
> a little French as well, and
> languages Monsieur Cuvier
> will never know have names.

Alexander also more powerfully draws on black feminist theory in order to inform Baartman's testimony.

> Since my own genitals are public
> I have made other parts private.
> In my silence I possess
> mouth, larynx, brain, in a single
> gesture.

The reference to being on public display but retaining the integrity of privacy evokes Darlene Clark Hine's notion of dissemblance, "the appearance of openness and disclosure but actually shielding the truth of their inner lives and selves from their oppressors."[8] Further, Alexander's comment about being silent evokes a common motif in the historiography on black women and slavery. As Farah J. Griffin perceptively argues, "silences, loopholes, interstices, allegory, dissemblance, politics of respectability—these are but a few of the terms that black women scholars use to help make sense of the silence that surrounds black women's lives and experiences."[9] Incorporating silence into the poem, Alexander suggests that many black women's voices might not be found in the archive. While historians have certainly recognized these and other forms of silence, they often assume that black women did not have the chance to have their voice recorded in the first place. Alexander, however, suggests the opposite: that Baartman avoided being documented.

The poem thus raises a critical issue for historians of sexuality and slavery to consider: when did enslaved women purposely avoid narrating an experience or conveying a feeling? While most historians certainly recognize that the openness and frankness with which we as scholars in the early twenty-first century discuss sexuality contradicts how enslaved people in the seventeenth, eighteenth, and nineteenth centuries articulated these desires and experiences, many scholars have been unwilling to recognize their silence as deliberate.[10] Although Darlene Clark Hine's brilliant theoretical formulation of dissemblance suggests that enslaved women deflected articulating their selfhood to those who oppressed them, scholars have not fully interrogated the reasons for the silences around enslaved women's sexuality. How did religion and spirituality, for example, impel many enslaved women from voicing issues related to their sexuality? In other words, did their moral, religious, or even cultural views of their bodies suggest a silence? Further, would these women approve of the ways in which historians, all of whom possess well-meaning intentions, dig up details about their intimate lives? Are there ethical limits to the historical recovery of sexuality? The poem suggests the extent to which Baartman would not want to be known or recorded in terms of her sexuality; this might be partially why Alexander insists on her silence.

Taking a cue from this poem, historians of sexuality and slavery can better interrogate the silences within the archive, not simply as limitations of the record keepers, but rather as concerted efforts by enslaved women to not be documented.[11] More to the point, while historians do not empower themselves with the literary license to ventriloquize historical actors in the way that Alexander as a poet can, the poem, nevertheless, can instruct historians on how to negotiate deep archival research with a skillful application of black feminist theory and an informed imagination to produce more detailed scholarship on enslavement. In this particular case, historians can do more to explain the silences within the record, to build on Darlene Clark Hine's important theory of dissemblance to actually annotate the range of reasons why an enslaved woman, like Baartman, might not chose to speak. Alexander's poem reveals the need for historians of sexuality to move beyond the tools employed by social, political, and economic historians to investigate the past and to consider more imaginative methods: to think about how the voice of the enslaved and of the historian can be in dialogue, and to make that part of the analysis.[12]

Similar to Alexander, Toni Morrison excavates a woman's experience from the archive that had not been fully explored as the basis for her award-winning novel *Beloved*.[13] Building on the actual story of Margaret Garner, the enslaved woman who murdered her child to avoid her from being enslaved, *Beloved* charts the story of a woman and her two daughters, one who returns as a ghost after her mother murders her. The novel includes many themes from the abuses enslaved people endured before the Civil War to the challenges of living in Ohio during a gloomy winter after the war. Throughout *Beloved*, Morrison includes a narrative of sexuality that includes romance, intimacy, failed marriages, sexual abuse, and reproduction. As Morrison explained about the writing of *Beloved*, "the absence of the interior life, the deliberate excising of it from the records that the slaves themselves told—is precisely the problem in the discourse that proceeded without us. How I gain access to that interior life is what drives me."[14]

With few records available to narrate the history of the past, Morrison turned to fiction. "Only the act of the imagination can help me," she writes, in the face of an archive that cannot. Her imagination enables her to think about sexual abuse not only as it terrorized enslaved women, but also how it affected enslaved men. Morrison, for example, creates a scene in a labor camp in which formerly enslaved men must perform oral sex on those who oppress them. She writes, "occasionally a kneeling man chose gunshot in his head as the price, maybe, of taking a bit of foreskin with him to Jesus." Here, she establishes a probable situation in which black men may have been violently forced into performing oral sex. Within the archives on slavery—state repositories, historical societies, and libraries—there is little surviving evidence that details how sexual abuse affected enslaved men, but Morrison's imagination provides a chance to broaden the definition of sexual abuse to include men during slavery.[15]

The novel contains other moments of abuse from the scene in which two young boys "took" the main character Sethe's milk in an act of unfathomable violence. Again, Morrison presents a shocking case of abuse, which may lack archival support, but it nonetheless reveals the multiple ways in which enslaved people remained vulnerable to vicious attacks. Morrison's novel urges historians to imagine the multiple and quite shocking ways in which abuse threatened the lives of the enslaved beyond the recorded cases of whippings, sexual abuse, and intimidation. Her novel also implicitly tests the boundaries of the archives by revealing moments too numerous, too macabre, and too ordinary to leave even an archival trace.[16]

Further, as a talented writer, Morrison creates complicated characters who simultaneously endure such abuse alongside love, intimacy, and motherhood. In theory, most historians recognize the many roles enslaved people experienced, but often the discovery of an enslaved person in the archive only details one fragmented aspect of their life. Historians then treat only that aspect, not taking into account the full biography of their subject. Certainly, limited records are the reason for not being able to probe their interior lives. But Morrison's claim about the need for imagination to narrate enslaved people's interior lives can inspire historians to use their imaginations when writing about people from the past. On the most basic level, Morrison's novel can serve as a generative model to avoid casting historical actors in scholarship as one-dimensional characters based simply on the fragmented evidence. This does not mean that historians should invent their subjects' biographies, but they should at least raise questions or attempt to explore the multitude of their experience, rather than simply propping them up to voice a particular historiographical argument. While historians of gender and sexuality often understand this point, economic and even social historians of slavery often overlook the intimate and sexual lives of bondspeople. Historian Daina Ramey Berry offers an important gendered intervention on the polemical intersection of slavery and capitalism by closely examining the thin surviving records. Throughout her book, Berry insists on referring to enslaved people by their names, which adds a human shape to historical actors who are often reduced to serving as statistics. Berry also uses their ages, which are often the only other marker left about their lives, to show how age influenced the economy.[17]

While historians consider these new methodologies or perpetrate older approaches, novelist Edward Jones and artist Kara Walker have used their genres to add depth and detail to the sexual lives of the enslaved. Their approaches could not be more different. In *The End of Uncle Tom and the Grand Allegorical Tableau of Eva in Heaven*, Walker creates silhouette images that depict Tom, the protagonist of *Uncle Tom's Cabin*, giving birth to Eva, a child in the novel who symbolizes the Christian ambitions of the abolitionist movement. Other scenes depict violent acts of sodomy and women suckling on another's breast, an allusion to Sethe's milk being taken.

While Walker's images depict fantastical images of sexuality on plantations, Jones reveals the banality of sex. In a novel that turns primarily on the unique concept of black people owning enslaved people of African descent, the story opens with a black overseer who masturbates as he sits under a tree. Like Morrison, Jones does not revel in this point but simply drops the sexual detail with the same narrative beat as describing the ordinariness of the landscape. Yet this simple description breathes new life into the vast historiography of slavery that depicts enslaved people working to the rhythms of the slaveholders' economic interests. Jones's brief episode of sexuality sidesteps both the logic and rhythm of plantation management, exposes the absences in the archive, and refutes the economic basis of slavery. Masturbating for self-pleasure, spewing semen that has no fecundity, touching his body in a way that has no economic value and instead produced uncommodified waste show how sexuality can retell the history of slavery from the vantage point of enslaved people's desires. It disrupts the constant rehauling of historical actors to the fields and farms and puts their bodies back to work, if only on the pages of history books, and instead it shows how their bodies moved according to their own desires and pleasures. Walker also depicts sex in her art that has no reproductive value, which further challenges the representation of enslaved people as laborers and raises questions about their intimate lives.

Walker and Jones can do what historians can't and that is to use their imaginations as the driving source of their narratives. Their work should not just be a supplementary study of slavery but rather a source to consider how sexuality unfolded on plantations. Both Walker and Jones see value in such depictions but the empirical archive will not yield evidence that substantiates these claims. So historians must work creatively to think about how various acts of sexuality cannot purposely be seen in the record, and remember that invisibility does not indicate absence. Both Walker and Jones have exquisitely imagined the historical conditions, settings, and scenes where that sexuality could have surfaced. Historians, in turn, can lean on their work to rethink how they describe the plantation South and the life within it.

Traditionally, historians considered it their responsibility to document the past, but Walker and Jones as well as Morrison and Alexander have done more than credentialed historians writing nonfiction to bring the history of slavery to the present. Their success can be traced, in part, to both the historical profession's limited understandings of historical writing and its provincial notion of what constitutes evidence. The profession's increasingly rigid definition of what constitutes history as a discipline and what counts as evidence has only made the work of academic historians that much more arcane and closed off to the public, inadvertently opening the space for novelists, poets, and artists to write the history of slavery and sexuality.

Yet, the historical profession's inflexible definition is a relatively new invention and does not reflect the objectives of the founders of the American Historical Association. When history as a field became codified in 1884, a diverse group of "professors, teachers, specialists, and others interested in the advancement of history in this country" met in Saratoga, New York, to form the American Historical Association (AHA), which grew out of the American Social Science Association.[18] At the time, history ranged from mere curiosity in the past to collecting various facts and objects to reading, writing, and teaching history. Within five years, the U.S. Congress recognized the importance of this dilettante enterprise and established a charter that incorporated the American Historical Association as a corporate body. At the time, the AHA consisted of six men who were charged with the duty to promote, collect, and preserve "the interest of American history, and of history in America."[19]

Over the last century, due to the influence of German scholars who emphasized the importance of empirical thinking in the writing of history, the practice of history in the United States developed into more of a social science than a self-made enterprise of collecting and writing about the past.[20] Historians, in turn, have become much more rigid and scientific in their assessment of the past. They must combine deep archival research with a systematic survey of the historiography in order to make the most minor points about love and physical intimacy. This methodology narrowed the practice of history to namely those who have earned doctorates (today, few with master's degrees continue to write and publish in a way that was more common less than half a century ago).

Due to the increasing professionalization of the historian's craft and the development of more inflexible methods in writing about the past, the recognition of novelists and artists as co-collaborators in the practice of history is unlikely. Yet, according to the founding mission of the AHA, there is no reason why artists and writers like Kara Walker, Edward Jones, Toni Morrison, and Elizabeth Alexander could not shape the historian's craft. The founding mission of the AHA seems amenable to literary and visual artists' commitment to the past.

When Congress sanctioned the founding of the AHA, it likely did not anticipate that the historical profession would evolve to such a state that it would remain locked off from the public, producing work that only appeared in academic journals or in inaccessible scholarly monographs. It's unlikely that Congress created a federal charter just for six dilettantes. Instead, it codified the AHA because it probably understood that the association would have a broader agenda that would engage a broader public. But historians have become too incestuously concerned only with what others who share their scholarly research interests think. As historians have been devoting all their talents and energies to fighting off other card-carrying members of the AHA, writers and artists have taken over as narrators of the past.

Novelists, poets, and artists engage the past by telling stories. They do not get lost in the minutia or the historiographical quibble; instead, they remain committed to making history legible. Historian Jill Lepore incisively charts when historians stopped telling stories and started to producing more scientific studies of the past. "Beginning in the 1920s, and intensifying in the post-Sputnik era," she writes, "a number of American and European professional historians began to insist they could and should investigate 'structures,' not events, by employing scientific methods." Lepore further argues that, to scientize history, "they quantified it . . . they used calculators. They made graphs. Their journal articles read like lab reports."[21]

The scientific turn engendered deep archival challenges for all historians, but particularly for scholars of sexuality and slavery due to the limitations of the archives and the paucity of sources. Historians of slavery and sexuality lack the raw data to track fecundity rates or to empirically analyze the raping of enslaved women across the antebellum South or to investigate intimacy and romance. When the historical profession made the scientific turn in the twentieth century, political and economic history dominated the historiography and the archive cohered with that historiographical vision. Political historians could count votes, measure voting districts, track an ideological movement from one region to the next, and obtain biographical information about leaders and membership, among other efforts to capture material. Similarly, the archive offered economic historians with financial sources from banks, plantation records, and notes from corporations that could be quantified, distilled, and inserted into scientific models of analysis.

As these changes were taking place in the 1960s, the historiography on slavery was rapidly growing, and the history of sexuality had just begun to emerge. Pioneering historians of slavery had to first counter the widespread racism that defined the traditional historiography on enslavement. They had to work against both the historical racism that characterized enslaved people in the sources as indolent and inferior and the contemporary racism that neglected enslaved people as historical actors.[22] They then needed to work against the logic of the archives in order to even find details about slavery, and they finally had to convince the academy that the history of slavery demanded to be studied on its own terms, not simply as a footnote in histories of the South. Some scholars cast their alliance with the burgeoning rise of social historians, who wrote history from the "bottom up." Similar to social historians' commitment to documenting the experience of women, laborers, and other ethnic minorities, historians of slavery validated researching and writing about enslaved people. Concurrently, the influence of Marxist theories on scholarship throughout the academy led historians of slavery to move away from the narrative urge to tell stories about slavery and instead compelled them to analyze larger power structures that undergirded the institution of slavery.[23]

Among the many books published on slavery is *Time on the Cross*, Stanley L. Engerman and Robert William Fogel's widely controversial study that drew on the scientific turn that had begun to dominate historical scholarship. The authors measured, quantified, and crunched enslaved people's lives into a digestible table of numbers. By drawing on clinometric methods, they argued that en-slaved people were more productive before the Civil War and possessed better medical care, living conditions, and food than after the war. While historians later discredited their findings by arguing that their calculations were incomplete and their evidence was not carefully analyzed, their approach to studying slavery along empirical and quantitative lines remains influential.

Despite this rebuttal, contemporary historians continue to value studies that provide statistical analyses over those that are more interpretative or even anec-dotal; they continue to denigrate studies that do not offer a clear set of numbers—which can range from the number of enslaved people on a particular plantation to the number that ran away to the number that died of a specific illness. Most historians today do not feel comfortable with an assertion about slavery unless it can be supported with some type of empirical or statistical proof. Each time that historians call for more numbers, more data sets, and more quantification, they unwittingly reify Fogel and Engerman's broader intentions and, in turn, move the field further away from telling history as a story.[24]

The problems with an empirical or scientific model in the study of slavery and sexuality are many. First, historians working in this field are often dealing with scraps of evidence. References to sexuality in the historical record often appear as clues, afterthoughts, and ellipses, which do not yield the kind of data that can be marshaled into a scientific model.

Second, when historians do—with herculean might—manage to unearth ev-idence of enslaved women discussing rape, intimacy, or motherhood, these cases accumulate only to what a skeptical critic would define as a rather small number. Finding a few cases of women, who for example ran away from slavery for love may only produce a relatively few number of cases.[25] From the vantage point of scholars of sexuality, the existence of this evidence that centers intimacy as a cause for action matters, but to historians who often count laborers or vot-ers, a few cases may appear inconsequential. Yet, as historian Jessica Millward poignantly explains, "any interpretation of slavery that omits love . . . may misrep-resent the motivations of enslaved women who pursued freedom for themselves, for their kin, and ultimately for their descendents."[26]

Third, historians of sexuality and slavery's questions push against the archi-val grain; questions that historians of labor and even politics pose seem to be in a more fluent dialogue with the archive than those that historians of sexuality raise. In other words, planters cared about labor, and they wrote about it; they cared about the southern economy and wrote about that, too. Therefore, when contemporary historians conduct research on labor or the economy, the archive, for all intents and purposes, has been organized and set up to answer those questions. Archivists also valued preserving accounting books, ledgers, and other documents relating to the circulation of capital. Historians of sexuality work against the archival grain in this respect: planters did not value, let alone understand, sexuality in the same way that contemporary historians do. Historians of sexuality and slavery begin their research by working with a vocabulary that planters and record keepers did not follow.[27] This is not to say that research in sexuality and slavery is impossible; it is simply to posit that the scientific model that most historians value as the litmus test to write history does not easily translate to the history of sexuality and slavery as it does for other subfields within the discipline.

Historians thus can learn more from the arts than the sciences. They could take more risks and develop better interpretations. The efforts to scientize history have discouraged interpretation and a healthy discourse of disagreement by deferring to empiricism. This does not mean that they should abandon the time-honored tradition of evidence, but they ought to rethink the use of evidence—not as a tool that could be counted and quantified and then added to a footnote but rather as an artifact that requires a closer inspection, a deeper meditation, with the hope that the document can generate more questions, introduce new perspectives, and open new paths of inquiry.[28] While some historians indeed treat sources in this fashion, many historians have been trained to be more scientific than interpretive and to file sources into a footnote rather than to interpret them rigorously and imaginatively.

What if, instead, historians held the source in their hands not as a scientist but instead as an artist? Handling the source in this way does not mean one should not be analytical or critical, it simply means analyzing the document for all its potential interpretive value. Elizabeth Alexander and Toni Morrison, for example, built full narratives with only fragments of evidence. While certainly much of their work was fictionalized, the contours of it remained tethered to the periods in which they wrote, and they both interpreted the evidence in multiple ways that expanded the history of enslavement.[29] Even for empirical sources, to understand these quantities or to visualize these amounts requires an imagination—the talents of storytellers, artists, and poets to provide the vocabulary to summon images that could connote and explain these numbers. Toni Morrison and Kara Walker likely do not count, measure, or quantify the facts of slavery in these works, but they produced a language that can illustrate these statistics, and make them known to audiences in a way that connects them more intimately to the meaning of enslavement.

In sum, writing the history of sexuality and slavery calls for an engagement with the archive and the current practice of historical scholarship. As it stands now, the study of sexuality and slavery will be continually marginalized if the dominant measures of historical scholarship remain in tact. Decades ago, racism, sexism, and other prejudices caused scholars to neglect exploring enslaved women's sexuality. Today, those issues, while still endemic, are not the only cause for the disavowal of the history of sexuality and slavery from being told; it also results from larger, more entrenched problems regarding historical practice, the notion of evidence, and the continual support of scientific methods as the most valuable tools in the writing of history. Rethinking these practices will not only usher sexuality and slavery into the dominant discourse in the history of the Americas, but it will also engender a broader reconceptualization of how all historians pursue their research and writing.

Those working in the literary arts have demonstrated the need to consider sexuality as a fundamental component in the history of slavery, and they have also modeled how historians can better develop their voice, use their imagination, and reach broader audiences in the study of the past. If historians do not rethink their craft, the more likely it is that those in the arts will become the official narrators of the past.

NOTES

1. Michel Foucault, *The History of Sexuality*, vol. 1, *An Introduction* (New York: Vintage, 1990); Jim Downs, "With Only a Trace: Same Sex Sexual Desire and Violence on Slave Plantations," in *Connexions: Histories of Race and Sex in North America*, ed. Jennifer Brier, Jim Downs, and Jennifer L. Morgan (Urbana: University of Illinois Press, 2016), 15–37.

2. Ann Stoler offers an example. See Stoler, *Along the Archival Grain: Epistemic Anxieties and Colonial Common Sense* (Princeton, N.J.: Princeton University Press, 2009).

3. Marisa Fuentes, *Dispossessed Lives: Enslaved Women, Violence, and the Archive* (Philadelphia: University of Pennsylvania Press, 2016), 6.

4. Gender historians have been most apt at avoiding these pitfalls, in part because their work inherently pushes against both the logic of the records and the values and concerns of planters. See, for example, Daina Ramey Berry, *Swing the Sickle for the Harvest Is Ripe: Gender and Slavery in Antebellum Georgia* (Urbana: University of Illinois Press, 2007); Stephanie M. H. Camp, *Closer to Freedom: Enslaved Women and Everyday Resistance in the Plantation South* (Chapel Hill: University of North Carolina, 2004); Thavolia Glymph, *Out of the House of Bondage: The Transformation of the Plantation Household* (New York: Cambridge University Press, 2008).

5. See Michel Foucault, *Language, Counter-Memory, Practice: Selected Essays and Interviews* (Ithaca, N.Y.: Cornell University Press, 1977); Stoler, *Along the Archival Grain*; Nell Irvin Painter, "Soul Murder and Slavery: Toward a Fully Loaded Cost Accounting," in *Southern History across the Color Line* (Chapel Hill: University of North Carolina Press, 2002), 15–39; Saidiya Hartman, "Venus in Two Acts," *Small Axe* 12, no. 2 (2008): 1–14; Jennifer L. Morgan, "Why I Write," in *Why We Write: The Politics*

and Practice of Writing for Social Change, ed. Jim Downs (New York: Routledge, 2006), 39–48.

6. Here I draw on Tera W. Hunter's incisive analysis of dance in post-Reconstruction Atlanta as a backlash against the regimented movement that domestic service demanded. Tera W. Hunter, *To 'Joy My Freedom: Southern Black Women's Lives and Labors after the Civil War* (Cambridge, Mass.: Harvard University Press, 1997).

7. Elizabeth Alexander, keynote address, "VENUS 2010: They Called Her 'Hottentot,' An Interdisciplinary Symposium on Sarah Baartman," New York University, March 27, 2010.

8. Darlene Clark Hine, "Rape and the Inner Lives of Black Women: Thoughts on the Culture of Dissemblance," in *Hine Sight: Black Women and the Re-Construction of American History*, ed. Darlene Clark Hine (Brooklyn, N.Y.: Carlson, 1994), 37.

9. Farah Jasmine Griffin, *Beloved Sisters and Loving Friends: Letters from Rebecca Primus of Royal Oak, Maryland and Addie Brown of Hartford, Connecticut, 1854–1868* (New York: Knopf, 1999).

10. Drawing on cultural theory and archival research, Marisa Fuentes and Aisha K. Finch each offer new ways of engaging these issues. See Fuentes, *Dispossessed Lives*. Also see Aisha K. Finch, *Rethinking Slave Rebellion in Cuba: La Escalera and the Insurgencies of 1841–1844* (Chapel Hill: University of North Carolina Press, 2015).

11. I develop this point further about enslaved women resisting being found in the archives in Jim Downs, "Harriet and Louisa Jacobs: 'Not without My Daughter,'" in *North Carolina Women: Their Lives and Times*, ed. Michele Gillespie and Sally G. McMillen (Athens: University of Georgia Press, 2014), 117–32.

12. Newer scholarship aims to do this. See, for example, Deirdre Cooper Owens, *Medical Bondage: Race, Gender, and the Origins of American Gynecology* (Athens: University of Georgia Press, 2017); Saidiya Hartman, *Lose Your Mother: A Journey along the Atlantic Slave Route* (New York: Farrar, Straus & Giroux, 2007); Hartman, "Venus in Two Acts"; Carla Peterson, *Black Gotham: A Family History of African Americans in Nineteenth-Century New York* (New Haven, Conn.: Yale University Press, 2012).

13. Historians have since written about Garner. See, for example, Nikki M. Taylor, *Driven Toward Madness: The Fugitive Slave Margaret Garner and Tragedy on the Ohio* (Athens: Ohio University Press, 2016).

14. Toni Morrison, "The Site of Memory," in *Inventing the Truth: the Art and Craft of Memoir*, ed. William Zinsser (Boston: Houghton Mifflin, 1987), 92.

15. Thomas A. Foster, "The Sexual Abuse of Black Men under American Slavery," in "Intersections of Race and Sexuality," special issue, *Journal of the History of Sexuality* 20, no. 3 (2011): 445–64. Also see Downs, "With Only a Trace."

16. In *Out of the House of Bondage*, Glymph offers one of the best detailed descriptions of the everyday forms of violence, intimidation, and abuse that enslaved people endured. Yet, despite Glymph's herculean excavation, her book is not the end of the conversation but perhaps the beginning of it. Morrison's novel imagines the multiple ways that violence could have unfolded.

17. Daina Ramey Berry, *The Price for Their Pound of Flesh: The Value of the En-*

slaved, from Womb to Grave, in the Building of a Nation (Boston: Beacon Press, 2017). Sowande N. Mustakeem also captures the intimate lives of enslaved people in her gendered analysis of the Middle Passage. See Mustakeem, *Slavery at Sea: Terror, Sex, and Sickness in the Middle Passage* (Champaign: University of Illinois Press, 2016).

18. American Historical Association, homepage, http://www.historians.org, accessed August 10, 2013.

19. "Brief History of the AHA," American Historical Association, https://www .historians.org/about-aha-and-membership/aha-history-and-archives/brief-history-of -the-aha, accessed December 7, 2017.

20. Peter Novick, *That Noble Dream: The "Objectivity Question" and the American Historical Profession* (New York: Cambridge University Press, 1988).

21. Jill Lepore, "Writing for History: Journalism, History and the Revival of the Narrative," in *Why We Write: The Politics and Practice of Writing for Social Change*, ed. Jim Downs (New York: Routledge, 2006), 85.

22. For more on how the present defined the past and the broader politics of writing social history, see Eric Foner, *Who Owns History: Rethinking the Past in a Changing World* (New York: Hill & Wang, 2003).

23. On the influence of Marxism, see Eugene Genovese, *Roll, Jordan, Roll: The World the Slaves Made* (New York: Pantheon, 1974). On the influence of social history of the so-called history methods, see Herbert G. Gutman, *The Black Family in Slavery and Freedom, 1750–1925* (New York: Pantheon, 1976).

24. Other fields have pushed for empirical analysis, which has resulted in only more confusion, as those counting often employ problematic methods. In the early American field, historians debate the number of Native Americans who died at the moment of contact. Henry Dobyns's scientific approach has proven to be flawed. Similarly, in the nineteenth century, historians continue to count the number of people who died during the Civil War, but the categories they employ to make this assessment reflect nineteenth-century models of analysis and omit the experiences of black people. Henry Dobyns, *Their Number Become Thinned: Native American Population Dynamics in Eastern North America* (Knoxville: University of Tennessee Press, 1983); David Henige, *Numbers from Nowhere: The American Indian Contact Population Debate* (Norman: University of Oklahoma Press, 1998); J. David Hacker, "A Census-Based Count of the Civil War Dead," *Civil War History* 57, no. 4 (2011): 307–48. James Downs, "Color Blindness in the Demographic Death Toll of the Civil War," April 13, 2012, *OUPblog*, https://blog.oup.com/2012/04/black-white-demographic-death-toll-civil-war/, accessed August 10, 2013.

25. Betty DeRamus, *Forbidden Fruit: Love Stories from the Underground Railroad* (New York: Atria, 2005). Also see Tera Hunter, *Bound in Wedlock: Slave and Free Black Marriage in the Nineteenth Century* (Cambridge, Mass.: Harvard University Press, 2017).

26. Jessica Millward, *Finding Charity's Folk: Enslaved and Free Black Women in Maryland* (Athens: University of Georgia Press, 2015), 74.

27. Further, many details about the inner lives of people from the past have been

discarded and thrown into the trash, as their descendants wanted to either conceal a relationship or did not recognize it as important. In Martha Hodes's nonfiction study, *The Sea Captain's Wife*, about an interracial relationship between a New England white woman and a West Indian black man, major chunks are missing from a trail of correspondence that likely revealed more about this relationship. While Hodes does not directly surmise why this void exists, one might speculate that a family member with political ambitions who was one of the last to own the letters, may have purposely destroyed the missing letters. See Martha Hodes, *The Sea Captain's Wife: A True Story of Love, Race, and War in the Nineteenth Century* (New York: W. W. Norton, 2007).

28. For more on the changing notion of evidence, see Marc Bloch, *Reflections on the Nature and Uses of History and the Techniques and Methods of Those Who Write It* (New York: Vintage, 1964).

29. Microhistory, narrative history, and cultural history have all in some way adhered to various iterations of these ideas, which likely became the first places where my thinking on this topic originated. See Hodes, *Sea Captain's Wife*; John Demos, *The Unredeemed Captive: A Family Story from Early America* (New York: Knopf, 1984); Carlo Ginzburg, *The Cheese and the Worms: The Cosmos of a Sixteenth-Century Miller*, transl. John Tedeschi and Anne Tedeschi (Baltimore, Md.: Johns Hopkins University Press, 1980).

CONTRIBUTORS

DAINA RAMEY BERRY is the Oliver H. Radkey Professor of History and African and African Diaspora Studies at the University of Texas at Austin. She is the author of *The Price for Their Pound of Flesh: The Value of the Enslaved, from Womb to Grave, in the Building of a Nation* (2017) and *"Swing the Sickle for the Harvest Is Ripe": Gender and Slavery in Antebellum Georgia* (2007). She is also an award-winning editor of *Enslaved Women in America: An Encyclopedia* (2012) and *Slavery and Freedom in Savannah* (coedited with Leslie Harris, 2014). Currently she is completing *A Black Women's History of the United States* (coauthored with Kali Nicole Gross, 2019).

SHARON BLOCK is Professor of History at the University of California, Irvine, and author of *Rape and Sexual Power in Early America* (2006). While she was developing *Colonial Complexions: Race and Bodies in Eighteenth-Century America* (2018), she and Stephanie Camp regularly shared their work on the cultural histories of racialized bodies. She is honored to help bring one of Camp's final pieces of writing to publication.

TREVOR BURNARD is Professor of History and Head of Historical and Philosophical Studies at the University of Melbourne. He is the author of five monographs and numerous articles and edited works on Caribbean history. His principal publications are *Mastery, Tyranny, and Desire: Thomas Thistlewood and His Slaves in the Anglo-Jamaican World* (2004); *Planters, Merchants, and Slaves: Plantation Societies in British America, 1650–1820* (2015); and *The Plantation Machine: Atlantic Capitalism in French Saint Domingue and British Jamaica* (with John Garrigus, 2016).

STEPHANIE M. H. CAMP (1967–2014) was a groundbreaking feminist historian of African American women's history who held the Donald W. Logan Family Endowed Chair in American History at the University of Washington at the time of her death. Her award-winning *Closer to Freedom: Enslaved Women and Everyday Resistance in the Plantation South* (2004) changed how scholars understand resistance, agency, and women's lives under slavery. With Edward E. Baptist she edited *New Studies in the History of American Slavery* (2006). Her chapter in this book is from her unfinished book manuscript, "Black Is Beautiful: An American History," which traces the intertwined meanings of race and beauty across American history.

CATHERINE CLINTON holds the Denman Chair of American History at the University of Texas (San Antonio). *The Plantation Mistress: Woman's World in the Old South* appeared in 1982, and her most recent book, *Stepdaughters of History: South-*

ern Women and the American Civil War (2016) is based on the Fleming Lectures she delivered at Louisiana State University in 2012. She is an elected member of the Society of American Historians. During 2016 she served as president of the Southern Historical Association and was awarded a Guggenheim Fellowship. She is an advocate for the Cassandra Project, an initiative to raise awareness about rape culture on campus and sexual harassment in the academy.

DAVID DODDINGTON is Lecturer in North American History at Cardiff University (U.K.). He has contributed to edited collections, including Paul Lovejoy and Vanessa Oliveira, eds., *Slavery, Memory, Citizenship* (2016), and published in journals such as *Gender and History*. He is the author of *Contesting Slave Masculinity in the American South* (2018). His edited collection, *Writing the History of Slavery*, is forthcoming.

JIM DOWNS is the author of *Sick from Freedom: African American Illness and Suffering during the Civil War and Reconstruction* (2012) and *Stand by Me: The Forgotten History of Gay Liberation* (2016). He coedited *Beyond Freedom: Disrupting the History of Emancipation* (with David Blight, 2017) and *Connexions: Histories of Race and Sex in North America* (with Jennifer Brier and Jennifer L. Morgan, 2016).

THOMAS A. FOSTER is Professor of History and Associate Dean for Faculty Affairs and Social Sciences at Howard University. He is the author or editor of six books on gender and sexuality in the United States, including *Sex and the Founding Fathers: The American Quest for a Relatable Past* (2014) and *Documenting Intimate Matters: Primary Sources for a History of Sexuality in America* (2013). His latest book, *The Rape of Rufus: Sexual Abuse and Exploitation of Enslaved Men*, is forthcoming.

MARISA J. FUENTES is the Presidential Term Chair in African American History and Associate Professor of Women's and Gender Studies and History at Rutgers University–New Brunswick. She is the author of *Dispossessed Lives: Enslaved Women, Violence, and the Archive* (2016), which has won prizes in the fields of women's and African American women's history and Caribbean studies. Fuentes's most recent publications include the coedited *Scarlet and Black: Slavery and Dispossession in Rutgers History* (with Deborah Gray White, 2016) and a coedited special issue of *History of the Present*, "Slavery and the Archive" (with Brian Connolly, 2016). She is currently working on a book about the slave trade, capitalism, and disposability.

LESLIE M. HARRIS is Professor of History at Northwestern University. She is the author or editor of the award-winning books *In the Shadow of Slavery: African Americans in New York City, 1626–1863* (2003); *Slavery in New York* (coeditor with Ira Berlin, 2005); and *Slavery and Freedom in Savannah* (coeditor with Daina Ramey Berry, 2014). She is currently completing a coedited volume on slavery and universities and a book on late twentieth-century New Orleans.

STEPHANIE JONES-ROGERS is Assistant Professor in the Department of History at the University of California, Berkeley, where she specializes in African American history, women's and gender history, and the history of American slavery. She is the author of "'[S]he Could ... Spare One Ample Breast for the Profit of Her Owner': White Mothers and Enslaved Wet Nurses' Invisible Labor in American Slave Markets," *Slavery and Abolition* (April 2017); and the forthcoming *Mistresses of the Market: White Women and the Economy of American Slavery*.

JESSICA MILLWARD is Associate Professor in the Department of History at the University of California, Irvine. Millward is author of *Finding Charity's Folk: Enslaved and Free Black Women in Maryland* (2015). She is currently working on a project that focuses on African American women's experiences with sexual assault and intimate partner violence through the nineteenth century.

BIANCA PREMO is Professor of Latin American History at Florida International University. She is the author of several awarding-winning articles and books on law, childhood, and the history of women, and on enslaved and native peoples in the Spanish empire, especially Peru and Mexico. Her most recent book is *The Enlightenment on Trial: Ordinary Litigants and Colonialism in the Spanish Empire* (2017).

BRENDA E. STEVENSON is the inaugural holder of the Nickoll Family Endowed Chair and Professor of History and African American Studies at the University of California, Los Angeles. Her single-authored books include *Life in Black and White: Family and Community in the Slave South* (1996); *The Contested Murder of Latasha Harlins: Justice, Gender, and the Origins of the L.A. Riots* (2013); and *What Is Slavery?* (2005). A past Guggenheim Fellow, she is completing a book on the black slave family in the United States from 1600 to 1860.

INDEX

Note: An *italicized* page number indicates an illustration or caption. A page number followed by a "t" indicates a table.

CPSIA information can be obtained
at www.ICGtesting.com
Printed in the USA
LVHW050005130121
676313LV00009B/925